A southern classic and a dazzling debut, at the Young Vic this autumn.

The Member of the Wedding
by Carson McCullers

07 September – 20 October

'Tender and devastating ... she has examined the heart of man with an understanding that no other writer can hope to surpass'
Tennessee Williams

A rare chance to see this great American play.

A major writer of the Deep South, Carson McCullers' much loved novels include *The Heart is a Lonely Hunter* and *The Ballad of the Sad Cafe.*

The Brothers Size
by Tarell Alvin McCraney

09 November – 08 December

'The thrilling sound, the beautiful music of a new voice'
The New York Times

There are two brothers Size. One owns an auto-repair shop. The other, fresh out of prison, always takes the wrong track.

McCraney plants Nigerian myth in the fertile soil of Louisiana with tough tenderness. Comic, lyric, passionate drama.

A Young Vic and ATC co-production

Book now 020 7922 2922
www.youngvic.org
Quote promo-code 401 when booking.

Under 26 £9.50

Young Vic, 66 The Cut
London SE1 8LZ

Photo **The Member of the Wedding / Flora Spencer-Longhurst by JP Masclet**
The Young Vic is a registered charity (no. 268876)

Lambeth Arts   LONDON COUNCILS   ARTS COUNCIL ENGLAND

GRANTA

GRANTA 99, AUTUMN 2007
www.granta.com

EDITORS *Fatema Ahmed, Liz Jobey, Matt Weiland*
EDITORIAL ASSISTANT *Helen Gordon*

CONTRIBUTING EDITORS *Diana Athill, Simon Gray, Isabel Hilton,*
Sophie Harrison, Blake Morrison, John Ryle, Sukhdev Sandhu, Lucretia Stewart

FINANCE *Geoffrey Gordon, Morgan Graver*
MARKETING AND SUBSCRIPTIONS *Lynette Jillians*
SALES DIRECTOR *Brigid Macleod*
PUBLICITY *Pru Rowlandson*
IT MANAGER *Mark Williams*
TO ADVERTISE CONTACT *Kate Rochester, ksrochester@granta.com*
PRODUCTION ASSOCIATE *Sarah Wasley*
PROOFS *Lesley Levene*

PUBLISHER *Sigrid Rausing*

GRANTA PUBLICATIONS, Crown House, 72 Hammersmith Road, London, W14 8TH
From November, Granta will move to 12 Addison Avenue, London, W11 4QR
e-mail for editorial: editorial@granta.com
This selection copyright © 2007 Granta Publications.
In the United States, Granta is published in association with Grove/Atlantic Inc,
841 Broadway, 4th Floor, New York, NY 10003

TO SUBSCRIBE go to www.granta.com
or call +44(0)20 8955 7011 or e-mail subs@granta.com
A one-year subscription (four issues) costs £27.95 (UK), £35.95 (rest of Europe)
and £42.95 (rest of the world).
Granta is printed and bound in Italy by Legoprint. The paper used in this publication meets the
minimum requirements of American National Standard for Information Sciences—Permanence of
Paper for Printed Library Materials, ANSI Z39.48-1984.

Design: Daniel Mogford
Front cover photograph: Joel Sternfeld, 1976
Back cover photograph: Nony Singh, 1966
Acknowledgements are due to the following libraries for permission to quote from the papers of
O. G. S. Crawford: the Bodleian Library, Oxford; the Rare Book Collection at the University of
Illinois. The quotation from the letter by G. M. Trevelyan is reproduced by permission of the
National Archives (UK).

ISBN 978-0903141-963

'DAVID PEACE'S DEPICTION

OF A WAR-TORN

METROPOLIS BOTH

CRUMBLING AND

ASCENDANT IS PEERLESS.'

James Ellroy

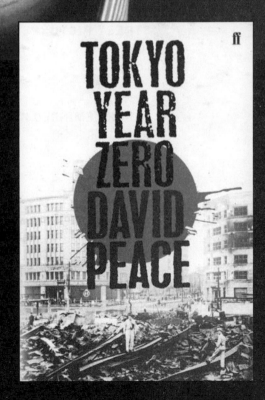

WHAT HAPPENED NEXT

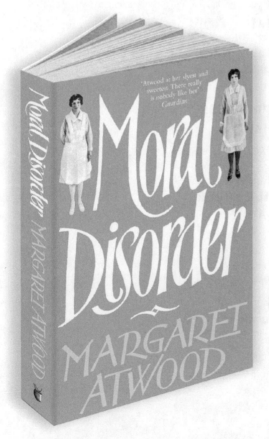

CONTRIBUTORS

Tim Adams was the deputy editor of *Granta* from 1988 to 1993 and is now a staff writer on the London *Observer*. His non-fiction piece 'Fantastic Mr Fox' appeared in *Granta* 90.

Chimamanda Ngozi Adichie was born in 1977 in Nigeria. She is the author of two novels, *Purple Hibiscus* (HarperPerennial/Anchor Books) and *Half of a Yellow Sun* (Fourth Estate/Vintage) which won the 2007 Orange Broadband Prize for Fiction. She first appeared in the magazine in *Granta* 88 with the story 'The Grief of Strangers'.

Nell Freudenberger is the author of a novel, *The Dissident*, and *Lucky Girls*, a collection of stories, both published by Picador in the UK and the Ecco Press in the US. She was one of *Granta*'s Best of Young American Novelists this year. She lives in New York.

Helon Habila won the Caine Prize for African Writing in 2001 and now teaches creative writing at George Mason University in Washington, DC. His most recent novel, *Measuring Time*, is published by Hamish Hamilton in the UK and by W. W. Norton in the US. An extract appeared in *Granta* 92. He is working on a book about Lagos.

Tessa Hadley's short-story collection, *Sunstroke and Other Stories*, and her most recent novel, *The Master Bedroom*, were both published this year by Jonathan Cape in the UK and by Henry Holt in the US. She teaches literature and creative writing at Bath Spa University and lives in Cardiff. Her story 'Matrilineal' appeared in *Granta* 94.

Kitty Hauser is the author of a book about the artist Stanley Spencer (Tate Publishing) and *Shadow Sites: Photography, Archaeology and the British Landscape 1927–1955* (Oxford University Press). She currently works at the Power Institute at Sydney University. 'The Earth from the Air' is taken from her book *Bloody Old Britain*, which will be published by Granta Books in May 2008.

Philip Hoare's books include biographies of Stephen Tennant and Noël Coward; *Wilde's Last Stand*, *Spike Island* and *England's Lost Eden*. 'Whaling' is taken from *Or, The Whale*, which will be published by Fourth Estate in spring 2008. A BBC documentary, *Arena: The Hunt for Moby-Dick*, directed by Adam Low and written and presented by Philip Hoare, will be shown in 2008.

Jon McGregor lives in Nottingham. He is the author of two novels, *So Many Ways to Begin* (Bloomsbury) and *If Nobody Speaks of Remarkable Things* (Bloomsbury/Houghton Mifflin). His first published story, 'What the Sky Sees', appeared in *Granta* 78.

Roberto Saviano was born in Naples in 1979. 'Naples '04' is taken from his book *Gomorrah*, which won the Viareggio Prize when it was published by Mondadori in Italy last year. It will be published later this year by Macmillan in the UK and by Farrar, Straus and Giroux in the US. Since the book's publication Saviano has been under police protection.

Nony Singh was born in 1936 in Lahore. She studied at the American mission school in Dehradun, India, and graduated from Delhi University. She married in 1960 and had four daughters. Her husband created a world record in wheat production and after his death in 1981 she took charge of his farm. From the age of ten until her husband's death, she photographed her family extensively. Her photographs will be collected as one of a series of books, *Dayanita Singh Sent a Letter*, published by Steidl in autumn 2007.

Joel Sternfeld's work has been widely exhibited internationally. He has received numerous awards, including two Guggenheim fellowships, a Prix de Rome and the Citibank Photography Award. His recent books include *Sweet Earth: Experimental Utopias in America* (2006), and *When It Changed* (2007), portraits from the United Nations conference on climate change, both published by Steidl.

Gemini Wahhaj was born in Bangladesh and grew up both there and in Iraq. She now lives in Houston, Texas with her husband and daughter and has just finished her first novel.

Josh Weil was born in 1976 in rural Virginia. 'The Tree Thieves' is from his recently completed short-story collection. He currently lives in Brooklyn where he is working on a novel.

THE ART OF
LEE MILLER

15 SEPTEMBER 2007–
6 JANUARY 2008

V&A

WWW.VAM.AC.UK
⊖ SOUTH KENSINGTON

GRANTA

AN INTERVIEW WITH RICHARD FORD

Tim Adams

An Interview with Richard Ford

The first story that Richard Ford wrote for *Granta* appeared in the eighth issue of the magazine, 'Dirty Realism', in 1983. At that time, Ford, who was born in Jackson, Mississippi, was about to turn forty and had published two novels, *A Piece of My Heart*, and *The Ultimate Good Luck*. Neither had sold in any numbers and when Ford's *Granta* story 'Rock Springs' came out neither was in print.

Alongside Ford in that 'Dirty Realism' issue were other writers who seemed, at least for the purposes of selling literary magazines, to share a similar take on the world, in particular Raymond Carver. If magazines could be said to have characters or souls (or even consciences) Ford and Carver did as much to shape those things in *Granta* as anyone.

A couple of years after 'Dirty Realism' appeared, Richard Ford wrote *The Sportswriter*, the novel that made sure that subsequently all of his writing would be in print. *The Sportswriter* introduced the character Frank Bascombe, a failed novelist, who, after his son had died and his marriage ended, had moved from the south of America to take jobs covering baseball and football in New Jersey. His was an indelible fictional voice: troubled, eloquent and stubborn in its hope.

Ford has continued to write stories, and many of the best of them have appeared in these pages. He has edited two anthologies, *The Granta Book of the American Short Story*, and *The Granta Book of the American Long Story*, which are not only wonderful primers in the art, but also a good guide to the rigour and generosity that inform his writing.

He followed *The Sportswriter* with a short novel, *Wildlife*, and then with another Frank Bascombe novel, *Independence Day*, the only novel to win both the PEN/Faulkner Award and the National Book Award. After two more collections of stories, *Women with Men* and *A Multitude of Sins*, the trilogy of Bascombe novels was completed by *The Lay of the Land* in 2006.

Richard Ford now lives in Maine, with his wife of thirty-nine years, Kristina Ford. This interview took place in July, 2007.   TA

When *The Lay of the Land* was completed you suggested you would never write another long novel. Are you still feeling that way?
I still feel that way, possibly even more that way. *The Lay of the Land* was, for me, a big effort and, as efforts go, entirely singular. And it requires a commensurate (if not exactly equal) devotion from its

readership. More than I can't imagine myself writing such a long novel again (and I can't), I neither can imagine wanting to write anything that would 'work on a reader' with anything like the same intense force—length, complexity, general largeness. I'd like to write another novel, yes. I'd like to write plenty of things. But I can't imagine another such undertaking as *The Lay of the Land*. Some things just don't need to be done twice—especially since I feel like I did it right the first time.

You set that book at the time of the disputed first Bush presidential election. Do you feel that election set America's fate?
It did set America's fate. No question. Insofar as the election was stolen by the Republicans, and insofar as the American electorate was sufficiently uninspired as to permit such a close race, and insofar as the two-party system (particularly the feckless Democrats) allowed a man of George Bush's astonishing incompetence and dishonesty to become the leader of our country—insofar as all these things are true and occurred at the heart of the 2000 election, then that set of events can be viewed as a direct cause of the unthinkable circumstances in Iraq today, the cause of so much loss of innocent life, and the cause of America's near-obliterated role as a potential force for good in world affairs. Is all this America's final fate? I surely hope not. It's the fix we're in today. And I hope we have a better, more wholesome fate than this. But there's no doubt about what was the initial event in the chain of events that landed us in this mess.

Why do you think so many American novelists—some surprising ones, John Updike, some less so, Don DeLillo—have felt bound to confront 9/11 so directly in fiction?
They were moved by those events. It's not very complicated. In the case of DeLillo and Updike, they're both supremely accomplished writers who're unusually confident of their abilities to make a subject their own. The fact that I wouldn't do it, didn't do it, probably just means I'm not their equal on either front. Otherwise I'd have surely done it. Right?

Much of Frank Bascombe's dislocation and hurt comes from the death of his son. All of your writing seems to have some of this

atmosphere of loss. **Where do you sense the source of that in your own life?**
First of all, I don't think that a writer who writes about loss (if I do) needs to have suffered loss himself. We can imagine loss. That's the writer's job. We empathize, we project, we make much of what might be small experience. Hemingway (as usual, full of wind) said 'only write about what you know'. But that can't mean you should only write about what you yourself have done or experienced. A rule like that pointlessly straps the imagination, confines one's curiosity, one's capacity to empathize. After all, a novel (if it chooses) can cause a reader to experience sensation, emotion, to recognize behaviour that reader may never have seen before. The writer'll have to be able to do that, too. Some subjects just cause what Katherine Anne Porter called a 'commotion in the mind'. That commotion may or may not be a response to what we actually did on earth.

That said, I probably experienced loss no more fully than most people. I was the child of older parents who I always was fearfully expecting to die on me. And the old Arkansas aunties and great uncles did start departing life when I was just a small child. One of my first vivid memories is of my Aunt Lizzie's funeral—in Arkansas—and of her lying in her casket. Vivid, yes; but also rather normal in life. Then my father died when I was sixteen—died in my arms, at home. That could certainly be seen as imprinting. We were a three-person family, very close and loving. So I experienced loss when he died; and probably, as significantly, I experienced the loss my mother suffered— of her one great love in life. How we experience what we experience is a complex business.

Did you, or do you, look back on the years before your father died, when there were the three of you, as a golden time?
No, not a golden time. I'm suspicious of 'golden times'. I think that right now this minute had better be the golden time, because it's what you've got. I had a happy childhood because my parents loved me and took good care of me. But my father had a very serious heart attack when I was eight and he was forty-eight. And that coloured a lot of life, because it scared him silly and he never felt entirely well after that—probably wasn't well. And he was gone a lot. His job as a salesman caused him to travel by car five days a week, and my

mother and I were left at home together. And we were both of us pretty volatile personalities. And I never did particularly well in school; was, as time went by, a kid who tended to get into trouble—stealing, getting into fights. I was dyslexic and never read very well. So, no. 'Golden' it wasn't. But it was good.

Did the stealing have consequences—did you get caught?
We're not talking about holding up Brink's trucks, here, or Manson Family capers; just, oh, stealing the odd car, some random breaking-and-enterings, and many lesser offences. And I *did* get caught, got hauled in front of the juvenile judge, put on probation—which was sort of awful but also sort of a badge of honour. It all scared my mother, though, made her miserable, in fact. And as far as consequence was concerned, I suppose I saw what consequence my behaviour had on her—which was bad. I was on probation at the time my father suddenly died; and my mother sat me down and told me that she wasn't going to be able to look after me the way she had up to then—because she had to go out and get a job—and that I'd better not turn up in jail or juvenile court again because she wouldn't get me out. That made a big impression on me. I guess that's consequence of a kind. But I wasn't a very committed felon. More of a little dickhead.

Do you think the dyslexia has shaped how you have read?
Absolutely. I read slowly, and as a consequence have definitely not read as many books as I *should've*—in order to be considered properly educated. But what I've read—because I've read slowly and attentively—I seem to have taken in pretty well. And, importantly, when you read slowly you also become available to those qualities of language that're other than the cognitive qualities. One becomes sensitive to what you might call the poetic qualities—rhythms, repetitions, sonorities, syncopations, the aptness of particular word choices—those qualities. They're important—at least they are to me. That's had a consequence not only upon my reading but also upon my aims as a writer of sentences.

Do you always know what a Richard Ford sentence sounds like?
I don't think there's any signature to my sentences. I've heard some people say there is, but that's just a gesture meant to flatter me.

Because I'm sure there's not. A sentence's style or manner, or a book full of sentences with styles or manners, is a response to a variety of forces operating on a writer: the writer's sensuous, instinctual relation to the material itself; the accumulated amount of material that precedes the writing; the writer's history with other books that may or may not have entertained some of the same subject matter, or books that the writer simply admires; the daily tidal changes in any person's mood and energies. And much more. All these things affect how sentences get written—how many words they hold, how syntactically complex they are, their diction and all word-choosings, what they undertake to elucidate. And in the course of any one book these stylistic characteristics can and often do change or modulate. It's certainly the case that over the course of any writer's life his or her grasp on sentences will also change—either from book to book, subject to subject, or just as one gets older. I think that *The Lay of the Land* has longer, complexer sentences because my mind (my older man's mind) was just fuller of things that interested me, and I didn't want to lose a lot of them. So, I devised sentences to keep all that stuff and put them in play. You can say that was ambition, or you could say it was poor judgment and an inability to discriminate. I'd say it was ambition, because I like the book a lot—like its thoroughness.

People can get preoccupied by such stylistic matters as 'voice': having a consistent 'voice', a true 'voice', a 'voice' of one's own. This conception of voice can have something to do with a writer's purported *signature*. But to me this isn't very important. To me 'voice' is probably just the music of the story's intelligence, how it sounds when it's being smart, or when it's working on the reader. And that music, like a story's style, can change, and does change. So. A Richard Ford sentence will usually be differently made from one piece of writing to the next. Which is fine with me.

How aware were you of Eudora Welty in Jackson while you were growing up?
Well, I knew her name. One did, in Jackson. I went to school with her niece, Elizabeth. But, Eudora'd grown up directly across the street from me on Congress Street, and I didn't even know that until I was far along into adulthood. I also didn't read anything of hers (or anything much at all) until I was in college and had it presented to

me on a syllabus. Eudora lived—on Pinehurst Street—not so far away from us when I was growing up. Walking distance. But it was in another, somewhat better 'old Jackson' neighbourhood than ours. My mother once pointed Eudora out to me at the grocery store—I might've been eight. She said 'Richard, that's Eudora Welty, over there. She's a writer.' I could tell from the tone of my mother's voice that she thought being a writer was good.

Did she write anything herself, your mother I mean?
Interesting—to me, anyway. When I was going through my mother's belongings after she'd died, in 1971, I found a notebook that had only one line written in it, on its first page, and in my mother's quite elegant hand. It said 'Les, A life'. Now my grandmother, her mother, was called Les—some version of her real name, which was Essie. My mother took care of my grandmother through the last years of my grandmother's life. And it was not an easy passage. My grandmother was capable of great, aggressive nastiness. And I know my mother got in the way of it a lot. We all did at one time or other. But it may have seemed to my mother that some act of writing—fictive or otherwise—was the best way to record or imagine her own experience. I'd guess, too, it was partly because she had a son who was a novelist that this began to seem possible to her. But. She never did it—which is all right. She didn't want to enough.

Do you think stories are created or discovered?
That's easy. Stories are created. It isn't as if they're 'out there' waiting in some Platonic hyper-space like unread emails. They aren't. Writers make stories up. It might be that when stories turn out to be good they then achieve a quality of inevitability, of there seeming to have been a previously existing and important *space* that they perfectly fill. But that isn't what's true. I'm sure of it. A story makes its own space and then fills it. Writers don't 'find' stories—although some writers might say so. This to me just means they have a vocabulary that's inadequate at depicting what they actually do. They're like Hemingway—always fleeing complexity as if it were a barn fire.

I've always thought of you as a Southern writer, but you have insisted in migrating north in your fiction. Why?

It's a long and not very interesting story. The first novel I wrote, *A Piece of My Heart*, I set in the South because I thought that's what writers from the South did. It was our job, so to speak. But I wanted my novel to be both set in the South but also to radiate its concerns out to anybody who could read—Southerner or not. In other words I wanted to use the Southern template to construct a larger than Southern novel. I suppose Faulkner and Flannery O'Connor and Welty were my models in this. But then when my book was published and reviewed it was only spoken of as a 'Southern novel'. And that frustrated the life out of me, and made me think I needed to write novels that wouldn't fall victim to that easy categorization. So, I wrote a novel set in Mexico, and once I'd done that I set about writing *The Sportswriter*, which is set in New Jersey and Michigan. And beyond that I wrote books set in Montana and France. And by this means the whole Southern issue was put to rest for me. I later came to think— but not when I was actually making this separation—that I must've intuited that all those great Southern writers (Welty, O'Connor, Percy, Faulkner, Styron, Reynolds Price, Barry Hannah) had already done the things I would've tried to and done them better than I could. So, why not then go off in the direction of things I could do best of all.

What do you think of when you think of home?
Home's not a natural subject for me. I have to specifically summon it up, first. But when I say the word, all sorts of 'home' referents do pop up. I was born in Mississippi, so that's one 'meaning' of home—probably the one most other people would nominate as the genuine one. I was also partly raised in Arkansas, so a part of what's home for me is that. I've also felt 'at home' (or at least enough that I can say so) in lots of other places: Montana, New Jersey, Louisiana, Maine. These last are all places I've chosen as 'homes'. So the essence of home for me is quite variable. Sometimes, when Kristina and I are out in the world and find ourselves staying in some hotel, we'll go to dinner, and sometime toward the end of the evening Kristina'll say, 'Let's go home now.' And she doesn't mean, *let's get on a plane to Mississippi or Montana or New Jersey*. She just means let's go back to the hotel. Home's what you say it is, I guess. Lately Kristina and I have been trying to decide where to be buried. We're old enough for such thoughts. But neither of us feels very certain about

where. I'd think that one's home might be the place where one would like to 'eternally reside'. But we're still on the fence about it.

Do you identify in any way with Frank Bascombe's unshakeable suburban optimism?
I probably don't identify with it very much at all—personally. The one note of exception I could sound would be the one that says *the suburbs interest me, and I'm always happy when I'm driving around in them.* But would I want to live in the suburbs again? No. I was a kid in the suburbs in Mississippi, and I was an adult in the suburbs in New Jersey. In both instances I couldn't wait to get out. And I did get out. But. When it came to setting a novel or two or three novels in the suburbs, when it came to projecting a made-up character into that made-up environment, I purely liked doing the writing. It was intensely pleasurable. And in so far as it was pleasurable, I became then interested in the suburbs and why it should be pleasurable to set things 'there'.

This caused me to 'use' Frank Bascombe as an agent for my own curiosity, and caused me to have him take on the suburbs as a subject of speculation. Using him, I think I did dream up some interesting (interesting to me, anyway) formulations about the suburbs. One was that by embracing the suburbs and all their metastatic commercialism and inert housing patterns and traffic nightmares—as Frank claims to do—one is, in essence, demonstrating a willingness to take credit for what we've created. We're all responsible, after all. And until we take that credit, we're just pointlessly pissing and moaning about what we don't like. Saying, as Frank does, that you like the suburbs is just a step in the direction of making things be better. But at heart Frank and I are not of one mind about the suburbs—in the sense, that is, that he has a mind.

You have written movingly of New Orleans, in memory of your feelings for that city, where you and Kristina have lived and worked; has that disaster altered your perception of loss?
I don't know that I ever had a previous 'perception' of loss. But the disaster in New Orleans surely didn't sponsor a new one. My sense of *permanence* has always included the likely demolition of all vestiges of permanence—houses, street corners, trees whereon we

carved our names in hearts, persons. It can all go, and will. In America we white people sentimentalize permanence—or at least we once could. But *Native* Americans certainly don't. Blacks probably don't either. Europeans of a certain age don't. I don't.

Has faith or church-going ever had any appeal to you?
Not church-going. But faith, well... There's the famous line in Hebrews 11: 'Faith is the evidence of things unseen'. I've always been attracted to that line. But for specifically ir-religious reasons. I deem that line to be a line about the imagination. I could almost say that, 'the imagination is the evidence of things unseen'. But again specifically I'd say that my 'faith' lies *in* the imagination and in the imagination's power to bring into existence essential experience that heretofore wasn't known to exist.

That reminds me of Frank Bascombe's line: 'The unseen exists and has properties.' Do you have an ongoing sense of that 'unseen', or only at certain charged moments?
I don't much think about the unseen. For lack of great erudition, or a great education, I suppose I've stored a fair amount of trust in my instinct. But as soon as I see that written down I start to think that instinct may just be another word for luck and for trusting to luck—which I've done. A favourite line I repair to is by the philosopher Daniel Dennett, who said: 'We have a built-in, very potent, hair-triggered tendency to find agency in things that are not agents.' I'm not sure if Dennett approves of that tendency or not. But certainly that's one of the things literature does—it ascribes agency where before no agency was noticed: it says this *causes* that, *this* is a consequence of *that*, etc. It may be that writing fiction, imagining agencies, is my most trusted way into the unseen.

There is a kind of unflinching morality in many of your stories. I'm thinking particularly of the tales of adultery in *A Multitude of Sins*. Trangression has consequences, even if only in pointing up the emptiness of lives. Does this moral sense grow out of characters, or does the moral engine come first?
I don't know a specific answer to that. In most of those stories I didn't start with a character. I usually don't. I usually start either with a

situation (a man meets his ex-lover's husband in Grand Central Station; a married couple are on their way to a party, when the young wife informs her young husband that she's had an affair with the host of the party they're attending—those are examples). Or else I just go looking for bits and pieces that I want a story to *contain*, and organize the story out of those bits. I suppose when I put it that way, and in terms of your question, the 'moral engine' may seem to come first, be an unspoken force in the choosings. But I'm entirely unaware of its being so. I hold with the notion that Martin Amis quoted Northrop Frye to say: that literature is a disinterested use of language; a writer must have nothing riding on the outcome. I set up situations and then see what I can have happen as a consequence, using language. And, at least in theory, the consequence could pretty much be anything.

Does that principle of disinterest apply equally in your novels, is it tough not to be rooting for Frank, say?
I'm always rooting for Frank to do something, or have something to say that's not expected, but interesting, given the conventional sort of man the reader may be imagining him to be—a real estate agent, etc. So, the rule of disinterest still applies. It should also be said, of course, that I'm not bound strictly by that rule. If by following it I write something that I don't like, or have Frank or any character say or do something that seems dumb or somehow wrong, I can just scratch it out and often do. I never saw Frank as a human being (although I'd like the reader to think he was pretty close to being a human being). Rather I saw him as an agency made of language. So, I wouldn't be 'rooting' for him the way you'd root for the kid with Hodgkin's Disease to see one last game at Yankee Stadium. It's different. I may be more rooting for myself to come up with something good.

Do you find your empathy with the weaknesses of your characters has deepened as you have grown older?
My empathy with every kind of weakness has deepened. Is it a matter of age? Maybe. More probably it's just a matter of experience. Graham Greene wrote—and I've always hated the idea—that morality comes with old age, with one's curiosity growing weak. That's a sourpuss's notion of morality. As something that's moribund. And I don't buy it. Maybe that's because my curiosity still seems strong.

In your introduction to the new *Granta* book of the American short story you quote Walter Benjamin suggesting 'We no longer work at things that can't be abbreviated', perhaps a factor of waning curiosity. What is your feeling for America's attention span?

That was Benjamin expressing his displeasure with modern times. Probably an observer could make, or could've made, the same claim about the contemporary attention span at any given time in history. But as for me, and as for now, I see lots of people on airplanes reading really long books; I see the 'young' of my country, as well as their beaverish parents, spending long, long, *long* periods of time in front of computer screens; I see athletes training and training until they drop. So, I conclude from this admittedly unscientific survey, that plenty of Americans have plenty of attention available—for something. It may not be for literary fiction. But then it's my job as a purveyor of literary fiction to tap into that otherwise wasted attention span. But it's there.

You have rarely written of childhood, in the way that, for instance, Tobias Wolff has; has that territory never tempted you?

Well, I'd say I *have* written about childhood. Several of the stories in *Rock Springs* are narrated by teenagers, as is all of *Wildlife*. And in the New Jersey books there are Frank's kids all around—especially in *Independence Day*. Maybe in your terms a teenager isn't a child; and maybe that's true. But I always think I've written about children—because I always brag that it's a lot easier to write about children than to have them. And I don't have any.

To what extent do you think your life was shaped by being an only child among big Southern families?

That's one of those questions that asks me to imagine another life from my own. I suppose I could—a life with brothers and sisters— but it's a bit like asking whether things have been different, do you suppose, if you'd been a girl. Probably would. Being an only child, however, shaped a great, great deal in my life. A psychologist could probably give a better answer than I could, and probably a truer answer, too. But I'll just propose one thing: that I was almost always around adults when I was quite young. Adult life was the 'important' life, the aspired-to life, and I could eavesdrop on it all the time, hear what adults thought was important, observe discrepancies in their behaviours and their pronouncements. It probably also intensified the faith that I had in parent–child relationships, inasmuch as my parents seemed to have wanted me, loved me, wanted good for me. It might've also caused me to fear loss more than would've been the case had there been others around. And I think that in myself (and perhaps evident in what I write) fear of loss and the corresponding instinct to protect myself against loss are potent forces.

Do you think that instinct to protect yourself against loss is one of the reasons you chose not to have children?
Doctor Freud might say so. But I just say that it was because Kristina and I didn't especially like children, didn't want to be saddled with the responsibility of them. We had our ideas about the future, and there was never room for children in those ideas. It was really the first important thing we ever agreed on when we were in our teens together, in Michigan. I remember the exact moment we first talked about it. It was great.

There are, you've said, two fixed points in your life: 'I always write and I am always married to the same girl.' In what ways does one depend on the other?
I've answered that question enough for one lifetime.

All right; you've also said that you consciously want your writing to be 'affirmative' of the possibility of love, closeness in a life, what makes you hold to that?
Not to keep on quoting famous men, but somewhere in Wallace Stevens there's a little fragment that says, 'we gulp down evil, choke at good'. That's always meant to me that it's more appetizing to decry, and less appetizing, maybe less simple, to find a vocabulary for affirmation. And also 'closeness in a life' and (if you will) 'love' seem immensely sustaining to me, and worthy of efforts at articulation. That said, I've written mostly stories that would have to be called 'cautionary tales', and that a lot of readers would not think of as conventionally affirming. However, I hold with John Gardner [the novelist and early supporter of Raymond Carver] who said that moral literature (by which I understand him to have meant good literature,

valuable literature) 'tests values and arouses trustworthy feelings about the better and worse in human actions'. To me, indeed, great literature is always affirming, even if it's grim—if only because it's a gesture by someone for the use of another in a future that's hoped to come. Sartre said even the grimmest literature is optimistic since it proves those things can be thought about.

So literature makes us want to be better men (and women)?
I don't know about that. I just know it gives a reader the chance to see life affirmed through literature's great concern with life. And it gives the reader a chance—in the sheltered environment of a book— to see the important consequences of events. Making one want to be better, well that's a private matter. I have some evidence that that may not be accurate—although *wanting* to be better and *being* better are obviously different things.

What did you make of being described as a 'Dirty Realist' by *Granta*?
I thought—we probably all thought—that 'Dirty Realism' was a wonderful marketing ploy. I don't think Carver or Toby Wolff or Jayne Anne Phillips or any of us ever thought it really described anything especially true or thematically consistent in our stories. Bill Buford just dreamed it up to sell magazines in Britain. And it worked very, very well. We're still talking about it, aren't we? At the time— the middle Eighties—I had no books in print, and no readership. This wasn't true for the other writers in the 'Dirty Realism' issue. But it was true for me. And Bill's scheme helped me find a readership for my stories. I can't thank him enough.

Did you ever think of giving up at that time?
I certainly did. I thought that I'd had my shot at being a novelist and it hadn't worked out well enough. I went over to *Sports Illustrated* and asked for a job. But the guy who was running it told me no. He said I was a novelist (cruel irony), and that I couldn't be a sportswriter. So I went home and wrote *The Sportswriter*. But if he'd given me a job I'd almost assuredly have taken it and been very, very happy. I'd be retired now and have a big pension. It would've been a great life.

Tim Adams

It seemed to me natural to group you with Carver and Tobias Wolff as writers to the extent that you had some kind of shared interest in a sort of lonely or alienated masculinity. Where do you think that came from?
I never think about that. At our best (if I have a best—and certainly they do), our stories weren't that much alike. And frankly I can't think about my own characters in those rather cosseted, conventional terms—alienated, lonely, even masculine. I'm not interested in 'masculinity'. I'd be surprised if Ray or Toby would've said much different. But. I do know that I inherited much of my sense of what a story could be and be about from my reading—from Frank O'Connor, from Sherwood Anderson, from Faulkner, from Isaac Babel, from Flannery O'Connor—alas, from Hemingway, who seems influential in only the most superficial ways. So, that's where my first ideas came from.

You've lived longer than your father, do you catch yourself making his gestures, or have a keener impression of his life now you have reached and passed his age?
I look like my father. I sometimes feel my facial features arranging themselves into visages that I know are like his. The long Irish upper lip lapsing over the poor lower one in a state of puzzlement; my tendency to sigh at moments of frustration; the fierce swarm into anger; the tendency to strike out at something (or someone) that threatens me. I saw all this in him when he was in my life. And I accept them in myself—which isn't to say I glory in them. That said, I have a paler and paler recollection of him as time's gone on. And I feel the poorer for that. I liked him very much.

Do you think men are born with more ways to fail than women?
I don't know what that means. But, no. Women and men seem a lot more alike than they're given credit for. A lot of 'interests', of course, are deeply and perniciously invested in keeping them apart and distinct.

You have written about your love of hunting. Does it inform your writing?
It's certainly informed *some* stories—the ones that're expressly about hunting: 'Communist', 'Great Falls', 'Calling'. But in general I think

it's just been a thing I like to do that hasn't much informed my writing. I don't like to read hunting stories. 'Communist' I wrote back in 1984, only because Tom McGuane and I were out hunting partridge in Montana, and he told me he knew a guy who was preparing an anthology of hunting stories and if I ever wrote a hunting story I should send it to this guy. I never had before. But I did. And 'Communist' was it. I probably never wrote a better story than that. Go figure.

Tell me about your relationship with your Harley-Davidson; it feels like an escape clause?
When I got back to owning motorcycles, in the mid-Eighties, I used to say (in my boyish way) that a fellow needed to have something around that could kill him. And at heart, once we get past the snapshot visions of oneself astride the rakish machine, and the appeal of the sound of the thing, and the wind-in-your-hair imagery, and the hoped-for effect on women—once that's all gone by, I guess I still feel the way I did in the mid-Eighties.

You don't strike me as someone with a self-destructive urge though —not at all?
I don't think I have a self-destructive urge. But the prospect of one's eventual end is pretty firmly fixed in my brain. And I'd certainly like to think I held my fate in my own hands should I be struck by some withering disease. I remember when my mother died—of breast cancer—and Kristina and I were sitting on her bed, getting dressed for her funeral, the phone rang. And it was one of my mother's old Arkie cousins, from up in the sticks. This woman was just calling up to express her condolences, I guess. I had no idea who she was, just a scratchy voice on the phone, there in Little Rock. She said a few consoling things. And then she said—and this woman didn't know me; she said, 'Now, Rich-ard. Your mamma died of cancer. So, hon, you're gonna get it, too. Don't forget that.' 'Okay, I won't,' I said. 'Thanks.' Just a kind sober thought toward the future to penetrate one's grief.

What did you learn in writing and in life from Raymond Carver?
I did learn some things from Ray. Sometimes people ask me if he was my teacher; but he wasn't. He and I were close friends, and were colleagues. But he wasn't that much older than me—seven years. We

27

were pretty much contemporaries. Though it's seems strange that he's been gone now for nearly twenty years. But. One thing that may seem insignificant, but wasn't, was that his parents and my parents came from pretty much the same place—west Arkansas. His parents had gone out west, and mine had gone down south—for work. And from that coincidence, and from admiring Ray's early stories very much, and admiring his own instincts for writing them, I think I drew some corroborative strength that my own inherited storage of what was interesting and what a story could be was, in fact, valuable and credible. Ray and I enjoyed a kind of unspoken confidence that we came from the same stock—possibly rough stock.

Beyond that, his early stories and our friendship—which began as he was writing his second book—definitely encouraged me to try writing stories again myself. I'd quit writing stories in the Seventies because I just couldn't do it very well. But Ray's stories seemed so natural, almost easy (many people have thought that to their ruin), that I thought I'd try my hand at it again. And I did. At least a couple of the stories in *Rock Springs* bear signs of his stylistic influence. He always encouraged me to write stories, although I'm sure he felt confident he would always be better at it than I'd be.

He must've learned things from you as well, though?
I don't know what he could've learned from me. There might've been something. We were friends, we talked about work a lot. We had that confidence that came from our family background. And I'm sure I re-enforced his confidence about his work. I also had opinions about some of the stories in his book *What We Talk About When We Talk About Love*—all of which he showed me in early drafts. But most of what I didn't like he rejected and later chided me for. Although there was that story, I think it's 'A Small Good Thing', that I and others (the poet Donald Hall and Geoffrey Wolff, probably Toby, too) complained to him about. He'd shown that story to us in an early, much more fully developed form. And then he published it in a rather harshly curtailed form. And we all told Ray he should restore it to its fuller self when he collected it in a subsequent volume. And he did. His work was growing, his sentences getting longer, more complex, his sympathies and intellectual reach expanding. Tess [Gallagher, Carver's second wife] had a big influence on him—probably the

biggest influence. I think that I—and again I was just one of a few people he trusted—I just told him work was wonderful, and that was probably the most of it.

You shared an absolute commitment to the business of writing stories: have you always had that work ethic?
No. I haven't. I always wished I had it—from an early age. But I didn't for a long time. It—the work ethic—just arrived during the summer of 1963, when I was nineteen. I'm not sure where it came from. I was working on the Missouri Pacific Railroad as a switchman, and making lots of money and having a pretty happy life. I was supposed to go to college in the autumn, and was giving thought to just staying working on the railroad. But I ended up going to school, instead.

Maybe seeing those working guys I spent my days with made an impression on me; or maybe it was that I wanted to impress Kristina. I don't really know. But when I got to school, in Michigan, I was just a changed boy. Whatever thresholds I'd not ventured to cross—with regard to my studies, for instance—I just barged across. And it's been that way ever since. But I should say—about myself and about a work ethic—it's pretty boring. That's why we associate the 'ethic' with Protestants, who're also pretty boring. It may lead one on to good, but it doesn't feel like much of a virtue, frankly.

A work ethic story, though. When I was in college I lived with a guy named Tom Candee, who's now a veterinarian not far from where I live—down in Massachusetts. And every term our grades came out, and Candee used to laugh at me—rail at me, really. He used to say, 'Look at Ford, he got all As, but had to worked like a pig to get it. Whereas me, I got all As and never turned a hand. I'm smart. He's not.' We eventually came to pretty serious blows, Candee and me, because that used to get under my skin real bad. But the truth was he was right. I did work like a pig. He barely lifted a hand. So, to me, a work ethic has always been a kind of blue-collar trait, something I have to embrace to do anything that's worthwhile—but spectacularly inferior to being able to waltz through life. I am, however, glad not to be a veterinarian.

I remember talking to Kazuo Ishiguro and he said he imagined the rest of his life in terms of how many novels he would be lucky

enough to complete, if he spent, as was his habit, five or six years on each. Do you have a powerful sense of finite time?

Well, the return on Ish's investment is quite wonderful, isn't it? So his attitude puts a much better burnish on those working virtues than I can hope to put. I suppose I do share a sense of finite time, all right. But I don't measure it in terms of how many novels I'll write, or might write. I agree that to get to write a novel at all is very, very lucky—to get to do one's best, to get to do what Dostoevsky and Faulkner did, to try to contribute good to the life of people you don't know. All that's a great privilege. But every time I finish a novel, or a book (and I've only finished nine), I ask myself if this isn't enough now. I've given this last effort—whatever it was—my very best. I've held back nothing. Have I not perhaps gone along this course as far as I can go? Are my returns not likely to begin to diminish? Could I really have anything as important as this to write again? Someday, I assume, my answer will be, 'Yes, this *is* enough.' I don't see writing as a profession, something I'm married to forever. I have to reinvent it every time. And I also see that there's more to life than writing. I see that portrayed in other people's lives all the time. I'm as curious about that as I ever was.

The greatest short story writers it seems to me are those with the clearest sense of an ending. Do you always know when you are done?
Yes, I always know when a story's finished. And I hope that makes me one of the greatest short story writers—if that's what it takes.

There's a line you once used: 'Your life is the blueprint you make after the building is built.' How do you think your own blueprint will look when the time comes?
Sketchy. Whatever there is of good in it is either private—something I shared with Kristina—or else it's all gone into what I've written. That seems just fine. □

GRANTA

OPERATION
Chimamanda Ngozi Adichie

L agos in June is steamy. But that Thursday afternoon at the *Champion* newspaper office, I did not notice how difficult it was to breathe or how the air was like a hot, moist blanket. I swaggered and smiled, too full of a sense of accomplishment. I had just had my collection of watery poetry published by a vanity press in London. I was doing my first newspaper interview. I was nineteen years old.

Kate, the woman who interviewed me, was squat, friendly, full of praise for the poems although she had not read them. After the questions—Where do you get your inspiration? Do you write indoors or outdoors?—she told me I was a role model for young Nigerians. I glowed. She took me downstairs to have my picture taken in a wide room that smelled of chemicals. Matt photographs were plastered on the wall. Most of them were of prominent people—Fela, Abacha, Gani—but it was the more mundane subjects, beggars under bridges and children playing football and soldiers by the roadsides, that I stopped to admire.

'They put up the best on the wall,' Kate said.

Later, as we left, I turned to glance again at the wall of photographs and that was when I saw it, the photo of Nnamdi. I may have let out a sound, I may have only shivered, but Kate noticed and asked if something was wrong.

I pointed. 'I knew him,' I said.

Kate shook her head in the way people do to show sympathy. 'Oh, sorry, sorry. It was an operation at the bank just across the road,' she said.

I remember the splashes of blood on Nnamdi's face, his head slumped against the front seat of the car; the blood was a deep grey in the black-and-white photo.

A t my university secondary school in Nsukka, there were two groups of students. The staff group, which I belonged to, was made up of students whose parents were university lecturers, who lived on the campus and had little money and spoke good English. The other group was the Omata. They came mostly from Onitsha and the name *Omata* somehow conjured the chaos of that large commercial town. Their parents were rich, illiterate traders; they lived in the dormitories and often missed the first week of term. Most of us staff students thought, smugly, that they aspired to be like us: their parents had sent them to our school so that our university polish would rub off on them after all. We mimicked their mixed-up tenses and their saying *SH* for *CH*: *sit down on that sheer*. We laughed at their poor grades, their bush manners. We mocked their bluster. And, secretly, we coveted what they had: the gold watches that we saw only on the wrists of adults, the priceless gullibility of uneducated parents, the imported sandals that cost more than our families made in a month.

Nnamdi owned such sandals; his were a sparkly brown, almost orange, and had wedge heels. Nnamdi was an archetype of the unrefined Omata student, down to his inelegant swaying-to-the-side strut and his trousers pulled halfway up his belly. Of course this made him unsuitable for me, particularly since I was an academic star of sorts, and of course I found him terribly attractive.

Nnamdi was in Form 4, a popular senior student, while I was in Form 2, a junior student. Still, he must have thought me intimidating because it was his friends who called me at first to say, '*Ima*, Nnamdi really likes you.' I was noncommittal, tough because I was expected to be. Finally, he came himself. I wish I remembered the first day I talked to him, or what we said. I remember his walking me home after school, though, and his saying very little. I knew him because he was the kind of student everybody knew and I had always thought him to be larger than life, taller than life. But there he was, shy beside me, looking down as we walked, reduced to a nervously solemn wreck. He had the strangest voice, so hoarse and scratchy it was barely audible, a voice that earned him a lot of jokes and that I would later fondly ape. That day, his shy muttering made it difficult to understand even the little that he said. I was attracted to this shyness. I was attracted, too, to his height; I barely reached his chest and there was something protective about his being so tall.

He took to walking me home. He took to calling me GB, like most of my family and friends. '*Bikonu*, please, GB, I want you to be my wife,' he said nearly every day, in Igbo. And I would say, in English, with a thoroughly false coolness, 'I have to think about it,' even though I wanted nothing more than to be his girlfriend. I have come to reject the rituals of pretence that females are taught to practise in courtship: to say no when we mean yes, to be bashful and evasive, to coat our intelligence in coyness. Yet pretence was magical during those weeks

33

when I said no although I meant yes. Nnamdi 'chased' me for a long time. Later, he would tease me about how I gave him a high jump to scale. I like to think now that he knew how much I liked him, from the beginning, and that we were both equal participants in the ritual.

The afternoon I said yes, we were standing in front of our garage and he went over and plucked a flower—one of my mother's carefully preserved yellow roses—and held it out to me.

'What is this for?' I asked sharply. (I had said yes, but it didn't mean I was no longer tough.)

'A sign. I won't leave until you take it.'

'I won't take it until you tell me what it means.'

We went back and forth until Nnamdi said, in English, 'It means love,' and I took the flower and he added, 'If your mother asks who plucked it, say you don't know.'

I left the *Champion* office and sat in a hot taxi and looked at Lagos inching past the window, the hawkers pressing sunglasses against my window, the buses spitting out thick, grey smoke, the cars stuck bumper to bumper in traffic.

'See this stupid man! He wan scratch me!' my taxi driver said, gesturing to the car beside us. Then he stuck his head out and cursed in rapid Yoruba.

I sat back, silent and sweating, and thought of Kate's words, of how we Nigerians used the word *operation* to refer to armed robberies and how it had taken on an ominous pallor. Buses were stopped and people killed in *operations* on the Benin–Lagos expressway. Houses were broken into in night-time *operations*. Banks were raided in *operations*. One Christmas when we were travelling to our home town, Abba, our driver made a dangerous U-turn in the middle of the expressway. 'There is an operation in front!' he said, and my mother praised him for being so quick. Other cars were turning as well and we heard gunshots and, soon after, the swift crunch of metal as two of the cars collided.

My taxi driver had stopped cursing and asked what I had been doing in the *Champion* newspaper office. 'Wonderful!' he said when I told him. 'Small aunty like you can write book. Well done!'

I thanked him. But my earlier glow was gone, my poetry forgotten. I was trying instead to remember what I had felt, to describe it to myself, when I saw the photo of the dead person on the wall and realized that it was Nnamdi.

My friends, my smug staff friends, were appalled by how much time Nnamdi and I spent together. Could he even make one decent English sentence? What did we talk about? they wanted to know. Even I hardly know now. He made me laugh. We kissed with me standing on the short steps in our backyard so that we could be the same height. We fought about things I no longer remember and sometimes, when I pretended to be angrier than I was, he would threaten to throw himself in the path of a car or to kneel, in apology, at the entrance of my class. He would say this so earnestly that I would laugh and laugh. Just as I laughed when he suggested we go to a *dibia* to do the *igba ndu*, a blood betrothal of sorts that would keep us from ever breaking up. I was not familiar with this; the people in my world did not do things like the *igba ndu* rite, they sniffed at the supernatural and had sanitized engagements when the time was right. But the simplicity of Nnamdi's faith intrigued me. Nnamdi intrigued me. I did not tell my friends that I had heard stories of his stealing money from his father, bribing test questions from teachers, getting drunk in town. Or that he never seemed to study or take exams. Or that he told the most charmingly transparent lies. Once, after he missed an exam, he said, 'As I was walking to school, I tripped and broke my leg and had to be taken to hospital, but they mended the leg right away and so I didn't need a cast or bandage. You can ask Ojay if you don't believe me.'

Ojay, his friend, corroborated this story and added that he had taken Nnamdi to hospital himself. Years later, when Ojay told me that Nnamdi had died, I remembered how people used to taunt him and call him Nnamdi's houseboy, Nnamdi's errand boy. It was Ojay who delivered Nnamdi's letters to me. It was Ojay who wrote them, too, until I refused to read any more unless Nnamdi wrote them himself. So in the following letters, I could see that Ojay had written in pencil first and then Nnamdi's shaky hand in ink had carefully gone over every word. It was Ojay who brought Nnamdi's red sweater and gave it to me one cold harmattan morning. 'Nnamdi thinks you look cold,' he said. And I slipped my arms, my self, into that huge red sweater and felt safe. When the bitter harmattan morning had given way to a sunny afternoon, I still wore that sweater. Never mind that sweat had collected in my armpits.

Before I went to the *Champion* office that June day, I knew Nnamdi was dead. Ojay had already told me some months before. 'Something happened to Nnamdi,' he had said. His eyes did not meet mine as he told me that Nnamdi had just been at the wrong place at the wrong time, that the operation was over, the armed robbers had finished stealing from the bank, but Nnamdi happened to have parked his car in such a way that he blocked their getaway. I didn't cry that day after Ojay told me. It seemed so distant, so unlikely, and I had not seen him in years, but as I walked past Freedom Square I stared at the grassy plains where, during the weeks of 'chasing' me, Nnamdi once bought me a whole pack of *suya* at a bazaar and then ended up giving it to a friend because he was too shy to give it to me.

It was in the taxi from the *Champion* office that I began to cry. I thought about the last time I had seen him. It was at a beach in Lagos and he was riding a horse and we had not seen each other since his father transferred him to another secondary school. We were both self-consciously, unconvincingly mature about things at first. He said he was trying to get into the University of Lagos. I said I was preparing to take my final secondary school exams. He had not changed; the tall, thin body, the narrow face and hooked nose, the hoarse voice were all the same.

'Do you have a boyfriend?' he asked finally.

'Yes,' I replied, although I did not.

He had a girlfriend, too, he said, many girlfriends in fact. Before we parted, he added, 'You can have as many boyfriends as you want to. But when it comes to marriage, it's me and nobody else. God made you for me. If we marry other people, thunder will strike us down.'

We were no longer young teenagers, we were old enough to be truly separated by our different interests, but he spoke with that old earnestness on his face and I laughed.

On my birthday, the last birthday before Nnamdi left my school, he gave me a scented satin rose in a gilded case. I hid it from my mother: it looked expensive and I feared she would ask me to return it right away. Later, when he gave me a ring, with gold strips that curved across my finger, I hid that too and wore it only in school. But I did not hide the card he brought when I was sick with malaria. It looked like an ordinary get-well card, one of the many my friends had sent. When you opened Nnamdi's card, though, it sang: an upbeat take on *Für Elise*. Inside the card, Nnamdi had written in his unformed, childish hand, 'To my one love GB. From your own Nnamdi.'   □

In memoriam: Nnamdi Ezenwa

THE TIMES

Cheltenham Literature Festival

5-14 October 2007

in association with

Waterstone's

Including:

Pat Barker
Stephen Bayley
Tony Benn
Simon Callow
Jonathan Coe
Douglas Coupland
Roddy Doyle
Terry Eagleton
Anthony Grayling
Germaine Greer
Christopher Hampton
Lucy Hawking
Stephen Hawking
Eric Hobsbawm
Armando Iannucci
Naomi Klein
Hermione Lee
Andrew Marr
Yann Martel
Blake Morrison
Michael Ondaatje
David Starkey
Juliet Stevenson
Claire Tomalin
Jeanette Winterson
Michael Wood
and
Margaret Atwood
via LongPen videolink

QUESTION · DEBATE · DISCOVER · ENGAGE · ENJOY

?
& !

ESTABLISHED IN 1949

**Box Office
01242 227979**

www.cheltenhamfestivals.com

Charity Number 251765

GRANTA

THE VIRGIN
OF ESMERALDAS
Nell Freudenberger

Nell Freudenberger

Onomatopoeia Poem
By Marisol Hernández

My stepmother is a witch.
She's the devil,
Even though she doesn't
Have a tail.

La Cuca:
Where other people have brains,
She has rusty
Nails.

She looks ugly
Because she's all rotted up inside
Like apples you get
From the cafeteria.

I wish my stepmother
Lived in North Korea
I'm sorry this poem doesn't have a
Onomatopoeia.

She wrote that a long time ago, last year, before her dad and La Cuca left for Ecuador. Her stepsister, Sandra, was still living with Jon Emmanuel then, and Marisol had her own room. Everything was okay until Marisol accidentally broke a china cup with a rose on it that her stepmother had brought with her from DR. The cup was special, for some reason, and if La Cuca hadn't been such a bitch about it, Marisol might have said sorry. But when she wouldn't say sorry, her stepmother had told her father, who'd beaten her (but only with a jump rope). La Cuca had watched the whole thing, and then she'd said that Marisol was lucky, because when *she* was a kid, her dad used to hit her with a bike chain. That was when Marisol had really lost it, and called her stepmother a *mamaciyalla*.

The next day, when Marisol got home from school, there was a line of blue tape on the floor, in and out like steps. Her dad's room and the living room were on one side of the line, and Marisol's room was on the other. Marisol could go into the kitchen and the bathroom, but she couldn't go into her dad's room or even into the living room to watch TV. When she told her dad that was crazy, he said she was lucky he hadn't kicked her out, calling her stepmother something like that.

'What the fuck?' she said, when Chewy got home that night (but quietly, because she knew when her dad was kidding, and this time she was pretty sure he wasn't). 'What is that?' And Chewy said, 'That's painter's tape,' and showed her how you could use it to make a straight line on the wall. You could pull it up and it didn't even leave a mark. Chewy sometimes worked for an Italian guy named Enrico who had a painting business, and that night in bed, on her side of the line, Marisol had thought about where La Cuca could've gotten the tape. But Chewy had looked so sorry while he was explaining, and she knew that even if he had given it to her, he couldn't have known what it was for.

Something like that would never have happened before her *tía* left them. It was her *tía* who first told her about El Cuco, the monster who stole children in the night. (Her aunt had laughed, when Marisol gave that name to her stepmother, even though she pretended to scold her.) Now that her *tía* had moved away, Marisol had no one to talk to, and maybe that was why she sometimes ended up telling things to Ms Reese. When Ms Reese heard that story (about the tape, not about what Marisol had called her stepmother, since she couldn't explain to her teacher that kind of Dominican word) she gave Marisol her cellphone number and said she could call any time she wanted to talk. Not that Marisol would ever call, but it was sweet, especially since she knew Ms Reese didn't do that for everyone. If someone was sweet like that, you could guarantee that they would leave. Ms Reese had gotten married in August; she had said she would be back after her honeymoon, and then she had never come back.

There had been a picture on Ms Reese's desk of her fiancé, who looked kind of Dominican but wasn't. He was Indian, like Rohanie. Except Rohanie said she wasn't Indian, she was from the West Indies—totally different. All the teachers at the school were white,

41

except for Mr Lee and Ms Wilson (who were new), and all the students were not. And how fucked up was that?

Those were the kinds of things Marisol used to think about, last year, but it was almost Christmas and she had bigger problems now. Number one: the camera. Chewy had paid $200 for a digital camera, so that they could take pictures of the house her dad and La Cuca were building in Ecuador. ('You from Ecuador?' Héctor asked her by the lockers yesterday. She told him to fuck off, she was from DR like him, but she could see how he got confused.) They were going for ten days at Christmas, and she wanted to take a couple of pictures at school to show to her dad when she got there. Yesterday was Red Carpet Day, everyone dressed up at school, and so Chewy'd said yes to the camera. He was nice like that, especially when Sandra wasn't around.

How could she have lost her brother's camera? She called Chewy her brother, even though he was only a half-brother. A half-brother was something, but a stepsister was nothing because you didn't share any blood. Thank God—she wouldn't want to share a drop with La Cucita, even if she was pretty. *Dos tetas tiran más que dos carretas*, was what her *tía* said, and then Chewy said, *El pelo de cuca jala más que un tractor*, which was funny until you thought of what it meant. It meant that Sandra's thing was pulling at Chewy—or at least that he had thought about it—nasty either way, even if Chewy and Sandra didn't share a single drop of blood.

She knew where she'd left the camera, on the bench at the bus stop: she remembered in the middle of first-period biology. Everyone was doing their Unit Two Quiz that was really a test (Mr Lee called all his tests 'quizzes' for some reason) and so she went up to the teacher's desk and whispered what happened. Mr Lee was skinny and wore checked shirts and was Chinese. Marisol gave him her best Red Carpet smile.

'It's only two stops,' she said. 'Maybe it's still there.'

'Miss Hernández, you know I can't allow you to leave school grounds. Why are you wasting your time?'

He called them Miss this and Mr that—as if he thought he was being funny, instead of just fake. 'It's an emergency. My brother's going to kill me. I'll be dead tomorrow, I'm serious. Think of how bad you'll feel.'

Mr Lee smiled in a way that did not make her hopeful. 'I'll have to take that chance. You only have twenty minutes left for the quiz, so I suggest that you sit down and finish it. Unless you've already finished?'

Fake, like that.

Ángel, who she usually liked, made a wildman face at her and shook his head back and forth. 'Fuckface,' she said.

'That's a yellow card, Miss Hernández,' Mr Lee said, and Ángel whispered something to Chanelle, who laughed. Mr Lee didn't even look at them! She wanted to smack them both. They were laughing because of her dress. Yellow card, yellow dress—ha, ha, very funny. It was her *quinceañera* dress, and it didn't exactly fit in the butt. She'd gained some weight, because all they ever ate was KFC, because Sandra basically lived with her boyfriend now and she was the one who could cook. Once Marisol had cooked, rice with *plátanos*, and Sandra had come home the next day and looked at the leftovers in the fridge and been like, *'What* is this?' And Chewy didn't say anything, even though he'd eaten two plates of it.

3) Define CAMOUFLAGE, giving one example of an organism that uses this strategy to survive.

She could picture the bench with the camera on it. The camera was a small silver box, and the plastic side of the bus stop was cracked, someone had smashed it and taken out the poster. Or maybe the city had taken out the poster so they could fix the plastic? Except they hadn't fixed it, and so the light came through and made patterns on the bench.

Maybe those patterns on the bench would camouflage the camera and keep it hidden from thieves? She could picture herself getting off the bus and seeing the camera still there. Or maybe she would get off the bus and the camera would be gone, but there would be a guy sitting there, young, without any beard or moustache—a cute black guy named Sean, who didn't go to Bronx Prep or know anybody she knew, and he would say, 'Hey, baby—lose something?' And she'd be like, 'Yeah, my brother's camera.' And he'd pull it out of the pocket of his parka. 'Then I'm waiting on you, baby,' he'd say, and then he'd ask her out to Pizzeria Uno.

4) Name three ASEXUAL methods of reproduction. Describe the
stages in the reproductive cycle of *Sarsia gemmifera*.

Sandra had sniffed her cooking, cussed her out, and made fun of
her jeans, but those weren't the worst things. That stuff was like
sisters—or so she heard, from people who actually had sisters. The
worst was one night when she came home from a basketball game—
their team, the Panthers, was playing Morris Heights down the
block—and she'd found all the lights out except for Chewy's room.
She wasn't supposed to bust in there without knocking, but the
Panthers had won and her then-but-not-any-more crush Ahmed had
scored twenty-three points.

'Guess what—' she started, and stopped, because Chewy wasn't
in there alone. For a second she froze, because he really would
murder her if she busted in on him and a girl, and then she realized
it was only Sandra. But that was weird too, because there was just
one, pinkish light on by Chewy's bed, and there was *bachata* on his
stereo, and they were both sitting on the bed, Chewy's back against
the wall and Sandra leaning up against him. When she saw Marisol,
Sandra didn't roll her eyes or cuss her out or anything; she just curled
up more and put her face in Chewy's chest, so that all you could see
was her soft, not at all kinky, Miss-Clairol-Burnished-Copper brown
hair. Marisol just stood there, and the worst was the way Chewy
lifted his left hand, careful not to disturb Sandra, and flicked it at
her, like a mosquito: Get Out. In the morning everything was exactly
the same, except that Sandra made eggs for all three of them and
when Marisol said she was sick to her stomach, nobody minded or
made her eat. That was when she really did start to feel sick.

The bell rang, and she started to write in the answer for one of
them at least. He was trying to trick them with that *Sarsia* stuff—
but they'd gone over it a million times, and everyone knew that
Sarsia gemmifera was just a jellyfish. Mr Lee said, 'Pencils down,'
looking at her, and so she stopped and picked up the fake quiz/real
test and crumpled it into a ball.

'Miss Hernández,' he said, but she ignored him.

'Oooh,' said Stephanie. 'You're in trouble, *Miss Hernández*.'

And so she just tossed the test into the trash can. She missed, but
she didn't go back for it. Let the Chink pick it up.

It was raining when they got to Ecuador and Marisol couldn't believe it, because she'd been picturing it for so long in the sun. In fact she'd been picturing DR without realizing it, and so the little airport in Esmeraldas was a surprise. She and Sandra stood and waited with mostly white people (everyone else had family) while Chewy went to look for their dad and the car. Sandra was wearing a white tank top with pink sequinned straps, and she had changed out of her boots in the terminal. Now she was wearing white leather sandals with a pattern of tiny holes, a wedge heel and a buckle. She'd gotten a pedicure, and her toenails were the colour of tangerines.

'Are you excited to see your dad?'

That was another annoying thing Sandra did: she spoke English to Marisol when they were in public, as if she'd been born in the Bronx instead of in DR. Now they were in Ecuador and she was still doing it, like she cared what the stupid tourists thought. Sandra had light skin and soft hair, and she was skinny like an advertisement model, but if she thought any gringo was going to mistake her for a white girl, Marisol had news for her.

'Are you excited to see your mom?' Marisol shot back in Spanish, just to annoy her.

Sandra sighed. 'Not really.' Marisol could understand that— because who would be glad to see La Cuca?—but she kept quiet. Chewy had promised to tell their father about the camera right away and Marisol was trying to imagine what his face would be like when he got out of the car.

Finally she saw her father and Chewy (La Cuca must've decided to stay at home) pulling up in a line of cars. They were driving a white Jeep that looked a little beat up, but was still a Jeep, and at first Marisol couldn't see her father's face through the windshield. Then Chewy rolled down the passenger window, and her father took off his sunglasses and leaned across Chewy and waved. Marisol was relieved and at the same time her stomach sank, because clearly Chewy hadn't told him.

'Hey!' her father called. He got out of the car and kissed Sandra, and then he gave Marisol a big hug. 'My baby.' He smelled different, like coconut oil, and he was wearing a wilder shirt than he would've at home, unbuttoned to the white undershirt.

'Like it?' he said, indicating the car.

'It's okay,' Sandra said, but she smiled.

'Your mother's waiting at the house—she hates driving these roads,' her father told Sandra, even though she hadn't asked.

Then he asked if anyone was hungry, and they all were except for Sandra, who was feeling sick after the plane. They drove for a little while on a good road (better than in DR), and there was a Quik Mart, and a Sunshine car rental, and also palm trees and green mountains in the distance. They stopped at a restaurant next to a gas station that her father said had the best *arroz con pollo*—Marisol's favourite. The restaurant had polished wooden tables and open sides, and behind it you could see some shacks with corrugated roofs, surrounded by bare, dusty ground. Marisol watched the rain freckling the dust, and then the freckles blending together into patches of mud, until the ground was more mud than dust. The food took longer to come than in New York, and while they were eating it really started to rain, so that the water ran in unbroken streams from the roof. The water was like a smashed windshield; you couldn't see anything past it except for splintered green, and then two wet, white chickens came inside from the dirt around the shacks and starting pecking at the concrete underneath the tables.

'Watch out,' Chewy told Marisol. 'You're probably eating his brother.'

Sandra groaned and put her hand on her stomach. She was drinking a Fanta that was making her tongue orange—to match her toenails, Marisol thought.

All of a sudden her father pushed his plate away and took a big drink of his beer. 'Let's see the car,' he said. And Chewy looked at Marisol, because the pictures of the car that he was thinking of buying were on the camera that Marisol had lost.

Chewy smiled (did he want to torture her?) and then he reached into his backpack and pulled out a camera. Not the same camera, because that had been small and square, and this one was a little bigger and rounder, but her father didn't know the difference. Chewy started showing pictures of the car he was thinking of getting, from the auto body place right around the corner from her school, with all the fancy hubcaps on the wall above the driveway. Her father was talking about cars again, not paying attention, and Chewy looked up and winked at her. You could tell Sandra didn't know about the camera, because she gave Marisol a funny look, and the fact that Chewy hadn't told her made Marisol almost as happy as the fact that he had saved her ass.

Her father paid for all of them, and they were about to get up when he said, 'Where are the pictures of the school?'

That gave Marisol gooseflesh, but it was easy enough. 'I forgot.'

'Red Carpet Day,' her father said, and she couldn't believe he remembered what she'd told him on the phone. Now she really wished she could show him the picture of her friends posing against the lockers in their long satin dresses.

'She took it to school, but then she forgot to take the pictures,' Chewy said, shaking his head. 'Girls.'

'There were a lot of cameras.'

'So how could you forget?' Sandra said suddenly, as they left the restaurant. The rain had stopped, but the parking lot had turned into a lake of mud.

'It stopped,' Chewy said, looking up. 'Maybe it's clearing up.'

'It rains this time every day,' their father said. 'Tropical climate.'

'You must've thought of it, when everyone else started taking pictures?' Sandra insisted.

'I thought of it, but there wasn't any time. By the time we took everyone else's pictures—'

'Oh,' Sandra said, stretching it out as if she'd just understood something.

'What?'

'Nothing.'

'I know how it is,' Sandra said. 'Girls are bitches—try to forget them.'

Marisol's words came out a hiss: 'I was in *everybody's* pictures. All of them. It was Stephanie, Jasmine, me and Yolanda and you should've heard the boys. They're all like, *Hey, check out the Dominican bitches—they mad hot.*'

'Okay, Mami,' Sandra said. And then in English, laughing, 'Calm down.'

Her father had said that the house was in the country, right near the beach. He said that Ecuador was warm all the time, like DR but better, and that the air smelled like the ocean. Marisol would sit in her room at home (which was still full of Sandra's things, even after her stepsister had gone to live with Jon Emmanuel) and imagine the room that was getting built for her here in Ecuador. In her imagination, you opened a pair of fancy white blinds and you were looking at the sea.

It was true that the house was in the country. There were trees all around, including some very strange ones with leaves so big that when they fell on the ground you wanted to pick them up and save them. There was a man who came and swept them away each morning; Marisol hadn't seen him, but the sound was the first thing she heard when she woke up in the morning: *scorch, scorch, scorch.*

You couldn't see the road (at least from the front of the house), but Marisol also couldn't see the ocean anywhere; she couldn't even smell it. She had told all her friends at school that the house was going to have two storeys, and when the Jeep pulled up she had to pretend not to be disappointed. Her father explained that the house was 'behind schedule', and that it was the fault of somebody named Miguel. Because of Miguel, there was only a flat concrete roof where the second storey should be, with stacks of concrete blocks. Even worse, you could see La Cuca lying up there in her green bathing suit, on a plastic chair, listening to Sergio Vargas on an old tape-player.

On the second day they drove to the beach. It took forty minutes, because the roads were bad, but their father said that it was really ten, as soon as the government fixed the road. At first Sandra said she wasn't going to go, because she didn't like to lie in the sun, and then La Cuca said she wouldn't go either, because of the road—and for a minute Marisol thought they were going to have the best day, just the three of them at the beach. She had wished for her *tía*, who would've been up early, making tortillas and chicken to take with them in the car. Of course, that was her *tía* in the past, before she left them; the now-*tía* lived with her daughter Patricia in Texas, where the warm weather might keep the cancer from coming back into her breasts.

When Sandra heard that her mother would stay at the house with her, she changed her mind, and so they all ended up going together.

'Do you want to borrow a razor?' Sandra asked, when they were lying under the umbrella on the sand. Her father and La Cuca had gone for a walk, and Chewy was way out in the flat, sparkling water, just a black dot. The beach was nice, she had to admit. They were the only ones there, except for a fisherman at the very end, casting from the beach, and a thin white bird standing on one leg in the foamy edge of the surf. There was a huge boulder at either end of the cove, all grown over with spiky green weeds; beneath the boulders were black rocks, probably full of tiny pools where you could find crabs and sand dollars. Marisol had thought about exploring those rocks, but instead she'd decided to stay on the beach with Sandra. Now she regretted her choice.

'No thanks. I don't shave.'

Sandra rolled over on her elbow: she was wearing a pair of huge tinted glasses with tiny rhinestones in the corners, and a long pink cover-up over her bathing suit. 'Don't the other girls shave?'

Usually Sandra liked to show off her body; her stepsister was obviously wearing that cover-up because there wasn't anyone else on the beach.

'No.' Jasmine didn't shave, and neither did Stephanie R; Yolanda did, of course, and so did Stephanie G. 'Not all of them.'

Sandra took off her glasses and looked at Marisol's legs, and so Marisol looked at them too: she hadn't noticed how dry her skin had gotten, a white and flaky layer on top of the brown. It didn't help that she'd gotten about a hundred mosquito bites last night in her room, but it had been too hot not to open the windows.

'At least use some sunscreen.'

'No thanks,' Marisol said. 'I don't need it.'

'You think you can't burn, just because you're dark?'

Marisol got up from the blanket. 'I'm taking a walk,' she said. 'See you.'

Sandra sighed and took out a magazine. 'Just don't come crying to me.'

It was one or two o'clock and there was no shade anywhere. The tide was as far out as it could go, and the only waves were little lapping ones that broke right on the beach. When she got to the boulder, she saw right away that it wasn't climbable: it had steep, slippery sides, dark grey with streaks of red and white. It was surrounded by smaller, sharper rocks that you could walk on, black and chunky as broken asphalt, but full of those scooped-out hidden pools.

Marisol cupped her hand over her eyes and picked her way out on the rocks. She could see the tiny crabs, only cockroach-sized, with red and yellow markings on their backs. If you were patient, and looked hard at the crevices between the rocks, you could find the bigger, greener ones, moving in their wave-like way: still for minutes at a time, and then hurling themselves all of a sudden sideways into the cracks.

She was going to try to wave to Chewy (she hadn't even had a chance to tell him thank you for the camera) and she got out almost to the furthest point of the rocks before she stepped on something sharp. She cried out and lifted up her foot, so she was balancing like one of those white birds. She turned to see if her stepsister was laughing at her, but Sandra was lying on her back with the magazine closed on her stomach: she had fallen asleep.

Marisol crouched down and looked at her foot. The cut was deep, and she couldn't believe how red her blood was: beautiful, the way it spread in its own bubble, refusing to mix with the water even when she dipped it in the pool. The cut stung, but it was all right once she sat down (the rocks dug into her butt and the backs of her thighs) and squeezed the sides of the foot, sole up. Now she could see something black in there, sticking out of the skin. Beside her on the rocks was a pair of black mussels growing out of the same spot, with streaks of white and bright blue at their base. One of the shells was cracked, missing a piece, and that was what had gone into her foot.

Was it possible to die in the middle of the day, in sight of two of your family members, at least one of whom gave a shit about you? The possibility made her heart speed up, and everything around her looked a little brighter. Sitting like this on the rocks, she was too low to see Chewy any more, and Sandra hadn't moved from her position on the blanket. Even if Chewy swam in, and Sandra woke up, and she sat here waving frantically, the two of them might ignore her, thinking she was calling them for some childish reason—to come and look at crabs on the rocks.

A pair of hands appeared just a few feet from where she was sitting, and she heard a low, rumbling noise. Marisol screamed—she couldn't help it—and then there was deep, delighted laughter, and Chewy's head popped up over the rocks. 'I'm coming to kidnap the princess,' he said. 'And take her away on the *Black Pearl*.'

'I hate you,' Marisol said. 'Look at my foot.'

Chewy hoisted himself up, as if it were only the side of a swimming pool. 'What're you doing all the way out here?' he said.

'I thought you were on the beach with Sandra.'

'I couldn't stand it any more,' Marisol said. 'She's disgusting.'

Chewy's legs were dark like the rest of him (like Marisol) and they were covered with black hair. Her brother wasn't handsome exactly (he was too short, and his face was too wide) but she knew that girls liked him.

'It's hard on Sandra,' Chewy said. 'You should try to be nice to her.'

'What's hard?'

'With her mother. They're having a fight.'

'She better watch it. You don't want to fight with La Cuca.'

Chewy grinned. She loved it when she could make him laugh.

'*You* better watch it.' Her brother took her foot in his hand: the place where the shell had gone in wasn't bleeding so much any more, but the skin around it had turned white.

'We've gotta get this out.'

'Don't touch it!'

'Okay, okay. Jesus, don't be such a baby. There look—Dad's coming back with your favourite person.'

Marisol looked, and while she was looking Chewy pinched the piece of shell and yanked it out. She screamed for real this time, but she was relieved too. Sandra sat up on the beach.

'Come on,' Chewy said. 'Now we have to swim.'

'Are you kidding?'

'That's the best way for you to get in, with your foot. Anyway, you could use the exercise.'

'What if there's a *Sarsia gemmifera*?'

'A what?'

'Or a rip tide?'

'I can almost stand here,' Chewy said. 'Believe me, you'll be fine.'

That night they left her alone. They were all downstairs at the table, drinking Pilsener—here you drank Pilsener, not Presidente—all except for Sandra, who never drank beer because it made you fat. Marisol was in the back, in her dad and La Cuca's room, where the TV was. She was watching a Mexican *telenovela* she hadn't seen before, but it was pretty easy to figure out. The young bride, Virginia, had inherited a lot of money from her dead husband, the General, and everyone was trying to get it away from her except for her one, loyal friend, the doctor's wife, who was terminally ill. The other problem was that Virginia was falling in love with the doctor, who was cheating on his sick wife with a slutty girl named Olga.

Olga was flirting with the doctor, and Marisol could guess what was going to happen next, when her stepmother knocked on the door. That was weird, since it was La Cuca's room, and if anyone should've asked permission to be in there, it was Marisol.

'Maritza? Honey? We're going out for a bit.'

Marisol looked for the mute button, but the stupid Ecuadorian TV didn't have one. Her stepmother came into the room.

'Oh—is this *La Esposa Virgen*? I love this one.' Her stepmother watched for a minute, until Marisol could feel herself getting even redder underneath her sunburn. She wondered if La Cuca could tell she was a virgin, just by looking at her, and whether Sandra could.

'Who's going out?' Marisol asked, to distract her stepmother from the television.

'Your father and me and Raúl and Sandra.'

It was stupid the way she called Chewy Raúl, as if she were his mother.

'Going where?'

'Down the road, to a restaurant. We'll be right nearby.'

'But we already ate.'

'To have a few drinks. Your father and I always go there. We'll take you for lunch one day.'

'You're all going without me?'

Her stepmother looked at Marisol as if she were ashamed of everything about her, including her bandaged foot, and her sunburn and the mosquito bites on her legs. 'You can't walk.'

It was true that her foot was swollen underneath the bandage, and that the only shoes she could wear were a pair of big pink slippers of La Cuca's, but she could walk, especially if Chewy helped her.

'And anyway, I don't want you going to a bar—especially here. You're too young.' She looked at the TV, now shut down. 'If you sit and watch this, and then the next one, we'll be back before it's over.'

'I have homework,' Marisol said. 'I can't just sit around watching TV.' She did have homework, since this vacation was longer than their actual break, but this was the first time it had occurred to her to do any of it. She couldn't believe they were going out without her.

La Cuca laughed. 'What a good girl.' Then she kissed Marisol on the head, and said, 'There's some shampoo in the bathroom, if you want to wash your hair.' The house was supposed to have three bathrooms, but so far there was only one.

'What if someone breaks in?'

'That's why we have Pedro. Haven't you seen him? He's the guard.'

'The guy who sweeps in the morning?'

'He watches all the houses on this road. You're safer here than in the Bronx.'

'Are there a lot of thieves in the woods?'

Her stepmother gave her a strange look. 'There's thieves everywhere, girl. You know that.'

She was going to work on her homework, just to show La Cuca. She went up to her room and tried to start reading *Siddhartha* for World Literature, but she couldn't concentrate. She could still hear them all downstairs but she wouldn't go down—let them hang out all together, if they loved each other so much. Sandra had given her a *People*, from the plane, and she was flipping through it when Chewy put his head around the door.

'Hey.'

Marisol didn't say anything.

'What's wrong with you?'

'Nothing.'

'I was coming to say goodnight. We're going out.'

'Good for you.'

'I save your ass, and you act like a brat.' Chewy shook his head. 'Typical.'

Marisol looked up from the magazine. 'Sorry,' she said. 'That was really nice of you. Thanks.'

She thought he would go, but instead he came in and shut the door behind him. He sat down on the folding chair, picked up *Siddhartha* and looked at the cover.

'That's the Buddha,' Marisol explained. 'He's like Jesus for Indian people. Not West Indians, but Indians from India.'

Chewy nodded, and for a second she thought he might have decided to stay, and let her dad and Sandra and La Cuca go out alone. They could play dominoes, the way they used to when she was a kid,

Nell Freudenberger

Chewy cheating a little so that she could get the double-sixes.

'Mami, do something for your Chewy? Okay?'

Back then she used to have daydreams that something would happen to Chewy. The danger was different every time—he had fallen on to the subway tracks, was stuck in a fire, was getting beat on by a guy with a knife or a gun—but every time, by some magic, Marisol was the only one who could save him.

'Let Sandra have your room for a while, when we get back? I'll make up the couch nice for you and everything.'

'The *couch*?' She had known Sandra would be back eventually. Her stepsister and Jon Emmanuel had a million fights, and even if things were okay now, there was no way it would last forever. She knew she'd be sleeping with Sandra again, and Sandra would complain about how she snored (in front of Chewy), even though Marisol slept on a mattress and Sandra got the bed. She knew Sandra's clothes would take up the entire closet, but if Marisol even touched one stupid shirt (which would never fit her, anyway) Sandra would scream at her. She knew she'd have to listen to Sandra complaining about what it was like for an adult to sleep in the same room with a child, and worst of all, never be able to come home from school and slam the door and know that no one would bother her as long as she didn't come out. She knew all that; she just didn't know she would get kicked out of her room.

'Sandra isn't feeling well, Mami.'

All of a sudden something occurred to Marisol. She thought of Blanche, the doctor's wife, who got whiter and whiter and stopped being able to eat. She remembered how Sandra couldn't eat at lunch the other day, or at dinner tonight, and how Marisol had thought it was a diet. But what if it wasn't a diet? What if Sandra was sick with the same thing Blanche had, and the doctors had given her only two months to live?

She was surprised to feel something hard just underneath her ribs. Maybe she didn't like Sandra, but she'd shared a room with her for three years; she was only a stepsister, but Marisol didn't want her to die.

'Is she really sick?' Marisol's voice came out in a kind of whisper, and she couldn't help thinking that if the director of *La Esposa Virgen* were there, he might think of putting her in one of his new *novelas*. 'Is she going to die?'

Chewy flipped through *Siddhartha*, as if he'd left something in there—money or tickets to a movie. Then he put the book on the floor and glanced up at the door, making sure it was still closed.

'No, Mami,' he said finally. 'But you're going to be an aunt.' And when she still didn't get it, he sighed and just told her right out: 'Sandra's having a baby.'

When they were gone, she decided to take a bath. The bathtub was pink, with dark red tiles around it; she'd been wanting to try it. While it was running, she hobbled into the kitchen, using the walls for support. She was going to see if there was any kind of dessert, some cookies or something, but all she could find was regular food and a stockpile of beer, filling up the bottom shelf of the fridge. There were some Marlboros, too, on the shelf where the butter was supposed to go, because her stepmother liked to smoke them cold.

She opened two beers (Chewy would kill her) and carried them back to the bathroom. She got undressed and was about to get into the tub when she thought of the razor. She wasn't planning to shave, just to try it out on a little patch, to see if she would cut herself. You were supposed to cut yourself the first time, and bleed, but she'd seen Yolanda's legs right after she did it and she didn't have any gashes. She'd heard the same thing about sex: some girls loved it right away, and others cried and bled like crazy.

She almost put her clothes back on, and then she looked in the mirror. She looked better without clothes; Sandra looked great in jeans (at least for now) but she had hardly any breasts. Marisol's breasts were perfect—she pinched the nipples, to make them stand up straight—and her waist was nice, too. The problem was her tummy and her ass, but when she sucked in her stomach, that mostly disappeared. She didn't turn around to look at her butt.

The lights were on; if not, she could've walked to Sandra's room completely naked. The switch was all the way across the room. On the other hand, they were in the country: outside the front windows were only trees, and the back windows faced the driveway. They were the last house on the road (so far, her father said) and the only person who could be out that way was Pedro, the sweeper.

Marisol stood just inside her father's bedroom and peered around the door frame: the outside light was on, but the driveway was empty.

She dared herself and, after a suspenseful interval, she accepted her dare.

She walked through the main room, not fast, not slow, as if she owned the house. It was her house, and she could walk naked if she wanted. The linoleum stuck to her feet, and she was sweating; she could smell herself. That was the thing about hair, Yolanda said: it made you stink. The razor was in a white plastic bag with butterflies on it, sitting on the floor next to Sandra's bed. Sandra would kill her if she could see Marisol going through her things without asking. She wondered if there would be anything in there to give it away, a pregnancy test, maybe (just to be sure), or some special vitamins. But it was the same old stuff Sandra always had: an eyelash curler, her Lancôme oil-free moisturizer, and a special pencil sharpened at both ends, black for your eyes and pink for your lips.

She heard it while she was shaving, different from the sound of the broom in the morning, just outside the front of the house: *hunch, hunch*. Her first feeling was disappointment: he hadn't been here until now. It was a relief that he hadn't seen her naked, of course, but what if robbers had come during that time? She planned to tell her father as soon as he got home from the bar.

She had finished the first beer and started on the second one: she had had a lot more than this at Jasmine's boyfriend's house two Saturdays ago, but when she stood up in the bathtub, she felt as if she'd had three or four. She looked down at her legs: one perfectly smooth (except for mosquito bites) and the other hairy and familiar. She decided that it was as far as she wanted to go, at least for tonight.

Marisol got out of the tub and dried herself. She wrapped the towel into a turban, the way Sandra did. She put on La Cuca's blue bathrobe, which was a little bit too small, and also too heavy for the weather, even though it was short. She looked at the bottom of her foot, but it seemed okay, not bleeding any more (neither was her single, shaved leg) and she stuffed the bandages in the pocket of the robe.

She walked into the main room, to test her foot, and that was when she saw him. He couldn't see her, now that the light was off, but she had a perfect view: at first, he was just walking up and down the gravelly driveway, and then he stopped walking and sat down on the swinging bench. The bench hung from two double chains, attached to the overhang of the roof; the chains groaned when he sat down. Marisol went a little closer.

Jasmine and Yolanda had both done it. Stephanie hadn't, because she was Christian (they were all Christian but Stephanie went to the Deeper Life Bible Church on 144th Street) and she was waiting until she got married. She wore a silver Purity Ring with a heart and a cross and a pink rhinestone to symbolize the Holy Trinity that she had ordered from the Internet. When Ms Bennett got all the girls together to talk about sex, Stephanie showed off her ring, and everyone clapped and said, 'You go, girl.'

'What about if you're not religious, but you still want to wait?' Ms Bennett had asked, passing around the Health Worksheet, and Marisol couldn't believe it when Yolanda's hand went up, because she was positive Yolanda had been having sex with Devon since the eighth grade.

'Yolanda?'

Yolanda hesitated, and for a second Marisol wondered if everything she'd thought about her had been wrong, and they had a lot more in common than she'd imagined. Then Yolanda said, 'Why would you *want* to wait?'

Of course everyone busted up, and that was basically the end of the class, even though they hadn't gotten to date rape or gonorrhoea on the worksheet.

It was boiling in the living room and Pedro wasn't doing anything interesting. It seemed as if he'd settled down to watch their house, but Marisol couldn't see any more of him than an ear and a shoulder, in a camouflage T-shirt. He was talking on a cellphone: she could hear his voice but she couldn't make out the words. She decided to go up on the roof.

The staircase was closed off with stacked-up concrete blocks. They were the same blocks they used to play with when they were kids in DR, making 'movies'. It was embarrassing to think of now: they would cover the opening of the block with paper—that was the screen—and stick those little plastic soldiers on the inside. Then they would light a candle behind the block, and all of a sudden there would be war. The movies always ended the same way, with the screen catching fire and everyone running for their lives. In the morning they would inspect the casualties: sometimes, thrillingly, a few of the soldiers would've been annihilated to puddles of wax.

As she stepped over the concrete blocks, Marisol realized she'd been hoping that the house in Ecuador would be built of some new and unfamiliar material. Until now, she'd tried to avoid even looking at the staircase, which led up to a square hole in the roof. The hole had a plain, plywood cover, where the second floor was supposed to be. She thought the cover might have something heavy on top of it, but when she tried she found she could lift it easily, with one hand.

The roof was a surprise. There was La Cuca's beach chair, and the tape-player, and a ladder she hadn't noticed, leaning against the side of the house. But when she looked up she couldn't believe how many stars there were. It was like she was in a different universe: there were thousands of them spilling everywhere, like God had ripped open a packet of sequins. She took the towel off her head, so that her hair could dry, and left it on La Cuca's beach chair. Then she went and sat cross-legged at the edge of the roof, looking out into the jungle that was for sale across the street. In the daytime, you could see monkeys there.

'Hey. You there? You there?'

At first she thought he was talking to her, and then she heard the static. What she'd thought was a cellphone was actually a walkie-talkie, like a cop's.

'This is Pedro. One, two, three—come in.'

She wondered how old he was. She felt older, now that she knew what she knew: it was funny the way that could happen. Chewy had said that she was going to be somebody's *tía*. But being a *tía* wasn't automatic, especially if there wasn't blood between you. If you were stepsisters, you had to decide whether or not you were going to be one, and Marisol hadn't decided yet.

She always told people that her *tía* was like her mom, since her actual mother had disappeared when Marisol was two. Her mom wasn't really Chewy's mom, but he'd known her a lot longer than Marisol had. Chewy didn't know his own mom, so Marisol didn't mind if he said 'our mom' when he was really talking about Marisol's. He had a picture of their mom in the kitchen of their *tía*'s house on the island, sitting at the table with a vase of flowers and a calendar behind her on the wall. The calendar had a picture of a horse, and you couldn't read the date, but Marisol knew it was 1993.

When she looked at that picture (there was a time, right after her *tía* got sick, that she would look at it every day) she couldn't believe the way she recognized the kitchen. Not the calendar, of course, which had changed, but the tablecloth and the colour of the paint on the walls (turquoise) and especially the vase. How could a shitty little vase, pink plastic with swirls in it, last longer than her mother? How could her father and her *tía* have kept the vase safe, but lost a grown-up woman?

She breathed in and smelled smoke, and for a moment she panicked that everyone was back, but she knew she would see the Jeep from a long way off. That would be enough time to hurry downstairs and hang La Cuca's bathrobe from the hook behind the bathroom door. Pedro had lit a cigarette. Marisol didn't smoke, but she loved the smell of it, especially when you were drinking a beer. She was glad she'd brought a third Pilsener up on to the roof.

'Hello?'

'Hello,' Marisol said. 'Is that Pedro?'

'Doña Renata?' He thought she was La Cuca.

'No!'

She heard the swing complain as he got up, and she started to move backward. He'd have to go all the way into the monkey forest to see her. She saw his flashlight making a half-circle in the road, and something moving in the dirt: the orange crabs that came out at night.

Why should she hide from him? It was her house. He moved out into the road, and she could see him better now, at least from the back. He was shorter and skinnier than she'd expected.

'Who's there?'

She pulled the robe around her, and retied the belt. 'Marisol.'

'Don Luis's daughter?'

'Maybe.' He pointed his light at her, and she covered her eyes. When she opened them, he had lowered the light to the road. She could see his face a little too, and she was disappointed. He wasn't ugly but he was young, maybe even younger than she was, and his jeans weren't baggy enough to look good. He was nothing like Dr José Guadalupe on *La Esposa Virgen*, with his thick eyebrows and black sombrero.

'Be careful, Miss.'

No one had ever called her Miss before, except for Mr Lee—and that was different.

'Of what? Monkeys?'

He didn't laugh. She could see him shake his head. 'Falling.'

'Hey,' she said. 'Stop looking at me.'

He shrugged and switched off the light, as if he didn't care. She had an idea of something that would be funny, only because he was so young. He was just a kid! Did La Cuca really think he could protect them?

Pedro stood there in the road for another minute, and then he went back under the roof. It was completely quiet, except for the sound of insects. She heard him light another cigarette. He used matches instead of a lighter.

'We can still talk,' she said, but he didn't say anything. 'Hey,' she called. 'Pedro!'

'Yeah.'

'Where are you from?'

'Esmeraldas.'

'You mean here.'

'Of course.'

She waited a second and then, because he didn't ask, she said, 'I'm from the Bronx. New York.' She knew what the next question would be—the question they asked every new kid, the minute they got to Bronx Prep: *But where are you really from? What are you?*

'Everybody knows New York,' Pedro said. 'Have you been to the Queens?'

Marisol laughed. 'Not *the* Queens. Just Queens.'

'You just said,'—he struggled to repeat it—'the Bronx.' He sounded like she'd hurt his feelings. At least his voice didn't crack like Angel's or Fat Manny's.

'The Bronx is the only one that has the "the". You don't say "the Manhattan" or "the Brooklyn", she explained, trying to be nice.

'My aunt lives there. In *Queens*.' He didn't have a *tía* like hers, of course—just a regular aunt he barely ever saw. Still, it made her feel like she knew him a little better.

'I'm going to be an aunt,' she said. 'I just found out. My stepsister's having a baby.'

'Uh huh.'

'She's moving back with us, so I have to give up my room.'

'We have a baby at home,' Pedro said. 'He cries all the time.'

'Whose baby?'

'My brother's. Now his wife lives with us, and it's like: *Pedro, can you hold the baby a minute? Pedro, I'm going out—can you keep an eye on the baby?* Drives me fucking crazy.'

'I'm not helping—it's not my baby. And I've got school.' She undid just the belt of La Cuca's robe. He couldn't see her, and it was still so hot.

'If you're there, they make you help. It doesn't matter whose it is.'

Marisol thought again about the thing she was thinking of doing. She took another drink of beer. She could hear the swing moving, and as long as she heard that, she knew where he was.

'How old are you?'

'Sixteen.' He didn't hesitate at all, but she wasn't sure she believed him. Some of the middle-schoolers were taller than he was. 'What about you?'

'Fifteen.' She could feel the warm air on her stomach, and between her legs, and when she took a sip of beer, it was warm too. 'How many girls have you had?'

'Fifteen,' came the answer immediately.

'Shut up.'

He didn't say anything, and then she heard him laughing for the first time.

'How many? On your grandmother's life.'

'She's already dead.'

'On your mother's.'

'Two,' he said. 'You?'

She believed him, and she didn't want to lie. But she also didn't want to tell him the truth.

'I haven't had any girls.'

The swing was still moving back and forth, but more slowly. 'Why not?'

'That's disgusting.'

'I think it's *sexy*.' That was his first English word so far.

She shrugged her shoulders and the robe slipped off, as if it had happened by accident. She looked down the road just to be sure, but there were no cars, no lights, no noise. Had she ever been naked outside before? She thought she had, but it was such a long time ago, when she was just a little kid in DR. She held the robe out in front of her in one hand.

'Pedro!'

The swing was moving very little now; it had almost stopped.

'Hello, Pedro?'

Was he just sitting there? Had he fallen asleep?

'Hey, Pedro. Look here.' She let go of the robe, which dropped in a black heap. She thought of the crabs moving over it, burrowing under it. If they came back in the Jeep now, there would be nothing she could do. La Cuca would trip over it on her way into the house, reach down to see what it was and have to brush the orange crabs off her own bathrobe.

'Pedro?' she said. 'Are you there?'

'No.'

She started and grabbed the edge of the roof. He was standing right behind her and he was laughing. He had come around the side of the house and climbed the ladder, completely silently, without her even noticing. He was not José Guadalupe, but he had had two girls. Now he'd climbed the ladder because he wanted her.

'Those jeans are too tight.'

'Nah. I think they look good. Girls like them.'

He was looking at her breasts. She turned her back to him and looked straight out at the monkey forest, sucking in her stomach.

'Not in New York,' she said. She couldn't believe she was one hundred per cent naked in front of a stranger.

Pedro touched her shoulder. 'Hey.' Then he took her elbow. She'd forgotten her foot, and she winced and grabbed his arm.

'You okay?'

'I hurt my foot. At the beach today.'

Pedro had very big, black eyes, and some acne on his cheeks. He had the kind of mouth she liked: full-lipped and sharply defined around the edges. Was it really going to happen right now?

'There's rocks,' he said.

'Yeah.'

He turned her around and pushed her very gently, so she was walking backwards towards La Cuca's plastic chair. That was good because he couldn't see the little dimples of fat on her butt, or the scrapes on the backs of her thighs. She could feel those scrapes, when she lay down on the chair: it seemed incredible to her that just this morning she had thought she was going to die on the rocks.

He took off his shirt and kneeled at the end of the chair, rubbing his hands up and down her legs. Then he felt her with his hands, and she was ashamed because she wasn't more wet. You were supposed to get wet down there; otherwise you were cold or a prude. She'd been relieved, in the past at night, to find she could get wet there without any boy, and she didn't understand why it wasn't working now.

'Girls in *the Bronx* only shave one leg?'

She was glad he couldn't see her face in the dark. She'd forgotten about her legs, or she might not've done what she did. Except he'd come up to the roof even before she dropped the bathrobe, so maybe it didn't matter. Maybe this was supposed to be the night—what did you say, *written in the stars*—and no matter what she did, it would've turned out exactly the same.

'Yeah, it's the style. You didn't know that?'

She wasn't scared, but there was something wrong. Was it the beers? She didn't think so, because all of a sudden she felt very sober. Now he had climbed on top of her and was touching her breasts and breathing fast. She could taste the cigarettes. He put her hand on his belt, and she knew she was supposed to undo it, maybe even flip him over and straddle him, toss her hair wildly, like a girl in a *telenovela*. The only problem was that she hadn't expected it would go so fast, or that it would be so hard to do anything. It was like school: before the year started, you could picture exactly how you would make girls' basketball, and do all your science homework, and be cool in front of Yolanda. And then all of a sudden everything had started up again, and you hadn't made the team; you were behind in science, and Jasmine was the one who was becoming best friends with Yolanda. And all you could do was watch it happen.

She almost screamed when he went inside her for real. She would've, if he hadn't all of a sudden stopped and said, 'You okay?'

'Yeah,' she said. 'You?'

But he was already doing it again. After a while it wasn't so bad, except for how hot it was with Pedro on top of her. They were both sweating, and she was thirsty, even thirstier than she'd been this morning out on the rocks, and the sky was as cool and unsatisfying as the flat, noontime ocean.

All of a sudden Pedro made a sound, and then he was outside of her, holding himself in his hand.

'I wouldn't do that to you.' He was breathing as if he'd just finished a race, and he seemed proud of himself. Did he think that was manly? She was glad he hadn't made her pregnant, of course, but she wondered whether it still counted, if he didn't come inside of you. Had she gone through all of that for nothing?

After a minute Pedro stood up and put on his jeans, and then he looked at her and asked whether she wanted his T-shirt. She did want it, but she could see it wouldn't fit: it would be embarrassing to put it on.

'Bring me my robe,' she said, and she thought he might make her climb down for it, but he went down there without saying anything and got it. He looked away while she put it on, and then he said he'd better get downstairs, before her father got back.

'I have to do some things inside,' she said, but she wished he wouldn't look so relieved. 'Can you open that?'

He picked up the plywood cover that hid the hole in the roof. 'I'll put it back,' he said, and waited for her to go down the stairs.

She thought about inviting him in for a beer—all of a sudden she wanted them to come back and find the two of them sitting together on the swing, drinking Pilsener. But she was pretty sure he'd say no.

'Goodnight,' she said. 'See you tomorrow, maybe.'

'Goodnight, baby. You're beautiful.'

But she wasn't ready to go inside yet.

'You know what?'

'What?' He was looking at the road, nervous.

'I'm going to help her.'

Pedro looked confused.

'My sister. I'm going to help her with the baby—be its *tía*.'

Pedro leaned forward and kissed her on the cheek, holding the plywood away from his body.

'You're a good girl.' He was pushing her, just like before, except he wasn't using his hands. Just like before, she went in the direction he wanted.

When she was halfway down the stairs she stopped: she was already forgetting his face. She turned around but there was only a black square, a snapshot of night-time sky, before Pedro shut the lid.

□

GRANTA

STREET PICTURES
Joel Sternfeld

Introduced by Liz Jobey

It is hard from this vantage point to realize how much colour photography was disdained among serious photographers in the 1960s. Black and white was the trusted mode of reportage and documentary, valued for its immediacy and its realism. But by the early 1970s, some photographers, particularly in America, had found that colour offered something new. On the one hand it could be seductive and painterly; on the other it reflected, far more accurately than black and white did, the surface of contemporary life.

Three photographers, William Eggleston, Joel Sternfeld and Stephen Shore, were among the vanguard of the new colourists. By the early 1970s, Eggleston had already made the colour snapshot his own. Shore had begun to document in colour the small towns of the Midwest. Sternfeld was interested in what colour could provide in terms of 'atmosphere and seasonal effect'. He wanted to explore the country in colour; to record the landscape, the sprawling suburbs, the desert and mountains, its inhabitants and their atomized lives.

Often, when we look back over the body of a famous writer's or photographer's work, it can appear that one project evolved from another in a seamless progression. The truth, more often than not, is that, instead, a path was made through a series of disparate projects, some successful, some not. One of Sternfeld's early experiments with colour was a series of pictures taken on the streets of New York and Chicago in the second half of 1976. He had been studying the colour theories of Josef Albers, and he was fascinated by the sight of people moving quickly through the crowd; he wanted to stop that action, mid-gesture, in a photograph—and, because there wasn't enough light, he used extra daylight flash, which only heightened the feeling of frenetic pace.

In the mid-1970s, America was suffering from a series of blows to its self-confidence: defeat in Vietnam, Watergate, the worst recession in forty years. Sternfeld was attuned to the atmosphere, and his pictures catch some sense of the anxiety and desperation, as well as the distracted aimlessness of people who make up a city crowd. At thirty-three, he felt the country had reached some sort of tipping point. As he wrote in his application for a Guggenheim fellowship the following year, it was 'as if I had been born into one era and survived to another'. He had grown up with a sense of 'classical regional America, and the order it seemed contain'. Now he

proposed a series of photographs, taken across America, that would look for 'beauty and harmony' in a country he found 'increasingly uniform, technological and disturbing'.

Two decades earlier, the Swiss photographer Robert Frank had used a Guggenheim grant to travel across the country, taking photographs for what became his famous book, *The Americans*. It had a deep effect on Sternfeld, 'I'd look at that book before I went to sleep, and in the morning I'd reach for it like a smoker reaches for a cigarette,' he said recently. When his Guggenheim grant came through in 1978, he set off on his own journey. He was not, like Frank, a recent immigrant, but a native, and he wanted to see how his country was faring. As he travelled in his VW camper van, he developed a distinctive personal visual approach. Changing from 35mm to a 10x8 view camera, he used a restrained colour palette, and he stepped back, as it were, to find a detached, slightly elevated position from which to observe the landscape. He moved from natural wilderness to city suburbs to the pools and gardens of private houses and back out to the prairie. But within this broader landscape, with the serendipity that comes to those who work hard, he found he was the witness to minor dramas. The most famous example is his picture of a runaway elephant, collapsed, exhausted in a suburban street, but there are many others that give his apparently benign pictures a surreal and often disturbing edge. Like a good short story, his pictures framed entire landscapes, but within them they captured a small event, or moment, that told a much greater truth. What he found were the signs of discontent and decay that lay beneath the superficial affluence of American life. In 1987, he published the pictures as *American Prospects*, a book which in its turn has become one of the important books of late 20th century photography.

Sternfeld has continued to examine aspects of America in other books, but only recently has he gone back to look at the series of street pictures he took in 1976. Some of the transparencies were never printed up; few of them have been published. But, retrospectively, it is possible to see their place in his development: a short, transitional, but nonetheless important period on the way to finding his mature authorial voice. As for what they show: in thirty years, though styles of clothing might have changed, little else is significantly different; we can still feel the energy of the street, as well as the familiar sense of communal desperation.   *Liz Jobey*

Akram Khan   **Sidi Larbi**
Antony Gormley   **Nitin Sawhney**

zero degrees

'Hugely moving and visionary'

THE DAILY TELEGRAPH

Tuesday 16 –
Saturday 20 October

GRANTA

WHICH REMINDED HER, LATER

Jon McGregor

And then there was the American woman he'd offered the spare room to that time, without question or thought or apparent consideration of the fact that Catherine might at least like to have been told. The first she'd known about it had been when she'd got home from work and found the woman standing there in the hallway, looking not at all surprised or uncomfortable, eating natural yoghurt straight from the pot and waiting for whatever it was that Catherine was going to say. Which had of course been nothing more than a faintly quizzical *hello?* Holding the front door open behind her, the rain blowing in from the garden and something like smugness or amusement lingering on the American woman's face for just a moment before she finally acknowledged Catherine with a quietly unconcerned *hello* of her own. And carried on eating the yoghurt. And made no attempt to explain herself.

A strange looking woman, she remembered. Very slim, and very pale, with rubbed-red eyes and mismatched layers of clothing; a long cotton dress, a man's checked shirt, a college scarf, a beige raincoat. Sandals. No make-up. She looked at first as though she might be in her sixties, but Michael said later that he'd thought she was closer to forty-five. Which was their own age at the time, in fact.

Can I help you? Catherine had asked, only slightly more pointedly—strange, this reluctance to come straight to the point, to say who the hell are you and do you mind getting out of my house— and the woman had shaken her head, and smiled graciously, and said, Oh no thank you, your husband's been very kind already. Holding up the yoghurt spoon to demonstrate what kindness she'd been shown. At which point Michael had appeared, loitering purposefully in the study doorway, and Catherine had understood the situation, had gone straight through to the kitchen without another word to take off her wet coat and sit at the table and wait for something like an explanation while the woman drifted away upstairs.

The woman had been in a bit of a situation, apparently. That was what she'd told Michael, and that was what he told Catherine when he followed her through to the kitchen and sat at the table to explain. She wasn't someone who went about asking like this, she'd told him, but she wasn't sure what else she could do. She'd come over for some medical treatment, she'd heard that the hospital here was a world-renowned centre for people with her condition, and obviously she hadn't thought she'd need worry about accommodation, it being a hospital and everything, only now there'd been some difficulty about being admitted, a difficulty she was never very clear about but which seemed to involve documents she didn't have, and she should have foreseen that, she knew she should, but people with her condition tended to grab at possibilities and this is a world-renowned centre we're talking about at the hospital here and logistics came second to hope sometimes, Michael understood that, didn't he? But the thing was she'd spent all her money getting here and so just for now she was in this sort of, well, this situation. If he knew what she was saying.

That first conversation had taken place at the church. People often went there looking for help, and Michael almost always gave them something; food, or money, or the address of somewhere else they could go. Sometimes it was enough that he didn't just shut the door in their faces, that he listened to their long explanations of funerals to be attended, school trips to be paid for, faulty gas meters and lost cheques and misunderstandings over benefit forms. He wasn't naive; he knew when to say no. It was just that he didn't always think being spun a yarn was a good enough reason for not doing what he could to help. It's the desperate ones who come up with the best stories, he used to say, and Catherine had admired him for this once, for his refusal to let cynicism accumulate with each knock at the church office door. She wasn't capable of such a refusal, she knew. She'd grown cynical in her own job a long time ago, listening to students mumble excuses about late and inadequate coursework, attending departmental meetings where people used phrases like *rebranding the undergraduate experience*. And then coming home from one of those meetings to find a strange American woman eating yoghurt in her hallway.

They'd had people staying before, of course. That wasn't new. Lodgers, friends of friends, people like this woman who just turned up at the church needing somewhere to stay. Catherine didn't usually mind. Vicarages were big houses, and they had plenty of spare rooms. Michael seemed to consider it as much a part of his job—and of his life—as the visiting, the prayer and the offering of communion. *What does our faith mean, if we don't do these things for even the least among us?* She'd heard him say that in his sermons, many times, and she'd been thrilled by how sincerely he'd seemed to mean it, once.

She'd asked him how long the American woman was going to stay. Not long, he'd said. A couple of nights, three at most. Maybe four. She'd asked him why he hadn't talked to her first, and he'd said he hadn't really had the chance and didn't she trust his judgment? She'd asked what sort of condition the woman had that would bring her all this way to find treatment, and he'd said that he wasn't sure, that the woman hadn't been specific, but that he'd got the impression it was some kind of bone disease. Something quite rare, he'd said, and she'd raised her eyebrows, and made a disbelieving face, and said that he wasn't making any sense, the story didn't make any sense. Which he'd pretended to ignore, and so when they'd made dinner then it had been in a bristling near-silence. Catherine boiling and draining and mashing the potatoes, adding butter and milk and salt. Michael turning the sausages under the grill, setting the table, stirring the gravy, disappearing upstairs to ask the woman to join them, coming back to report that she'd said she wasn't hungry and she didn't want to put them out. Moving around each other with a practised ease, passing forks and spoons and stock cubes from hand to hand without needing to be asked, and by the time they were sitting at the table and giving thanks her irritation had faded enough for her to be able to ask what the woman's name was. Michael said he didn't know. He hadn't asked, or she hadn't said, and the whole time she was there they only ever referred to her as this woman or the American woman or most of the time just a shorthanded her or she. When are you going to talk to *her*. What's *she* doing here. How much longer is *she* going to stay.

The whole business should have been the final straw, Catherine thought.

The day after she arrived, the American woman went back to the hospital—they knew this because she left a note in the hallway which said GONE TO HOSPITAL in thick capital letters—and when she came back, early in the afternoon, she went straight up to the spare room without telling Michael what the result of her visit had been. The same thing happened, complete with a second note—GONE TO HOSPITAL, AGAIN—the day after that. On Sunday the woman stayed in her room all day, and when Catherine knocked on her door around suppertime she was met with a sudden taut silence, as if the woman had been pacing around and had now stopped, her breath held, listening. Catherine knocked again.

Who is it? the woman said. Who's there? This said suspiciously, almost aggressively. Catherine hesitated.

It's Catherine, she said. She half thought, since they hadn't been properly introduced, that she should add something like *Michael's wife*, or possibly even *the vicar's wife*, for clarification. But she didn't. The American woman jerked the door open and stepped forwards, standing a little closer than Catherine would have liked, wearing the same mismatch of clothes she'd been wearing when she arrived. She didn't say anything. She seemed to be waiting for Catherine to speak. It was infuriating, this misplaced sense of—what was it, self-assurance? Self-possession?

We were just wondering if everything was okay, Catherine said. Speaking calmly, she hoped. We were wondering if you needed anything, she added. The woman seemed to relax slightly.

I'm fine, she said. Thank you for asking.

Have you had any luck at the hospital? Catherine asked. With your documents and everything? The woman smiled.

Oh I think I'm getting somewhere, she said. You know what these places are like, she added, waving her hand dismissively; it's all forms to fill out and papers to sign and documents to produce, it's all just bureaucracy isn't it?

Catherine looked at the woman, and noticed again how thin and pale she was. A little powder would have helped, a spot of colour, something around the eyes. She looked so drained. But she was probably the sort of woman who would disapprove of make-up.

Do you mind if I ask what your condition is exactly? Catherine said, speaking more abruptly than she'd intended. The woman looked at her a moment, blinking fiercely, as if she had something in her eye.

I'll be going back there in the morning, she said, ignoring the question. Maybe I can resolve the matter then and be out of your way.

Oh? said Catherine. Do you know how long you'll be? Because Michael and I will both be out until quite late. The woman smiled, and started to close the door.

Oh no, she said, it's okay. I can let myself in, thank you.

Catherine found Michael downstairs, sleeping in the armchair, and asked him if he'd given the woman a key. He stirred slightly, and sections of the weekend paper slipped from his lap to the floor. Catherine repeated the question, and he opened one eye to look at her. It seemed like a good idea at the time, he said.

Which had reminded her, later, of the morning after the first night they'd spent together, and of him lying in bed with one eye open just like that, watching her dress. Because he'd thought he was dreaming and didn't want to wake up, he'd said. That's not what it looks like, she'd told him, buttoning her blouse and looking around the room for her stockings. She'd loved him watching her like that, then. No? he'd asked. No, she'd said, it looks like you're spying on me. And you a man of the cloth as well. This said when the idea of him as a vicar was some kind of joke still, before he was ordained; before they were married even, although there'd been some prevarication around that *before*, around whether they hadn't better wait, which they'd settled by deciding that engagement was a commitment in itself and they were as good as married in God's eyes. She remembered their haste over dinner that night, once the decision had been made; barely tasting the food, barely even speaking, catching a bus back to his friend's flat while most people were only just heading out for the night. And then the heat and hurry of first sex, collapsing all too soon under the weight of expectation. The realization that this, after all, was something else which would have to be learned, considered, practised.

And what were they then, twenty-one, twenty-two? More than half a life ago now. Graduates, just, and already moving on to the next thing. Michael at theological college, preparing for ministry, talking about curacies and parishes and the discernment of vocation; Catherine less certain, knowing only that she wanted to carry on studying English, that she didn't want to fall into teaching the way so many of her friends had done. No more than two years since they'd met, volunteering together at the chaplaincy's soup run—Michael overflowing with the thrill of new belief, Catherine looking for some way to rekindle a childhood faith which had been more inheritance than choice—and already the thought of them not being together had seemed puzzling and unreal. As if they had been brought inevitably together. Which she'd believed, then. Their life together had been so filled with purpose that it had felt like something more than chance:

the soup-run project, and the Christmas night shelter they'd help set up; the prayer vigils they'd organized, the twenty-four-hour fasts; and that summer in Europe, sleeping in train stations and parks, going to free concerts in bombed-out churches, sharing open-air communion with Germans and Italians and Norwegians and thinking that this was how life would be for them now, that this endless sense of possibility was what her faith could finally come to mean.

And then there was marriage, ordination, a first curacy, a flat. A masters degree, a PhD proposal, a funding problem, and falling into teaching term by term. All these things decided, settled, while they were still too young to know any better. You can go back to the research later though, Michael had said, when the PhD fell through and she found herself accepting teaching work after all; there's no rush. Trying to reassure her. Keeping one eye on what she was doing.

On Monday morning they found the yoghurt spoon outside the American woman's room, with a note. THANK YOU FOR THE SPOON it said. Catherine knocked at the door, and waited a moment before peering inside. The bed was made, and the holdall the woman had brought with her was gone. But there were still clothes in the wardrobe, and a scarf hanging on the back of the door.

She hasn't left then, Catherine said.

Doesn't look like it, Michael said, already turning away.

She might have just forgotten to pack everything, she said.

Maybe, he said, in a tone which suggested it was unlikely, and went downstairs. She closed the door and followed him, picking up the post and putting it on the kitchen table while Michael put the kettle on to boil. She cut two slices of bread and put them in the toaster, and Michael fetched plates and knives and butter and honey from the cupboard. Unthinking, this routine. Unbreakable, almost.

I don't like her, Catherine announced. Michael looked at her strangely.

Like her? he said. You don't even know her. Why would you like her or not like her? The toaster popped up before the toast was ready, as it always did. Something was wrong with the timer, apparently. Nothing that couldn't be fixed. Catherine reached over and put it down again.

There's something about her, she said. She makes me uncomfortable.

The way she looks at me. The way she seems to be taking us for granted. Michael filled the teapot, put it on the table, and sat down.

The way she looks at you? he repeated. He seemed amused. The toaster popped up, and she put it down again.

And the way she won't answer my questions, she added. Michael made a noise in the back of his throat, something like a snort or a stopped chuckle. A harrumph, people would once have called it. She'd married a man who harrumphed at her across the breakfast table. The toaster popped up a third time. She brought the toast to the table and passed it over to him. What's she doing here, Michael? she asked, sharply. What's she doing in our house? She could be anyone. We don't even know her name. He finished buttering his toast before replying, and she saw, in his expression, that same infuriating self-assurance which the American woman had shown her.

First, he said, it's not our house. It's a vicarage. It belongs to the church, and we're guests here just as much as she is. Catherine tried to cut in, but he held up a finger to stop her. Actually held up a finger. When had he started doing this? Why had she never said anything?

Second, he continued, this woman came to me asking for help, and regardless of whether she's odd or evasive or whether she's even telling the truth I don't see that any harm can come of offering her a room for a few nights. It's not as if we need it. He poured the tea, sliding hers across the table and reaching for the pile of post. But if you think I've made a mistake, he said, you're welcome to ask her to leave.

There was a word for this, for the way he was being about this whole thing—superior? Supercilious? And there was a word for women like her who put up with this kind of behaviour for as long as she had—a word like, what, weak? Not weak exactly, it was more complicated than that, but not decisive, not assertive. Not when it mattered. She stood up, leaving the tea on the table and her toast uneaten. She'd given up slamming doors a long time ago, so instead she just left it gaping open and went upstairs to get ready for work.

Work was a lecturing post in the English department at the new university. She hadn't ever got back to the research. There weren't all that many research positions available in the English departments of new universities. She wrote the odd paper here and there, did her bit to keep the external assessment scores at a respectable level, but mostly she concentrated on shepherding her students through the set texts and critical literature; giving lectures and seminars, setting essays and marking essays and trying to keep up with all the paperwork which had lately crept into the job.

It was a good job though. She liked it. She couldn't remember, now, why she had once been so determined to avoid teaching. She enjoyed standing in front of a group of students and helping them to work their way towards an understanding of what literature could do, what it did do. *Developing the analytical tools*, it was called these days, although she preferred her first departmental head's description of it as *turning the lights on in there*.

She liked being in an environment where people enjoyed what they were doing, valued it, even if they tried to pretend they didn't. She liked having colleagues at all—she'd seen how Michael's solitary, self-directed work had isolated him at times, turned him in on himself—and she enjoyed just sitting in the staffroom with them, drinking coffee, talking, listening to gossip. Of which there seemed only to be more the older they got; some of her colleagues were divorced already, and over the years there'd been regular talk of goings on behind marital backs. She'd even, once, found herself in a situation where it had been made clear that something like that had been an option for her. But the idea had seemed absurd, a caricature of any discontent she might have been feeling, and she'd declined. She wondered if that had ever been gossiped about around the coffee table there, with the curled-corner posters of fat new novels Blu-tacked to the walls and the ring-binders stacked in the corner behind the door. It seemed unlikely.

When she got home that afternoon, Michael showed her a note he'd found on the desk in his study. WOULD APPRECIATE FEWER QUESTIONS, it said; MY CONDITION DOES NOT REACT WELL TO STRESS.

You have to ask her to leave, Catherine said. Michael made a non-committal sound, an *mm* or an *umm*, and Catherine waited for something more.

It's quite a statement though, isn't it? he said. What did you say to the woman?

Michael, please. I'm just not comfortable with her being in the house, Catherine said.

Do you think she's on some kind of fast? Michael asked. Catherine took the note from his hand and looked at it again.

What? she said.

Do you think she's fasting? he repeated.

I don't know Michael, she said, I really don't know. She was suddenly very tired.

Because as far as I can see she's only eating yoghurt, he said. Have you noticed her eating anything else? She hasn't asked to use the kitchen. She's never joined us for dinner, she keeps insisting on not being hungry. Haven't you noticed? He seemed fascinated by the idea.

Michael, Catherine said. He looked up. She can't stay, she said.

The woman came back late. They heard her letting herself in while they were clearing away the dinner things, and by the time Catherine had got out to the hallway she was halfway up the stairs.

Hello again, Catherine said. The woman turned round, the holdall in one hand and a carrier bag filled with pots of yoghurt in the other.

Hey, she said. Her hair was hanging limply around her face, and her skin was even paler than it had been before. She looked exhausted, ill.

No luck at the hospital? Catherine asked. The woman stared at her.

Does it look like it? she said, turning away. She was almost at the top of the stairs before Catherine could take a breath and respond.

Excuse me, she said, raising her voice a little. Sorry? The woman stopped, but didn't turn round. Sorry, Catherine said again, trying to soften her voice with a laugh; but I was just wondering. I mean, we don't actually know each other's names, do we? Waiting for the woman to turn round, feeling her fists almost clenching when she didn't. My name's Catherine, she called up.

Hello Catherine, the woman said, flatly, and continued on up the stairs to her room.

Catherine stood in the hallway, waiting for something, unwilling to go straight back to the kitchen and have Michael ask about her day and what they might watch on the television as if nothing untoward was going on. As if the woman wasn't staying longer than he'd said she would. As if the woman had been open and straightforward with them and given them no cause for concern.

She prayed about it later that evening, sitting in the front room with a lit candle and a Bible on the coffee table, a confused prayer in which she asked that they all be kept safe, that her fears about the woman prove unfounded, that the woman find what she was looking for at the hospital, that Michael or herself might find some way of resolving the situation, that she could be less suspicious and more trusting of the world and the people who came her way, that God might grant her more love and faith and empathy in situations like this, that Michael might listen to her a little more, take her fears more seriously, that God might watch over them all in this situation.

She opened her eyes, and saw the woman standing in the doorway, still wearing the long beige raincoat and holding another spoon. Smiling.

I'm sorry, the woman said. I didn't mean to intrude. I just thought I heard something.

Well, Catherine said. Only me. She felt as if she'd been caught out, exposed somehow. The woman smiled, and that self-assurance, self-contentment, self-whatever-it-was, was there again.

Yes, she said. Only you. She noticed Catherine looking at the spoon. Oh, she said, I hope you don't mind. I helped myself to a spoon, for the yoghurt. Pronouncing yoghurt with a long *oh*, and in Catherine's irritable state this only felt like one more appropriation.

Oh no, Catherine replied, lifting her hands in an attempt at nonchalance, letting them clap down on her thighs; that's fine. It's only a spoon. A weak smile, met with a shrug. The woman glanced down at the Bible, the candle.

Were you praying? she asked. Catherine nodded, and the woman looked puzzled, tilting her head as if she was about to ask something. Well, she said, finally, I won't keep you. It sounds like your husband's gone to bed already.

Goodnight, Catherine said. The woman left, closing the door behind her, and Catherine watched as the candle flame flapped and fluttered and eventually stilled.

She shouldn't be angry though. It wasn't fair. She shouldn't have been angry at the time, and she should have learned not to be still angry about these things now. He was dedicated to his job. He cared about the church, about the redevelopment, about the new community services he wanted to offer, about enthusing the congregation with a sense of mission. These were all good things to care about, to spend every waking moment worrying about. But she was tired of it now. She was tired of being towed along while he did these things.

At least people didn't come calling to the house, generally. That was one thing. It happened to other vicars—it had happened in previous parishes—but it hadn't happened here. The vicarage was too far from the church, too anonymous looking, and so they hadn't had people banging on the door at all hours asking for money as they had elsewhere. People went to the church, and Michael dealt with them there. Which was good. It gave them some separation, mostly. It meant Michael could relax a little once he was home, and it meant Catherine had to worry a little less about always being The Vicar's Wife. There were still the phone calls, and the members of the congregation who knew where they lived and would insist on calling round with messages, paperwork, problems, and would talk to her when Michael was out as if she was his secretary. She'd minded it more in the early days, before she'd felt established in her career. She'd resented the idea that her role in the world might amount to no more than being The Vicar's Wife. I married you, she'd snapped at him once; I didn't marry your job. I didn't marry the Church.

That had been their first crisis. There had been others; his muted, slow-burning reaction to his mother's death, when he'd shut her out so completely that she'd almost walked away; the string of burglaries in the last parish; the incident that never was with her colleague in the English department. And there was the business of children, of course, but they'd stopped talking about that eventually, once it had become more or less academic.

And then there was the American woman he'd offered the spare room to that time, six years ago now and she couldn't help thinking it was too long ago for her to be still thinking about it like this. It wasn't as if they'd ever seen her again.

That Saturday, when the woman had been in their house for more than a week and was showing no sign of being about to leave, Catherine had been woken by the sound of Michael making his breakfast. She usually tried to have a lie-in on Saturdays, and was usually woken like this, by the clatter of knives and plates and mugs, reflecting each time that for such a big house sounds did seem to carry awfully well, that the two of them seemed to rattle around in there sometimes. She heard the toaster popping up, and Michael putting it down again, and she turned over to go back to sleep.

In the kitchen, Michael was taking the butter and the honey down from the cupboard and waiting for the kettle to boil. The American woman appeared in the doorway—this was Michael's account of it, later—and said she hoped she wasn't interrupting but could she ask him something? Michael said yes, certainly, and she came into the room and sat down. Her situation was more complicated than she'd expected, she told him. It seemed she would have to go back to New York to get copies of her medical records, a referral from her doctor, her insurance documents. Which was a problem because she didn't have the money to go home and come back again. Wasn't there someone she could ask to send the documents? Michael asked. Couldn't they be faxed? The woman looked at him, and ignored his interruption. She didn't have that kind of money, she repeated, not to go home and come back again. She didn't even have the money to get down to Heathrow, ha ha—this said as if it was all a big joke, according to Michael, or rather as if she wanted him to think that she was bravely trying to make it all into a big joke—and so she knew it was a lot to ask after all the kindness they'd already shown her but did Michael think there was any chance he could help out at all? Financially?

Michael said he was sorry but he didn't think he could do that. Which seemed to surprise her, he said. Seemed to nudge her off-balance. Something in her expression changed, was the way he described it. But all she said was fine, okay, sorry to have troubled you. And then, as they were both moving into the hallway; can I ask you something else? A nod or a shrug from Michael, and she asked if anything was wrong, that she'd noticed, that she'd wondered if there were maybe some problems between him and his wife. And the answer heard by Catherine, as she stood in their bedroom doorway at the top of the stairs, was that he didn't think that was an appropriate question actually, ha ha; whereas the answer in the account he gave her later was a far less equivocal no.

He'd left for a meeting at the church then, and the American woman had gone back to her room, and she must have already started packing because by the time Catherine had been to the bathroom and washed her hair the woman was gone, the room empty, a note left on the bed beside a heap of stripped sheets and the front door key.

She stood in the empty room for a few moments, feeling the blessed silence settle around her, and then she went downstairs to set the table for lunch. She scrubbed and pierced two jacket potatoes and put them in the oven. She washed and drained and mixed a salad, and made a dressing. She looked in the kitchen drawer where they kept their bank cards and passports and housekeeping money, and made sure everything was there. She checked that Michael's new laptop computer was still in the study. She ran the vacuum cleaner around the spare room, emptied the wastepaper basket of yoghurt pots, straightened the rug. She took the crumpled sheets downstairs and put them in the washing machine, and when she went back upstairs she checked through her jewellery box.

It wasn't that she'd thought the woman would turn out to be a thief. Not really. She just wanted some rational explanation for the way she'd felt about her, the suspicion and unease which she couldn't bring herself to admit might have been unfounded.

It felt like a long time before Michael got home. He started telling her about the meeting almost before he'd opened the door, tugging off his shoes in the hallway and rattling on about misplaced funding priorities and a Dean who cared more about church buildings than putting the gospel into practice. She waited for him to finish talking before telling him that the woman was gone, by which time they were sitting at the table with a dressed salad and two steaming baked potatoes between them. She showed him the note the woman had left, unfolding it from her cardigan pocket and smoothing it out on the table. THANK YOU, it said, SEE YOU AGAIN SOON. He smiled, and nodded, and draped a napkin across his lap.

What do you think she means? Catherine asked. *See you again soon?*

Oh, I'm sure it's nothing, he said. Just a figure of speech.

Really? Catherine said.

Really, he replied. He straightened the napkin on his lap, and fiddled with his knife and fork. Crisis over, he said. He poured out two glasses of water. Did she take anything? he asked.

No, she said. I looked, but I don't think anything's missing.

Did she say anything when she left, besides the note?

No, Catherine said, nothing.

They shut their eyes and said a prayer of thanks and cut open their potatoes, the steam rushing out into the room and filling the space between them for a moment while they each waited for the other to reach for the butter and the salt.

Well, he said. He was almost smiling. He felt vindicated, she supposed. I imagine that's that then, he said.

Yes, she said. I imagine you do. □

GRANTA

THE EARTH FROM THE AIR

Kitty Hauser

O.G.S. Crawford in 1931, dressed for an Ordnance Survey expedition.

At particular times of day when the sun is low, the contours of trenches and craters from the Western Front can still be seen pock-marking the fields of Flanders and Picardy. Seen from the air in certain seasons, ghostly lines of the old front line wind across the landscape. When the fields of Thiepval are ploughed over in the winter, the trench lines of the Leipzig Redoubt show up pale against the dark soil where, ninety or so summers ago, German soldiers dug tunnels and communication channels in the chalky ground. Trench warfare transformed this landscape into a mud that sucked up corpses, releasing long-buried seeds into surreal outcrops of flowers, burying dead men's bones, weapons, military buttons and mess-tins for future archaeologists, farmers and souvenir hunters to find. Every year, they say, ploughing brings forth an 'iron harvest' of rusted military hardware. Buried shells and grenades have a habit of working their way to the surface; as the earth repeatedly freezes and thaws over decades any solid objects buried in it move upwards. Stone-age axes regularly appear here too, for the same reason. Much like the Thames valley, with which it shares certain geological and archaeological characteristics, the whole area around the Somme valley was the site of prehistoric and Roman settlement. An excavation of the front line at Serre not long ago uncovered the remains of a German soldier with a Bronze Age flint scraper in his bread bag. Men living below the surface of the earth must have become intimate with it to the point of madness.

Among the first draft of British soldiers sent to northern France in the winter of 1914 to reinforce the 1st Battalion was Osbert Guy Stanhope Crawford. Crawford had not long since graduated with a diploma in geography from Oxford University; as a keen archaeologist he was more familiar with the surface and contents of the earth than his fellow territorials. Crawford had spent the first six months of the year in the Sudan, working on excavation sites funded by the pharmaceutical millionaire Henry Wellcome, but in September, before the war was a month old, he had enlisted with the London Scottish regiment. He was not particularly patriotic, but he had acted on the advice of older friends, who had urged him to 'get going early, before the rush'. By December, his regiment was ankle-deep in mud that froze, then thawed, then froze again, while they tried to keep the structure of the newly dug trenches in shape. On December 21 the

London Scottish had been sent to relieve the Coldstream Guards who were trying to prevent German reinforcements reaching Arras. They were billeted at Givenchy, in the Pas de Calais. In the four days of fighting round Givenchy, 6,000 men died, twice as many on the British side as the German. Crawford survived, but early in February he was invalided home with flu and malaria (picked up in the Sudan). Trench warfare was not something he wanted to repeat, and while he convalesced he looked for another area in which he might put his skills and his enthusiasms to more use. When his application to join the Royal Flying Corps was turned down, he wrote to the War Office applying for work in the army's map department and was more successful. After a period of training and a leisurely leave, which he spent sculling on the Thames at low tide looking for stone and bronze implements that might have been washed up on the river bank, he was sent out to Beauval, near Doullens, where he reported to Major Winterbotham, who was in charge of the Third Army Topographical Section.

Crawford was already a practised field archaeologist. From his childhood in Hampshire he had been intrigued by the earthworks near his home; and at school at Marlborough he visited nearby ancient sites and explored the landscape on long cross-country runs over the Downs. These early expeditions and runs gave him a particular kind of physical knowledge of the surrounding landscape, a knowledge through the feet as well as the eyes, of pathways, contours, distance, junctions and alignments, the opening up of views. He also had a passion for photography. These particular skills, combined with the rapidly developing technology of aerial surveillance, meant that after the war he would be one of the first people to read the history of the earth from the air.

Crawford's main job in the Topographical Section was the distribution of maps, and the supervision of a small printing press. Contributing to the war's artillery of images, his duties also included taking panorama photographs of the front line, covering its length from the Somme up to the north end of the Vimy Ridge. He took great pride in these photographs, describing them on occasion as 'quite artistic'; but they had the most utilitarian of functions, being used, alongside maps, in the planning of attacks. To take the photographs he positioned himself at observation posts, high up in chimneys or half-ruined church towers, or sometimes from the front line itself. He made himself vulnerable to the extent to which he was visible to the enemy, and so he often used a little periscope to see above the parapet. The camera he used revolved on a tripod to survey a scene, and he had to change its plate between exposures. Like his periscope, Crawford's camera was an extension of bodily vision, a revolving eye on a stick; and when it was hit by a sniper at Fricourt he photographed its damaged bodywork almost as if it were a surrogate of himself.

Crawford was particularly interested in the batches of aerial photographs that were delivered to the map office at regular intervals by the Royal Flying Corps from behind enemy lines. Aeroplanes were still a recent invention in 1914, and the photographs they brought back from the field must have constituted a kind of visual shock, showing the landscape in a way often imagined but never before seen with anything like such clarity. This was how the earth and its features might appear to a disembodied, astral eye. The most familiar of things seen from a human perspective—trees, fields, church towers, towns; the receding orders of earth and sky, foreground, middle-ground and distance—were all made unfamiliar from the air. The aerial view flattened out the landscape, pictured it like a map, and with such resolution, such detail. In the right hands, aerial photographs could be read like maps; but unlike maps they were records as well as diagrams, containing photographic information that was sometimes unexpected, and always up-to-date. An officer in the front line might not be able to see much beyond his sandbagged parapet, or have knowledge of the state of the trenches further up the line. An aerial photograph could show just how far away the enemy was, how complex its earthworks were, and what effect any recent shelling might have had on both sides. It brought visual news from beyond the frontier of natural sight.

This wasn't just the identification of enemy positions, manifested to the eye through graphic, coded signs. Aerial photographs also revealed networks, distances and connections that existed but which couldn't be seen by earthbound mortals. As such they lent their viewers a thoroughly modern but somewhat inhuman sense of visual mastery of space, something Modernist artists such as Malevich and Marinetti found very exciting. Crawford was excited too. Not long after arriving at Third Army Maps, he wrote home enthusiastically about the aerial images of German trench lines he'd seen. He was astonished to see how plainly the trench lines showed up, being dug in chalk. 'One could hardly believe the trenches were full of men,' he added, 'they looked so peaceful and lifeless.' As W. H. Auden later remarked, it was precisely this sort of effect of the aerial view—its tendency to desensitize human values, reducing history to nature— that enabled the aviator to drop his bombs.

It was the aeroplane—along with the tank—that rescued the First World War from stalemate, adding a vertical dimension to the field of battle. As a tool of observation and reconnaissance, aviation revolutionized the field, even if commanders were slow to realize its full potential. Military intelligence, after all, had always looked to the highest vantage point. Before aeroplanes there were information-relaying balloons anchored on the battlefield (these were still being used in 1914–18); before balloons there had been watchtowers. The principle is primitive enough: it was the same impulse, at root, that propelled early man to a high point in the landscape from which to survey the territory, looking out for predators, enemy tribes, or searching for better pasture. Military intelligence is always looking for the point from which the whole picture is visible, while camouflaging itself. It has a horror of perspective; it wants nothing to hide from its sights. Its history is the search for an Archimedean point that has been pushed ever further into space, residing now in the remote sensing capabilities of spy satellites; in 1914–18 the closest approximation to that point was an airborne camera just underneath the clouds.

Thanks to his geographical training, Crawford had a strong sense of the importance of a good visual sweep, seeking out the highest and best observation posts for his panoramas. In fact he soon wanted to go higher. In the autumn of 1916 he went up in a plane 3,000 feet over the Somme front as the battle raged below. 'It was a wonderful sight,' he wrote, 'especially flying over the battle area. The whole country there is brown, there is a great brown belt all along the front, about a mile wide, where the ground has been turned up by countless shells.' The experience of flight was so thrilling that in January 1917 he applied to join the RFC as an observer. 'I am very excited about it,' he wrote to his aunt. After a course in aerial gunnery at Hythe he was posted to the 23rd squadron, stationed at first near Beauval, and then at Baisieux. His stint as an observer did not last long. On his maiden observation flight Crawford's plane was attacked and had to make an emergency landing after gliding northwards to the right side of the frontline, guided by the dark outline of Adinfer Wood. Crawford and his pilot were safe, but Crawford's right foot was 'a gory mess'. An enemy bullet had cut across his instep, breaking the bone of every toe except one. For the rest of his life the right sole of his shoes wore out most quickly in the middle where there remained a bony lump in his foot.

He was out of action for the best part of six months. In May 1917, after passing through a series of hospitals in France and England, he was sent to convalesce at the RFC Auxiliary Hospital at Heligan House in Cornwall, before the legendary gardens there were lost. Here he had a lot of time on his hands, and he started to write a book. The book, as he explained in a letter, was ambitious enough. 'It deals with the classification of knowledge,' he wrote, 'and the place of archaeology in that classification—then its aims and methods.' He proposed to look at the evolution of civilization from a geographical viewpoint and to consider how this viewpoint might shed new light on historical and archaeological problems. After that it would get round to 'more practical things like town-planning and garden cities'. He'd been thinking about all these things for some years, and his enforced leisure at Heligan gave him an opportunity to write them up. But it was H. G. Wells who was seemingly the immediate catalyst and ongoing inspiration for his book.

As a young man Crawford was particularly susceptible to social prophets, especially those who, like him, had rejected a religious upbringing in favour of Science. So it is not surprising that he had long been a fan of H. G. Wells, whose Utopian fiction and other writings were propelled by an understanding of evolutionary science promoted with the passion and the rhetoric of an evangelist. Science, in Wells's work, would quite literally save the world. Following apocalypse and mass destruction, only a higher intelligence—in the form of extra-terrestrials or scientists—could redeem the planet. Wells had a big following amongst the middle-class young in the closing years of the nineteenth century and the early years of the twentieth, and it's not hard to see why. In an age when, as George

Orwell wrote, 'science was faintly disreputable and religious belief obligatory', Wells's vision was exhilarating:

> It was a wonderful experience for a boy to discover H. G. Wells. There you were, in a world of pedants, clergymen and golfers, with your future employers exhorting you to 'get on or get out', your parents systematically warping your sexual life, and your dull-witted schoolmasters sniggering over their Latin tags; and here was this wonderful man who could tell you about the inhabitants of the planets and the bottom of the sea, and who knew that the future was not going to be what respectable people imagined.

Crawford was just such a boy; Wells's influence was, he said later, 'profound and lasting'. He wrote his first fan letter to the great author from the stifling confines of Keble College in 1908, thanking him 'for the encouragement your books are to the lonely wayfarer who feels that he is not, as he feels in Oxford, the only one who does not bow the knee to Baal; and hopes some day to do some service to the only living cause.' Eight years later he got to meet his idol when, in the autumn of 1916, Crawford showed Wells around the map section at Arras, explained aerial reconnaissance to him and gave him some panoramic photographs. The following May, after Crawford had been invalided home with his wounded foot, he spent a weekend at Wells's home at Dunmow in Essex; and it was soon after this that he began work on his book.

Wells was by this point becoming very vocal in the British press on the subject of the war and the future. He had begun to envisage a world in which the various nations would be replaced by a single Federal World State. The nationalist rivalries that had caused the First World War were superfluous in a world increasingly united by science and technology, according to Wells; they were the hangovers of an evolutionary tribal stage that had already been superseded. Fresh from the front, in his 1917 book *War and the Future*, Wells expressed his vision with the fervour and language of a preacher:

> I think that mankind is still as it were collectively dreaming and hardly more awakened to reality than a very young child. It has these dreams that we express by the flags of nationalities and by

strange loyalties and by irrational creeds and ceremonies, and its dreams at times become such nightmares as this war. But the time draws near when mankind will awake and the dreams will fade away, and then there will be no nationality in all the world but humanity, and no king, no emperor, nor leader but the one God of mankind. This is my faith. I am as certain as I was in 1900 that men would presently fly.

Wells realized that it was going to be impossible for a new world order to be conceived, and nationalism to cease, unless history started to be thought about in a different way. National histories would have to stop being taught in schools and Universities, since they perpetuated nationalist sentiment, and gave a skewed picture of the whole. They should be replaced by a new 'Universal History'. This would not be just a collection of histories of, say, modern America, medieval France, the British Empire, and so on, but a synthetic History of the World, from its beginnings to the present day. Such a history would need to be written; and so, astonishingly, Wells embarked on what would be published in 1920 as *The Outline of History: Being a Plain History of Life and Mankind*; followed in 1922 by *A Short History of the World*.

Wells's history books turned out to be a huge and apparently unexpected publishing success, which their author put down to an untapped public thirst for world history in a digestible form. Among writers and intellectuals some, notably Hilaire Belloc, were appalled, but others were pretty impressed. George Bernard Shaw recommended *Outline* to Trotsky as a thoroughly new kind of politically sound history; but Trotsky was not convinced. He described Wells's book as the product of an uninformed and unrigorous so-called historian 'roaming far and wide over the history of a few millennia with the carefree air of a man taking his Sunday stroll'. Crawford, however, saw an affinity between Wells's conception of history and his own. History—as he told him—was Crawford's gospel as it was becoming Wells's; and he too took the big scope, putting nations and empires into perspective. Crawford was thrilled to hear that Wells took seriously the influence of geology and geography on the history of civilization; and he too sensed that discoveries in the realms of archaeology and palaeontology were rewriting that history. What's more, he was in line with Wells politically. He agreed that 'universal history' was 'the necessary educational fore-runner of a world-federation', as he told Wells in a letter in 1919, and he effusively justified to the great writer his devotion to archaeology, an apparently

> ... useless branch of knowledge by the thought that it will provide new material for the education of future generations—material that, if it is used at all, must help to weaken the consciousness of nationality and strengthen that of universal brotherhood. It has done that for me at any rate.

Crawford was delighted to think that religion, superstition and jingoism were to be swept away by the great and unstoppable tides of history, making way for a brave new world of scientific reason; and he was keen to play his part.

The seeds of *Man and his Past* were planted at Heligan in the spring of 1917; but by the autumn Crawford's foot was healed, and he was ready to return to the front. In September he joined the RFC No. 48 Squadron as an observer. The planes flown by this squadron were the new Bristol fighters, in which observer and pilot sat back to back, both of them armed. Crawford's main job was to escort the naval squadron as it carried out bombing missions. He went out on reconnaissance missions, too, taking photographs, and recording the locations of enemy positions. He turned out to be uncommonly good at this kind of work, recording so many more details than the other observers that the Wing Commander suspected him of faking them. Crawford put his success down to a novel method he had devised, in which he recorded his observations direct on to a hand-drawn map, rather than using map references. He also made full use of his geographical and archaeological knowledge, using the straightness of Roman Roads, for example, to help orientate himself at times.

Every day in the autumn and winter of 1917 he went up, recording some of his impressions of flight in a diary. From above, the cloud layer 'looked like a vast snowfield, and the shadow of our machine was visible upon it, surrounded by a small circle of rainbow light'. Flying at 20,000 feet or so with no enclosed cockpit may have been spectacular but it was also chilly, and Crawford made himself a face-mask from a black catskin after his nose got frostbitten. The icy temperature could be hazardous. Crawford's mounted Lewis gun often used to freeze up, and on one occasion this happened when his plane was under attack. It landed with a dead engine, covered with ice, but Crawford and his pilot were unhurt.

Once again, Crawford—who was by now Squadron Intelligence Officer—had had a lucky escape; others in his squadron were less fortunate. In these early days of aerial reconnaissance, observers were at the mercy of darkness, fog or cloud. They were obvious targets for anti-aircraft guns and fighter planes. As a result, observers had a short life-expectancy and were therefore only allowed to do it for six months of continuous service. Even with this safeguard, there were many casualties. Some were recorded in Crawford's diary without much apparent emotion, but when one observer named Hardie and his pilot, Maclaren, were killed, it had an impact that made its way on to the page. Crawford glimpsed Maclaren's burned body through the door of the mortuary, alongside 'several forms wrapped up in blankets and sewn tight'. 'I ... felt very much upset for some time afterwards,' he wrote. 'The image has photographed itself on my mind.' Hardie and Maclaren had been flying beneath the clouds, where they were particularly vulnerable to attack from above. After seeing their bodies in the mortuary Crawford was more nervous when flying under clouds: 'I sit the whole time with my eyes on the clouds behind and above and my finger on the trigger.'

As he got towards the end of his six months Crawford was entrusted with a reconnaissance mission that involved going deep behind the enemy lines, to collect intelligence on preparations for a major German offensive. The plan was to fly above the clouds, calculating the direction and distance to get to the destination, coming down at that precise spot to carry out the reconnaissance under the clouds. Crawford and his pilot would head for Le Cateau, where they would descend, then along the valley to Hirson, on the river Oise, and back home, guided by maps. They waited for the right conditions, and on a day in February, when the cloud cover seemed adequate, they set off. After flying in what they had calculated was the right direction, for what they believed to be the right duration, they came down at a dramatic tilt through the clouds.

Their calculations were wrong. Crawford later blamed his pilot, who had not taken into account the plane's retardation of speed in ascent. Emerging from the clouds they saw a German soldier hanging out his washing. They had no idea where they were; and they began to be shot at. They landed and set fire to their aeroplane, with no one in sight. Escape was not possible, and before long they had both been taken prisoner.

Ten days later, and weak from lack of food, Crawford was taken to a camp on an island at Landshut in Bavaria where he was to receive various regulation inoculations. Within a week or so he began to feel stronger, and started to think about how he might escape. He hatched a plan; and on March 6 he attempted to carry it out; the escape attempt, including a map, is described in his autobiography. Disguising himself as best he could by turning his army tunic inside out, he hid himself in a ditch until nightfall, having put a dummy in his bed. During an especially noisy evening sing-song by his fellow prisoners (who were in on it), he got across the yard and squeezed through the barbed wire that surrounded the camp. His plan was to swim across the river Isar to the mainland, but the current was too strong; he was carried downstream, and ended up back on the same shore. He set off again by foot; when challenged by a sentry he pretended to be a drunk German soldier, but he was soon found out. He was taken to the civil prison at Landshut, where he was put in a cell. He stayed there for a week. He tried, he said, to start work on his book again; but he was too hungry to think.

Not long after returning to the camp from prison, Crawford was sent to the POW camp at Holzminden, near Hanover. It was at Holzminden that the biggest mass escape of the war took place; when Crawford arrived there, the secret tunnel was still being dug. As a recent arrival, Crawford wasn't allowed to join in, but he helped out as a 'soil consultant' to the tunnellers, and, after the big escape in July when seventy or so captured officers tried to get away, he smuggled food and news to those who had been caught and were returned to the camp. Despite the fact that Holzminden was described in the British press as the 'worst camp in Germany', its inmates 'at all times' the 'victims of brutal treatment', Crawford found it not only companionable, but also remarkably conducive to studying. He read books on psychology and 'semi-philosophy', anthropology, archaeology and town planning; he read Samuel Butler, Jung, and more H. G. Wells. He wrote down extracts in a notebook, 'fine, confused stuff', as he later called it; and he discussed his reading with a major who was teaching him German.

Crawford remained at Holzminden until the end of the war in November, a total of seven months. He returned home to Newbury. He was thirty-two; he had no job (Henry Wellcome's work in the Sudan had been indefinitely postponed), but he had his war gratuity and some back payments. Alongside finishing *Man and his Past* he spent the next year or so doing fieldwork, first in Wiltshire and then in Wales, under the auspices of the Cambrian Archaeological Association. He camped out alone in a sheepfold in the hills above the Merionethshire coast, where there were chambered cairns, stone circles and a hill-fort. When members of the Cambrian Archaeological Association—'a motley crew of amateurs', according to Crawford—visited his excavations on their annual outing, they found him eccentric in dress and diet. The geologist Boyd Dawkins explained to the group that he had surely been traumatized by the war. Crawford later laughed off the incident as an example of a bourgeois distaste for working attire. But it's possible that the war had taken its toll. Fresh air was the best tonic; and, unlike the visiting amateurs, it passed no judgment. After packing up camp in October 1919 he walked home to Newbury, a journey that took several days over the Welsh hills and across western England, following the Roman Road from Gloucester to Boxford.

During this period Crawford made full use of the fact that the Ordnance Survey had issued six-inch maps free of charge 'to certain qualified persons' in exchange for archaeological information inserted on them, to add to and correct what was already there. Just as in his wartime observation work, Crawford located and marked many new sites on these maps. He also pointed out a large number of 'archaeological errors and deficiencies' on them. So regular a visitor to the Ordnance Survey offices did he become, and so many corrections did he make, that apparently Sir Charles Close, the Director General 'thought that he might do worse' than offer him a permanent post. After more excavations in the summer of 1920 in Hampshire (where he was again accused of wearing 'funny clothes'), and then on the Isle of Wight (assisted by an ex-serviceman badly injured in the war) Crawford went to Southampton to start work as the Ordnance Survey's first Archaeology Officer.

His official task was to correct and update the archaeological information of each county as it was revised. No one expected him to leave his office much. The antiquities marked on OS maps were patchy. Too often untrustworthy sources had been accepted without question. In some cases, sites identified in books had been inserted on the map without their position and identity being checked on the ground, or their names—often inventions—given a second thought. At worst there were sites that were named with wild inaccuracy as 'Druids' Altars' and the like. Crawford found plenty of work to do. Mindful of his vulnerable and unprecedented position, perhaps, he made it his business to broadcast the need for a centralized authority—himself—who would weed out the errors, fill in the gaps, and rationalize the entire operation.

The Director General was 'rather taken aback', Crawford wrote later, when he asked him for permission to do fieldwork. But there were so many blank spaces on the map, so many dubious attributions lent authority by the permanence of printed text. The map had to be returned to the terrain it was supposed to represent, paper and print checked, wherever possible, against earth and stone. Gloucestershire was being revised when Crawford started his job, and in the autumn and winter of 1920 he claimed personally to have inspected 208 ancient sites in and around the Cotswolds, many of them unmarked. Eighty-one new barrows were added to the map. Encouraged by this early success, and having established a precedent, Crawford made fieldwork an essential part of his job, even though his long absences from the office were often frowned upon. As each county's turn came up he went out, in all weathers; he visited Roman sites in Scotland, and prehistoric sites in the Scilly Isles, plotted long barrows and megaliths against geological and vegetative features; he compared symbols with monuments, maps with views, and views with old records found in county archives; he pencilled in his corrections and additions, filed his report at the end of each year.

His preferred mode of transport was the bicycle, with which, when adapted for his use, he claimed he could survive for a month or more at a time. Two lamp-brackets fixed to the handlebars enabled him to carry up to five bags at once. A curved hook stopped the bags from knocking against his knees as he cycled. He strapped a raincoat on to the back carrier, and wrapped the all-important six-inch maps around the crossbar. His trousers were tucked in and the outfit was completed by furry mittens and a pilot's helmet, presumably left from his war service. Decked out in a similar fashion, he said, he once cycled the seventy-two miles from Stonehaven, south of Aberdeen, to Blairgowrie, in a day. Substitute a Bristol fighter for the bicycle, and it was not so different an activity from Crawford's wartime observation work; and certainly—in his eyes at least—no less urgent.

He got help, of course; from regional antiquarian societies, and from a network of so-called 'honorary correspondents' who knew their corner of the country, and who supplied information in exchange for maps. Crawford called them his 'ferrets'. Some of his prize ferrets were barely out of short trousers, and were inspired by Crawford's example to become archaeologists themselves. Other correspondents were retired surgeons, ex-colonels, landowners and country curates, drawn from those ranks of the middle and upper classes which had long maintained antiquarian interests, and who took upon themselves the responsibility of recording antiquities in the shires. This they continued to do—but now when their identifications were questionable, the new Archaeology Officer made it his business to double check their work in the field—'a very necessary but very thankless task', as Crawford reported to the Royal Geographical Society in 1922.

It was as an attempt to reduce the need for such double checking that Crawford drew up some Field Archaeology 'Notes for Beginners', first issued by the Ordnance Survey in 1921 and reprinted many times throughout the following decades. Like the bird-spotter's field guide, instructing the amateur ornithologist how to tell the difference between, say, a marsh and a reed warbler, Crawford's 'Notes' issued guidelines on how to know an antiquity when you see one, and how not to mistake for it a logan stone, rabbit warren, or chalk pit.

Field archaeology as promoted by Crawford's 'Notes' was an activity as much as a body of knowledge. In principle, it was most democratic—as long as you followed the rules, of course, and didn't go imagining that dolmens were altars built by Druids or Ancient

Egyptians. It encouraged participation, with no special equipment required; and it implied that discoveries by informed non-experts might well be possible. It had as much in common with rambling, bird watching, scouting and landscape appreciation—pursuits with which it could easily be combined—as it did with scholarship. And so it found favour in a nation that was notoriously both suspicious of abstraction or bookishness and convinced of the wholesomeness of outdoor activities of all kinds. 'Field archaeology,' wrote Crawford later, reflecting on its development in this country, 'is an essentially English form of sport.'

Field archaeologists look at the landscape differently; they have to see—really see—and see through superficial appearances. They try to perceive the outlines of ancient fields beneath modern ones, the old roads that might, or might not, coincide with roads that are still being used; they keep their eyes peeled for evidence of old boundaries or ditches, the slight contours of burial mounds, the buried foundations of Roman villas, or the ground-down ramparts of hill forts. 'The surface of England,' wrote Crawford, 'is a palimpsest, a document that has been written on and erased over and over again; and it is the business of the field archaeologist to decipher it.'

The archaeologist's 'field sense' involves all of the senses, sharpened like the hunter's. His eye is trained, and like Sherlock Holmes he is alert to things that are invisible to others. He may spot, for example, a belt of gritty soil in a ploughed field, and it may be all that is left of this portion of a Roman road that is visible as a raised causeway in the neighbouring meadow. He may know, too, the best season in which to detect different kinds of site in different types of landscape. Fieldwork is impossible in parts of Wales after May, wrote Crawford, since bracken hides the surface of the ground. A dry afternoon in March is the best time anywhere, since vegetation is low, and 'every fold in the ground is plainly visible'. January in Scotland might be cold but, wrote Crawford, 'the low, yellow sunlight in midwinter is ample compensation for the slight discomforts endured, and ideal for photography.'

And how beautiful they are, the photographs Crawford took in the field. How well he knew the way in which the Scottish sunlight could illuminate a scene, how the light shone differently in a denuded Fife wood on a February morning to a leafy Southampton suburb on an afternoon in July, how shadows are the result of a unique meeting of time and place, and how they had history in them. Clarity of information was their purpose, not beauty. Yet Crawford's photographs make it seem as though he had a particular knack of finding the remains of the past, however inauspicious their guise; as if he knew that it was here, where there is now a line of trees, that there was once an earthwork, and that it would be at just this moment that the sun's rays pierce the canopy of leaves that the telltale ledge would be illuminated. His photographic eye seems oracular, reminding us of Walter Benjamin's remark that photographers are all the descendants of 'augurers and haruspices', those who read omens and portents in the stars, in the flights of birds and the entrails of animals, uncovering guilt—and foreseeing the future.

The eye of the field archaeologist is evident in Crawford's photographs. And he was, by all accounts, astonishingly observant. The artist John Piper and his wife once shared a car with him and were amazed by how much he saw in the landscape that passed by their windows. But it was not just a question of seeing, the action of the trained eye in the landscape. The observation of the field archaeologist involved tactility as much as vision, feeling the land as well as just looking at it; like the time that Crawford took soundings with a walking-stick along the bottom of a ditch on the Silchester–Speen road in Berkshire, looking for the rounded hump of a Roman causeway. What is sought is a visceral knowledge of the land that is as intimate as the farmer's knowledge of his fields. Crawford knew that field archaeologists had to acquire and develop the sort of knowledge possessed as a matter of course by countrymen, and he often consulted local people about the land they lived on. A woman who lived in a cottage in Avebury on the old road—long since disappeared—to East Kennet told him that the plants in her garden grew differently in the place where the road was said to have been. What was important to field archaeologists was to know different kinds of landscape—chalk downs, fenland marshes, or gravel flats; how they behaved in different circumstances, how fast and in what manner old monuments might degrade in them. They sought to know how, for example, tracks in chalky country might sink over time; how, after rain, silted-up ditches hold moisture for longer than the surrounding earth; or how ploughing on an incline—as was the case in the Somme valley—creates visible banks known as lynchets.

Unlike his famous contemporary, Mortimer Wheeler, Crawford did not do a great deal of digging himself. 'His prime interest,' recalled the archaeologist Glyn Daniel, 'was the face of the countryside in its archaeological aspects.' It was not just where ancient sites and monuments were to be found that interested him; it was how they related to each other, what constellations they formed, and how the siting of those constellations related to topography—geology, vegetation, trade routes, sources of water.

Working at the Ordnance Survey was, in this sense, ideal; for he was at the very source of the most up-to-date cartographic expertise. Crawford could build up a database of sites and plot them on the maps that it was his employer's business to produce. Not long after he began work at the OS, on his own initiative Crawford revived a plan to produce so-called 'Period Maps'. He drew up a model for a map of Roman Britain, plotting all the known routes of Roman roads and the settlements they connected against a background of physical features, and submitted it for approval. The Director General was not pleased, apparently, to discover that the new Archaeology Officer had used office hours to pursue what was an unsanctioned project. The map, though, went ahead; it was published in 1924. The *Daily Mail* described it as 'one of the most wonderful maps ever produced', suggesting, rather surreally, that it would open up 'a new era in motor touring'. It sold out so quickly that the Director General was forced to concede. This sort of success was, in fact, just what the Ordnance Survey needed. After the First World War the Survey was under considerable pressure to broaden the market for its maps. The artist Ellis Martin had been brought in to design map covers, part of the popularization drive of the 1920s; he designed the cover of Crawford's *Map of Roman Britain*, which was quickly reprinted, and a second edition produced in 1928.

More Period Maps followed in the 1930s, and Crawford considered these maps to be the chief accomplishment of the Archaeology Office during his time there. It was not just that they sold well, although this was important to Crawford as part of his own popularization drive. It was also that they were, for him, works of art, and the very embodiment of the sort of non-textual history that he had long believed in.

Crawford's office at the Ordnance Survey became the first port of call for workers in the field. He built up a collection of photographs of cadastral maps, old maps of country estates which often included invaluable archaeological information that had since been lost or built over. After coming to an arrangement with the Air Ministry that any RAF air photograph showing archaeological information would be transferred to the OS Archaeology Office, he created a centralized archive of aerial archaeology of the entire British Isles, accessible by archaeologists and members of the public. He encouraged young archaeologists to use these resources, and to add to them. And in 1927 he began his own journal, *Antiquity*, as a publication in which new work, and new findings, both on the ground and from the air, could be published.

Crawford conceived of his work, and the work of a select group of his fellow archaeologists (described by him as a 'heroic band'), as a new wave in archaeology. He felt that for too long archaeology had been in the hands of gentlemen amateurs. It required a scientific outlook, a clear mind, and a willingness to get your boots dirty; it also required the knowledge of basic and established facts. Training was required. Effectively Crawford and his 'heroic band' represented the professionalization of a field that had hitherto been the province of just about anyone with the leisure and the inclination to pursue it. As the historian Adam Stout has shown, these archaeologists sought to establish authority in a hitherto largely unregulated field. And they pretty much succeeded. Theirs was a kind of archaeological modernism that left its mark on just about every major ancient site in Britain.

In the meantime, the volume of Crawford's work at the OS was increasing enormously, largely thanks to his own industry and initiative. The build up of the archive of aerial photographs collected from the RAF, the production of Period Maps, the listing of megalithic monuments, the rounds of fieldwork for county revisions, communication with honorary correspondents; all of this kept him very busy. The volume of letters received by the Archaeology Office by members of the public increased enormously, too. Correspondents from all over the British Isles wrote with questions about their localities, suggestions for identification, requests for information, or for work experience. Crawford tried to answer them all, although—as the poet Geoffrey Grigson found out when he approached him—he did not have much patience for whimsy or wild ideas. His successor Charles Phillips wrote later that Crawford was likeable but exasperating, and that the Archaeology Office was much more peaceful when he was out of it.

For all Crawford's complaints— and there were many, from the illiteracy of its typists to the bureaucracy of the Stationery Office— there were advantages to being part of the State machinery of the OS and he knew it. He had been keen from the start to democratize archaeology as an activity, and to make its findings available to the broadest public. The OS was a place from which he could carry out these ambitions, with its cartographic expertise, its privileged access to the RAF, and, from the 1920s, its marketing drive. If he received little official encouragement for the projects that would become his legacy—aerial archaeology, the Period Maps—the fact that the administration took so little notice of him ensured an environment in which he could largely do his own thing.

It was aerial archaeology that—with Crawford's encouragement—really kick-started British field archaeology in the 1920s. Seen from the air, this old country certainly showed its age. Old pathways, ploughed-over burial mounds and the craquelure of ancient field systems might not be visible from the ground, but in an aerial photograph they could be seen with extraordinary precision. Seen from the air it was easier, too, to distinguish old networks from subsequent developments. The ridged outlines, or 'ribs' of older cultivation-systems, in Crawford's words, showed up through the network of modern field boundaries 'like the bony skeleton of an old horse'. The surface of the British landscape could be read like an ancient text, especially in the deforested regions of southern and central England. The gravel flats of the Thames Valley, the marshy fenlands of East Anglia, or the chalky Southern downs all gave good results. And how spectacular and strange it looked, this country that we thought we knew so well; how astonishing it was to see through this most modern of lenses these ghosts of history. It was quite literally a kind of revelation. As the historian G. M. Trevelyan told Crawford in 1929, 'I think the discovery of these old Celtic fields, from under the palimpsest of later agricultural systems, is the most romantic thing that has come to stir our historical imaginations since the first Cretan finds.'

Crawford's experience of flying in the First World War had reinforced his conviction that aerial photographs might be of quite some interest to archaeologists. But it wasn't until 1922, when his friend Dr Williams-Freeman showed him some RAF photographs of Hampshire that he realized just how interesting they could be. Pictures of Windmill Hill, near Crawley, taken at ten thousand feet revealed an entire system of ancient field boundaries, or lynchets, which was insensible to the earthbound observer. This was just the kind of thing that Crawford had dreamed of. So clearly marked on the photographic plate was this pattern that Crawford could make a map out of it, in the same way as enemy trenches had been mapped during the war. This map—as he announced to the Royal Geographical Society in March 1923—was nothing less than an accurate plan of the 'fields of a group of communities which ceased to exist about 1,500 years ago'. It was like having access, for the first time, to a lost world. The invention of aerial photography, Crawford announced, would be to archaeology what the invention of the telescope was to astronomy. It was the instrument archaeology had been waiting for.

If the lynchets had turned up as if by accident on the RAF pictures of Hampshire, how many more faint constellations of ancient settlements might turn up, almost casually, on the practice aerial photographs of the RAF? Crawford lost no time in finding out. There was an army school at the Old Sarum airfield on Salisbury Plain, where pilots were trained in the arts of aerial reconnaissance and artillery spotting that had been developed in the war. Looking over their practice negatives, Crawford found something remarkable on some shots taken over the fields near Stonehenge. Nobody in 1923 knew for sure the course of the Eastern branch of the Stonehenge Avenue; nobody had known for hundreds of years. What Crawford thought he saw on these negatives were the faint lines of the bank and ditch of the Avenue leading away from the famous stone circle towards the river Avon. The corn grew differently over this bank and ditch in the dry summer of 1921 when the photos were taken, and whilst the difference was so slight that it could not be seen from the ground, it was clear enough from the air. Back on the ground, Crawford and the archaeologist A. D. Passmore used the aerial photographs as a guide to where they might look for the remains of the Avenue. 'It was like steering a ship by means of sounding,' wrote Crawford; for there was no sign on the ground of where the Avenue might be. Trenches were excavated in three places, revealing the chalk ditches filled with soil they hoped to find, along with a whole load of flint scrapers pocketed by Passmore for his collection, later left to the Ashmolean Museum in Oxford. Out in the stubbly fields in the autumn of 1923 other archaeologists who came to have a look were 'quite satisfied' that the course of the Avenue had been proved. The advantage of aerial photography, as Crawford announced, was not just visual revelation, thrilling though that was. It was also that it provided a key to excavation; X marks the spot where to start digging.

It was as a result of reading about these aerial discoveries in *The Observer* in 1923 that Alexander Keiller, heir to the family marmalade fortune, wrote to Crawford. Keiller was a trained pilot with antiquarian interests who had worked in intelligence during the war, and he proposed to finance an aerial survey. Crawford and Keiller hired a plane, installed a captured German camera in the observer's cockpit, and set up their headquarters at Andover. In the spring and summer of 1924, accompanied by a pilot, Captain Gaskell, they flew over Berkshire, Dorset, Hampshire, Somerset and Wiltshire, looking out for visible remains. They mounted the photographs resulting from these sorties on cardboard, and walked over the ground each covered, looking out for evidence at ground level, drawing up a schematic map for each one. The photographs and the plans were compiled and published, with commentary, as *Wessex from the Air* in 1928, a strange and beautiful tome. It turned out to be too wet for crop sites to appear, but Crawford and Keiller learned how to catch the banks and ditches of hill forts or ancient fields either early in the morning, or just before dusk, hours of the day they called 'lynchet time'. 'On a June morning before breakfast the greater part of Salisbury Plain is seen to be covered with the banks of abandoned Celtic fields,' wrote Crawford, in his introduction to

Wessex from the Air, 'but afterwards they "fade into the common light of day".'

The quotation is from Wordsworth's 'Intimations of Immortality'; it is one of the moments in which Crawford's Romantic sensibility surfaces in what is otherwise the spare prose of a die-hard empiricist. Such moments appear throughout Crawford's writings and in the visual logic of his photographs. They formed a link between professional archaeologist and non-specialist reader, something he was keen to maintain; but they also betray a poetic imagination that was sometimes at odds with, and sometimes in marvellous tune with, his professional activities. He saw the astonishing beauty of aerial archaeology no less than those artists in the 1930s—John Piper, Paul Nash—who were so fascinated by it; but he had little time for visual art himself. Aerial archaeology, unlike art, had a purpose from which its beauty was inextricable. Perhaps it was precisely because he saw the perfect beauty of aerial photography—its exquisite fitness to the purpose of archaeological revelation, a Vision Splendid—that he picked it up in 1922 and ran.

The basic premise of aerial archaeology is the fact that when earth has been disturbed, when a post-hole or ditch has been dug, or a bank built up, that ground is never quite the same again. This is true whether the disturbance happened recently, or thousands of years ago. Under certain conditions the difference becomes sensible to an aerial observer. So-called 'soil sites' appear when the disturbed earth retains more moisture—or less—than the surrounding earth, and so appears darker or more pale. 'Crop sites' appear when surface vegetation registers the difference in the underlying earth. The roots of plants will not be able to penetrate the earth so deeply where there are subterranean remains, for example, and as a result the plants will grow stunted. In times of drought these stunted plants will dry out more quickly than the others, and will appear pale to an aerial observer. Likewise, plants that grow over silted-up ditches will grow more luxuriantly, and will be the last to wither in a drought, retaining their colour when the others have become pale. Surface vegetation can act like the dust of the detective, or photographic developing fluid, but only under circumstances that are not always easy to predict. Barley is a more sensitive 'developer', for example, than oats, wheat or grass, but only in certain soils. Dry spells can bring about remarkably sharp crop sites, like the outline of the medieval tithe barn, complete with buttresses that appeared in the grass at Dorchester in June of 1938. But sites like this one are only spectacular if there is an observer to see them. The aerial archaeologist has to be in the right place at the right time; he is a geomancer in collusion with the sun, the weather, and the crops in the fields.

It was Crawford who categorized sites according to how they reveal themselves to an airborne camera—shadow site, soil site, crop site—or, more rarely, through the patterns of melting snow. Crawford explained and showcased the discoveries of aerial archaeology in two buff-covered Ordnance Survey pamphlets in 1924 and 1929, by which time his name was firmly identified with the new technique. He did not take many aerial photographs himself; flying in these days was largely confined to the military forces. But he encouraged the RAF to look out for sites on practice flights, and he tirelessly publicized the new technique and its findings, not least in *Antiquity*.

One of the most exciting things about aerial photography was that it showed mysterious lines and shapes that had not been seen before and that could not at first be identified, like the large rectangular enclosures that showed up in the Thames Valley, at Dorchester, Benson, and Sutton Courtenay. Another new type of site revealed by aerial archaeology was Woodhenge, found by Squadron-Leader Insall, a pilot stationed at Netheravon on Salisbury Plain. Flying near Amesbury in the winter of 1925 he spotted a circle with a curious series of concentric white dots within it on a ploughed field. Returning late the following June the field was full of wheat, and now both the circle and dots appeared dark. The site was later excavated, and the dots Insall saw turned out to be pits that had once contained wooden posts, in a structure thought to be like nearby Stonehenge, but constructed from wood rather than stone. Prehistoric timber circles owe their discovery to aerial archaeology, since their scant traces are rarely visible from the ground. It was discoveries such as Insall's that caused Crawford to encourage any 'young archaeologist who wants to make discoveries' to 'join a flying-club and learn to fly. Not until then,' he said, 'will the harvest be reaped... England is still, for the archaeological aviator, an almost unexplored country.'

Woodhenge, oblique view from the south, taken by
Squadron-Leader Insall, June 30, 1926

Someone who heeded Crawford's call to explore this unknown country was Major George Allen. Allen was the wealthy managing director of Messrs. John Allen and Sons, his family's engineering firm based in Cowley near Oxford. He had his own plane, with its own private airstrip at Clifton Hampden, and he was willing and able to respond quickly as sites were identified, or when the circumstances were propitious for discovery. In consultation with Crawford and other archaeologists he went on photographic expeditions all over the Thames Valley in the 1930s. Time and money were of little object, and so he could return again and again to the same site under different circumstances. In July 1932, for example, he photographed the big circles—due to the silted-up ditches of a prehistoric henge monument—that had appeared in the arable fields at Dorchester between the Abingdon and Oxford roads; and he returned again and again between April and August of the following year as the circles slowly emerged but only in certain fields; and again in the summer of 1938 when, since the entire site was planted with cereal crops, the whole monument was visible from above. (There is nothing there now; the site was turned into a gravel pit and flooded.)

Allen's circumstances meant that he could fly at a moment's notice. 'There is a plum waiting to be picked,' Crawford told Allen in a letter of April 1933, 'and that is Castor, near Peterborough.' Allen sped off, although, as he told Crawford a couple of weeks later, 'I doubt if the plum was quite ready.' Later that dry summer he had more luck. 'I have been overwhelmed with air work,' he told Passmore in a letter. 'The whole of the Thames valley and its tributaries have come out in a violent rash, circles and marks everywhere.' A single photograph of Stanton Harcourt showed twenty-six new circles. Crawford was delighted by Allen's results, such as the lovely photograph he took in 1936 of Headington, near Oxford, where medieval strip-lynchets line up like waves on a petrified sea, about to break over an orderly line of villas and their gardens. As he told the Prehistoric Society in 1938, 'When I see his handwriting on a large packet amongst my morning letters, I know that there will be no work done until the contents have been examined and the new discoveries duly gloated over.'

The photographs that Major Allen took in the decade before his sudden death, in a motoring accident, in 1940, were taken with a large camera that he designed and had built himself. This camera, now in the Ashmolean Museum, was made out of aluminium; it was fitted with two large handles on either side, and took one plate at a time—the plate had to be replaced after each exposure. Allen flew his plane single-handed, Ordnance Survey map across his knees. Flying hands off ('there is no risk,' he wrote 'in letting go the controls') he would lean out to take each photograph. This resulted in an oblique image, rather than the vertical shots—much better for mapping purposes—that were taken for *Wessex from the Air*. Allen's technique was novel; but the results were stunningly beautiful. There is a photograph of fields near Royston, taken in the winter, just after rain. Two lines divide the image horizontally; one is the railway line from Royston to Baldock, and a train is just passing, a plume of white smoke drifting behind it. Parallel to the railway line is a modern road, a solitary car making its way along it. It is a scene of modernity and movement; but other landscape features, invisible to the driver of the car or passengers in the train, can clearly be seen.

Iron Age ditches, silted up over the centuries, bisect both the road and the railway; they have absorbed the rainfall and so appear as dark stained lines across the ploughed fields. And just below the road, and running alongside it, are the ruts of the old Icknield Way. What is astonishing to the point of being uncanny is the way in which these ancient features, invisible from the ground, secretly share the landscape with the living, as they go about their business. The appearance, in a photograph, of these traces of the past is like the casual way in which ghosts appear alongside the living as they pose in their drawing rooms in Victorian spirit photography. Perhaps this was why, in the early days of the new technique, Crawford was at pains to tell the audiences he lectured on the subject that there was nothing magical about it, and no photographic tricks involved. The camera simply recorded what the aerial observer saw.

When Allen returned after a month to the same fields, the marks of the ditches were gone; more rain had fallen and the dampness of the field had been levelled out. Similarly elusive was the double enclosure known as 'Caesar's Camp' on Greenfield Common in Middlesex. The antiquarian Dr William Stukeley had known of this site in the eighteenth century—he recorded it, and gave it its misleading name—but by the twentieth century its precise location was unknown. Flying back from Scotland in June 1930, Crawford spotted the site—he recognized it from Stukeley's drawing—in a field outside Staines. He had no camera with him, however, and the moment was lost. Not until the spring of 1933 did Major Allen manage to photograph it, a faint figure in a ploughed field. The back gardens of a strip of new suburban villas abut the fields in which this strange figure persists, after so many centuries; but the occupants of those houses presumably do not know that they are living in such proximity to a site that was there long before they were. They cannot see what the aerial viewer can see. It is a disjuncture of perspective that has revealed the ghost. And yet here it is, this ghost; and the uncanny thing is that while it may have been unperceived, it was there all along.

All his life Crawford was fond of cats. And his analogy for the disjuncture of perspective of the aerial view was that it was like the difference between a cat's view of a patterned carpet, and a man's

view of the same carpet. The man, standing over it, can see quite clearly the pattern on the carpet. The cat, however, has only a blurred awareness of the pattern, being so close to it. So pleased was he with this analogy that Crawford took photographs of a patterned carpet, as seen by a cat, and the same carpet as seen by a man, and published them in his contribution to a scientific volume on aerial archaeology. It's an analogy that reinforces a sense felt in front of the photographs of Royston and Staines that aerial archaeology defamiliarizes the landscape, making the familiar scene of roads, fields and suburban life strange. And it implies that we earthbound humans are like the cat on the carpet, with only a partial perception of the earth we tread upon, and live in. It takes another kind of eye, another viewpoint to reveal to us the truth about the world. And does this not have a theological resonance? Does it not remind us, once again, that there may be a vantage point—God's, surely, and the great eye in the sky—from which things are perfectly clear? If anything, Crawford would have claimed a military rather than a theological precedent, the lessons of the battlefield in the First World War when it became clear that only from above was the mazy network of trenches visible and intelligible. It's the same logic as that which underpinned the dream of Universal History. The participants in history may not have a clear view of the vast processes of which they are just a tiny part. Yet seen, as it were, from a great distance, the pattern of those processes comes into focus.

One of the most remarkable things about aerial archaeology is that very few human processes will completely remove a site from view forever. It might be decades—centuries even—before the right combination of crop growth, rain, sun and aerial observer result in a site manifesting itself and being photographed. But unless deep excavations or quarrying are carried out, removing all traces of the site, the possibility remains that one day, under new conditions, it will reveal itself. As the President of the Society of Antiquaries told his listeners in 1925, aerial photography had 'emphasized one thing, not quite appreciated hitherto, namely, how sensitive the soil is, how slowly nature heals the wounds made by man'. For all that it depends on chance, human ingenuity, and practical restraints of finance, technology and skill, there is a sense in which aerial archaeology suggests that we just have to wait for the right combination of circumstances for the revelation of even the most elusive traces of the past. Certainly more recent technologies of remote sensing have captured images of sites that are not only invisible from the ground but are also invisible to the ordinary aerial observer. But a sense of this possibility was there from the start, at least in Crawford's less guarded writings on the subject. Describing two aerial photographs taken over Woodbury in 1929 showing an Iron Age crop site, Crawford described them as 'heralds of innumerable queer resurrections. They assure us that no site, however flattened out, is really lost to knowledge.' Aerial archaeology was the perfect visualization of a faith that the past is never quite lost to us, for all that our desires to find it may be thwarted. It implies that history—like the secrets of astronomy and molecular biology—will surely reveal itself, given the right tools, the right technological aids, the right viewpoint. Nobody, surely, hoped for this more than O. G. S. Crawford. And perhaps this is why, in his 1933 book *The Shape of Things to Come* (a vision of a future World State ruled over by airmen), H. G. Wells had a survey aeroplane named Crawford locate the ancient wreck of the mythical glider of Icarus under the sea in the year 2104. What was lost shall be found, even if it takes hundreds or thousands of years. □

GRANTA

TREE THIEVES
Josh Weil

Up ahead, in the thick, tumbling derangement of jungle, someone was sawing. Noah heard it first: a dry sound filing at the hot, wet air. He stopped and glanced behind him down the trail. His father hadn't heard it. He was too caught up in talking to Noah's brother, as usual.

The two of them had started at it as soon as they'd entered the jungle—erosion control and ecosystems and deep mysteries of groundwater. Noah had tried to take part, wedged in what he could remember of the Earth Sciences course he'd just finished, but by the time they were far enough from the Uyole road to have left behind the ox carts and wood-loaded women, his father and brother were passing ideas between them that seemed designed to remind Noah he was only fourteen. He'd spent his birthday in the air. Their father picked them up at the airport in Dar es Salaam, handed Noah a birthday mango, and started asking Wes about his newly conquered first year of college.

In another six weeks they'd fly home again. The plan was that their father would be back by Thanksgiving. *Do you think he really will?* Noah had asked his brother in the electricless dark of last night, whispering beneath the cries of the dogs outside. *It's his work*, Wes answered; in a few years, when Noah started thinking about what he wanted to do with his life, he'd understand.

As far as Noah could tell, their father had always known what he wanted to do with his life: sustainable agriculture, subsistence farming, helping the starving to eat. It had been nearly a year since he had left for Tanzania on his sabbatical to study potassium deficiency in village fields. Two weeks ago Noah and Wes had arrived to see him. Today was the first full day their father had taken off to spend with them, and they were hiking to the lake. On the map it was a small blue eye on a vast expanse of yellow and brown: a crater and a mountain and a scant forest of trees the government had made it a crime to cut down.

Noah listened to the saw and waited for his father, or Wes, to hear it. They talked on. He couldn't make out the path behind them—just peeled bark and swooping vines tangling in a camouflage of sun-touches and shadows and giant bamboo shafting upwards toward the hidden sky. What had started as a path had become a foot-tamped trail that he could hardly find even around his own boots. He turned back towards the rise. Ahead, the last of the trail disappeared. There was just the hint of something large having pushed through the foliage.

'Noah.' His father called his name with just enough firmness to make him stop. When he looked back, his father and Wes were standing perfectly still. The sawing had ceased. Above, a monkey, or a bird, or some other thing he didn't yet know made wheezing sounds in the canopy.

'Don't go so far ahead,' his father whispered.

'Who is it?'

'It's okay,' Wes said. He was whispering, too.

Their father held up an open, shushing hand. His eyes searched the woods.

A shout. A man's, Noah thought, but before he was sure it was smothered under a violent crashing of branches, tearing louder and louder until it thundered to a stop. The boom shook through the jungle all the way to where they stood. Slowly, it rolled away down the slope and was swallowed in the quiet woods below.

'We should go back,' Wes whispered. He looked behind them at the way they had come, or from where he thought they might have come, or what looked like it could be the trail as much as any of the other places that looked like they could be the trail. 'Shit,' he said.

'It was a tree,' Noah said. He was whispering now, too.

'I know,' Wes said. Then, to their father, 'Maybe we should cut up around them.'

'Why are you so scared?' Noah asked him.

'There's no reason to be scared,' his father said. 'Wes's just...'

Somewhere in the distance behind the wall of woods, a man said something—the round, soft-lipped sounds of Kiswahili.

Noah leaned close to Wes. 'What did Dad tell you?'

'Nothing.'

Their father spoke without taking his eyes off the woods: 'I told your brother they might be poachers. Lumber. But it could be rangers. Or some kind of selective logging.'

'They allow logging?' Wes said.

'No.'

'In the protected forest?'

'No, Wes.'

'Well, then—'

'Well, then, we don't know yet, do we? Let's not get anyone scared.'

'I'm not,' Noah said.

A hollow, hard knock. Then another. The three of them stood listening to the sounds of the axes.

After a while, Noah said, 'Why should we be scared?'

'It's very valuable wood,' his father said. 'There's hardly any forest left in Tanzania. These trees, if they can get them down the mountain and out without anyone seeing them...'

'Or hearing them,' Wes said.

'...they can make a lot of...'

'What happens to them if they get caught?' Noah asked.

'Well,' his father said, 'they don't want to get caught.'

'Dad,' Wes said, 'do you know how to get back?'

Their father looked behind him. 'Probably,' he said. 'But I'll tell you what. I wouldn't worry about this, okay? Chances are it's not a problem. The important thing is to act like we don't care, make it clear to them their business is their business and...'

'You're going to talk to them?' Wes said.

'Look, whether we go up or down it would be good to have a guide.'

'They're gonna shoot us,' Wes said.

'I don't think so.'

'I read the paper, Dad. Every day there's another—'

'Three dead Africans they might get away with. Three *mzungus*? One of them a kid?'

'What about that white woman they found all chopped—'

'That was in Kenya. Put yourself in their shoes, Wes. You think poaching lumber would get them in trouble... Okay? But a little extra cash? For leading a few friendly guys up to the crater? Actually, we're pretty lucky. I don't know if we could have gotten all the way up if we hadn't found them.'

'Dad,' Noah asked, 'do they have guns?'

The distant knocking of the axes came together into one rhythm— whack-whack, whack-whack, whack-whack—and then lost it again.

'Come on,' Wes said, 'he's not a kid.'

'You're the one acting like a kid,' their father snapped.

Noah could feel his father looking at him with the same look he had the day he left for Tanzania, almost ten months ago, when he had made Noah promise not to grow *even another damn shoe size* until he got back; the same look he had had in the airport in Dar es Salaam, when he had chastised Noah with a grin and a pointed finger—*Look at you! I ought to give you what for!*—and that same wistful expression.

'No,' his father said. 'They won't have guns. Now, Wes, you come with me. Noah, you're going to stay back, okay? Just in case. If you hear something—shouting, or one of us calls out, or gunshots, which isn't going to happen—I want you to go back as fast as you can to the road, okay?'

Sometimes, over the past year, when he was alone in the house after school, Noah would put on the cassette-tape letters his father sent from overseas and study the voice, mimicking it, training his own until he thought he could shape it into a sound almost the same. His voice had dropped that winter. 'Okay,' he said now, exactly the way his father would have made the word.

His father looked at him as if his voice had shaken. 'No, no, no. Just in case, Noah. Just on the off chance that they're not friendly.'

'You want me to just wait here on the trail?' Noah said.

'Well, maybe a little off the trail.'

A minute later, they were gone.

As soon as they had left Dar es Salaam, his father had turned in the driver's seat and warned Noah in his eye-smiling, beard-serious way: always swat a stick through the grass in front of your feet; if you get bit lie still to keep the heartbeat slow, send Wes for help. *What if Wes is bit?* Noah had asked, and Wes had told them about the green mamba, from *drop out of trees* to *thirty seconds* to *chop off whatever part it bites*, as if he were an expert on snakes. They have small mouths, their father had assured him, too small to close around anything bigger than a finger. Noah had sat silently in the back seat, waiting for them both to stop talking to him as if he were a child.

His father should have taken him instead of Wes.

He climbed towards a snarl of vines and upturned roots and, crouching behind the blind, peered at the place where they had gone. He tried to listen through the clacking of the bamboo, the rustling of leaves. His hair stuck to the skin behind his ears. Insects crawled through his sweat. He was careful not to move even enough to slap, but silently pressed a finger, a palm, to wherever he thought he could feel them. The jungle was all stillness, time kept only by the markings of his breath.

After five minutes, he told himself, if he didn't hear anything, he'd follow them. He thought he might have heard voices, and spent another five waiting to hear them again. Then he stood up. He'd just follow them until he was close enough to hear. He'd keep low, and quiet, and to hell with snakes, and he'd get just close enough to see them, just to make sure... Then he was imagining what might have happened—the flash of hatchet-heads, shoulder meat-cleaving, shatter of bone; he tried to think, instead, of how he would stop it from happening. Gorillas always attacked from uphill. If he came down at a fast enough rush, making enough noise... He scanned the forest for the best weapon, trying to decide if bamboo would splinter, when he suddenly dropped back to a crouch.

It was the sound first—a tearing of foliage, then quiet, then another ripping noise—and then he saw him. The man was coming up the path, fast and easy, looking straight ahead instead of at his feet, swinging a machete as he went. His face glistened black beneath the dusty green of his cap and his sweat-darkened shirt. He wore the uniform of a Tanzanian soldier. A rifle was slung over his back. With each step, the curved ammo clip jutted out and disappeared and jutted out as the barrel slapped against his thigh.

The only thing for him to do was get up and run, run up the path until he found Wes and his father, run and warn them. His legs ached; he could feel the ligaments pulling at his bent knees. The soldier was talking to himself, in a low mumble of Kiswahili a dozen feet away. He could shout to them. If he shouted now... The man was swinging by, machete hacking. If he waited until the man was past, got out fast, hit him in the back...The man was almost out of sight, blending into the green. Then he was gone, all but the glint of his machete blinking back at Noah through the undergrowth. He could still climb up and go around, warn them, at least. At least he'd be with them when the man came through the woods with his blade and his gun. In the distance the machete hit something with a dull clang. Shout, he told himself. That was the least, last thing he could still do. The machete was quiet. The man was listening for him, had heard him stir, was waiting.

Noah didn't know how long he stood, but he was still standing there when the soldier returned. Beside him, was another man: African, shirtless, wood dust pasted to his chest. He held his machine gun in his hand. Noah was about to run, back down the path towards the road, when he saw his father. Wes was with him, coming through the woods behind the others. They were talking to the shirtless man. Noah heard one of them—he couldn't tell which—laugh.

The only people looking at him oddly were the African men. They stopped and gestured towards him. He heard his father answer back, 'Sick,' showing them with his hands on his belly. The men nodded and talked with his father about their own children as they waited for Noah to come down.

The whole walk up to the crater, Noah stayed silent. His father and Wes were talking science again. He left them to it, tried to listen past them to the conversation of the Africans, their low voices making sounds he did not understand, words he would never have to know. When they got to the top, his father paid the men to leave.

The three of them stood on the bright bare rock of the rim, looking down. The lake was so far below that it didn't even look like water; it might have been a hole punched in the earth's crust and showing the other side of the sky.

'It must be at least a thousand feet,' his brother said.

'More,' his father said.

They discussed the distance, worked their way towards certainty using some kind of math Noah knew he would eventually have to learn. He wandered back down the rock and stood in the shade at the edge of the jungle, looking into the trees for a hint of the retreating men. He wondered if they would gather their saws and axes now and leave the jungle to itself again for one more year. Back in town, he knew, his father would have to decide whether or not to turn them in.

'Noah,' his father shouted to him, 'look at this.'

'What kind are they?' he heard Wes say.

'They're huge,' his father said. 'Noah, come look. They're larger than eagles and they have…'

'They have horns,' Wes said.

'They have a beak that looks like a horn,' his father said. 'They're just gliding. Around and around, right along the crater's edge. Amazing. We'll look them up at home. Noah? Kidd-o? Don't you want to know what they are?'

He didn't. He wanted to stay down by the jungle, but he could feel the two men looking at him and eventually he turned, started the climb back up the rock. He went as slowly as he could. He was still below Wes, below his father, the stone ridge still between him and the view of the lake, when he heard the birds. A strange keening sound, unknown as all the rest of this African crater's woods and yet, too, familiar as the geese back home calling out the Octobers of each year.

They left the research station two days before the ceremony, in the early blue of morning, roadside dogs scavenging through the trash. From the back of the Suzuki Noah gazed out at the road that he and Wes had taken to and from Uyole market every day for the past two months: the auto-repair shop full of broken bikes, the Maximum Miracle Center, the perpetually moulting eucalyptus trees. As they passed a line of young girls balancing heavy drums on their heads—garish plastic blues and oranges against the dry brown rest— he remembered how he had once found unthinkable so much effort to transport something as simple as water. Wedged on the seat between two five-gallon jerry cans, their own drinking water sloshing beneath his forearm, he could hardly imagine being a boy who had not understood even that.

They drove north through Masai Land, past the Mara, beyond Mt. Kenya, towards the Samburu Hills. It was two days of hard driving. But Noah's father was hoping to use the village in a new experiment; and the village chief had invited them to the ceremony; and, despite their father's promises, they had not taken a single trip since their arrival—not to Kilimanjaro, not to Zanzibar—and now there were only a few days left.

That evening, as they had neared the village, Noah's father had described how it would happen—the fainting when the trance hit; the nakedness at dawn so the cold could numb the pain; the moment when the knife would come out and the boy would have to stand utterly still and silent until it was done. But now, sitting in the hut with the old man, Noah knew that his father hadn't prepared him for any of it.

The old man was telling them how he used to hunt buffalo. He would say something in Samburu and his young son would translate into Swahili and Noah's father would make that into English. Even in English he called the chief *mzee* with the respect due such an old man. There was no light other than what curled up from the embers beneath the kettle and all Noah could see of the *mzee*'s face was the glint of metal in his ears and, if he was speaking, his teeth. One of the bottom front ones had been knocked out. *They do it when they're very young*, his father had told him. *In case they get lockjaw. So they can be fed through the hole.*

Wes sat next to him on the raised bed of dried skin. On his other side, a Samburu man's arm pressed against his. Noah could hear the close crowd shifting their feet on the dirt floor, the clearing of a nostril. But mostly he could smell them. The scent of the hut was so thick it clung to Noah's skin: smoke and goat stink and the rancid fat they smeared in their hair and the smell of the people themselves, which was strongest of all. Flies crawled on everything.

'Before they got too close to the herd,' his father was saying, 'they would dress up as...I don't quite...' His father spoke to the *mzee*'s son. 'He says they put on the skins of lions they had killed.'

In the darkness across the kettle, the crouched old man dropped his shoulders; his head dipped and rose; his entire body seemed to drift on the sway of his spine. He grinned.

'They approach the buffalo moving like—moving like that. They keep low in the grass and pretend they're lions stalking so...'

The *mzee* leaned over the coals and rolled his head so that his mouth stretched wide and let out a leonine sigh that rumbled into an air-shaking roar.

For a moment, silence. Then the *mzee*'s boy was talking again. Then Noah's father: 'Ah, ah, I see. They do it to draw out the bulls. The biggest ones come to the front of the herd to protect... The bulls are angry now, and closing in to charge—Good God, to draw one of those things on you on purpose—and that's when, at the last moment, they jump up from the grass and reveal that they're men and shoot them. With arrows.' Noah's father said something in Swahili that made the few who could understand him laugh and, as the boy translated it into Samburu, the *mzee* joined them. His laugh was so warm that it seemed to Noah he could suddenly see the old man's eyes. When he looked harder, though, he couldn't.

'What if they charge after they're shot?' Noah whispered to his brother.

'What's that?' their father said.

'Nothing,' Wes said. Ever since they had arrived at the village, Wes had shrunk into monosyllabic deference, all careful motions and watchful eyes.

'I told them we *mzungus* also think it's brave to shoot buffalo,' their father said. 'But we do it with very big guns from very far away.'

Noah could tell his father wanted him to at least smile. Instead, he said, 'What if the arrows don't kill it?'

All the eyes in the hut found him. Wes stiffened.

'*Aaeh*,' the *mzee* said as his son translated, '*Aaeh*.' It was the noise they all made to show they were listening, and, when the old man spoke again in Samburu, Noah felt sure that he was watching him now, instead of his father.

'They dip the tips in poison,' Noah's father said. 'It kills very quickly.'

'How?' Noah said.

'Well, I suppose it gets in the blood.'

'If it's in the blood how can they eat the meat?'

'Jesus,' Wes said.

The *mzee* pushed closer to the fire and Noah could see the dark gap in his smile, and then the *mzee*'s eyes trained on him. Speaking quickly, the old man used his hands to shape a ball in the smoke above the fire, then smashed the shape into his chest.

'It's a coagulant,' Noah's father said. 'It causes a giant blood clot.'

The old man had his knife out. The blade carved another circle in the smoke.

'They cut out the clot,' Noah's father said. 'The poison stays in the part they throw away.'

Even as Noah's father finished speaking, Noah could see the *mzee*'s son looking at him as if he expected Noah to begin the chain of speech now. The boy was the *mzee*'s youngest son and he looked a year or two younger than Noah. He had warm eyes and felted thick hair that Noah knew would be scraped off tomorrow with a knife. Noah couldn't remember his name, even though he was why they were there.

The old man's wife—or one of them—saved Noah from having to say anything else. She came from outside with a bleating of goats and made her way through the crowd, flashlight tucked under her arm, a tray full of metal cups and a plastic thermos rattling in her hands. She poured from the kettle, brushing flies off the cup rims.

Just before entering the hut, his father had warned them both not to drink the tea and now his father tried to describe lactose intolerance to the *mzee*'s wife. Wes pressed his palms together and repeated one of the two Samburu words he had learned: '*Ascheoling, ascheoling*'—thank you so much, thank you so much.

After a moment of mass confusion, the *mzee*'s wife simply shifted the cup towards Noah. His father began the whole explanation again.

'It's okay,' Noah said, and took it from her hand.

While she poured for the others, he held his palm over the cup, trying to keep the flies out. The steam was burning his wet palm and the insects were tickling all over his fingers by the time his father raised a cup in thanks and took the first sip. He did the same. It was hot and sweet and he sipped from it, watching the *mzee*'s son through the dark, until he realized that, over the rim of the boy's own steaming cup, he was staring back.

They were at the campsite, making lunch on the cooler, when they heard the singing. It was coming from a group of boys that had just left the *boma* and started on the road. Through the thorn trees and cacti, Noah watched them. The loose cluster rose in height towards the front like a bird's crest—younger boys trailing behind, taller ones ahead. In the very front walked the *morani*, flashing colour and glint: red wraps, beaded chin chains, brass earrings, machete-sheaths sun-bleached to pink. The dyed feathers and bright plastic roses with which they dressed their long, ochred braids quavered in the afternoon light. *They're the ones who've been warriors since the last circumcision*, his father whispered the first time Noah had caught his breath at the sight of them. Now, in the middle of them all, strode the *mzee*'s son. His scalp had been shaved that morning and it glistened with the red-ochre grease his mother had spread on. He was wrapped in a black cloth and, amid all the gaudy flashing of the others, a thin green chain of beads glinting across his shoulder blades was his only hint of colour. Among the entire group, there were no women, no men, as if every boy in the village was heading for something, or somewhere, that did not allow any adults at all.

He caught up to them just as they were turning off the dirt road into the trackless bush. A few of the small boys in the back eyed him warily, then went on talking among themselves. They didn't turn to him again, didn't offer a smile, and, stepping through the thorn-spiked brush, Noah watched their bare feet and wondered if they resented him: mute *mzungu* following.

Three massive boulders rose out of the brush, the tallest higher than the roof peak of his mother's house back home. The smaller boys scrambled up past the *morani*, who climbed with the unhurried ease of adolescents. Noah hung back. He could see how it would be on the open rock face: their dark silhouettes made of grease and wraps looking as right against the sky as the rocks, and him— awkward, floppy hat and quick-dry pants. If he were one of them, he would resent him, too.

So it was a surprise to see the hand stretched towards him across the crevice between two rocks. Watching, waiting for his grip, was the *mzee*'s. Noah waved off the help, leaped on his own, but on the other side the boy gripped his wrist anyway and didn't let go until they had made it up the rest of the rock together.

From the top, Noah could see all the way to the purple mountains, the dry flatness of the plateau from which they'd come, and, twisting below, the broad back of a river he had not even known was near. The earth sloped down towards it, darkening with trees and tanglements until, along the river banks, it was engulfed in a forest so verdant it seemed in bloom with green.

The *mzee*'s son pointed at the trees. He said something in Samburu, touched the knife in his belt. Noah shook his head to show he didn't understand. Dropping his wrist, the boy drew back an imaginary bow and fired an invisible arrow at a wisp of fast-moving cloud.

Down again, and into the deepening woods, Noah followed the *mzee*'s son in what he soon realized was a hunt for just the right trees. The group spread out, until it was only glimpses of movement, the occasional hacking of a knife at a branch. Every one of them was consumed with the task of gathering shafts. The *mzee*'s son showed Noah how to select a branch, where to cut, the way, peering down its length and turning it, you could tell if it would fly straight. The boy had gathered and skinned four already before Noah found a branch he thought might work. He was trying to break it off with his hands when the *mzee*'s son appeared behind him. He handed Noah his knife.

After the arrows, they all went down to the river, stripped, swam, dressed in rock-warmed clothes, and walked back wet in the sun. The group's dust clung to Noah's skin until it was a paste on his arms and neck and face and he could feel it crusting in his nostrils. As they neared the village, they began to sing. It was a high, piercing tune cried out by a *moran* at the head of the group and swelled by the rest in a low chorus that Noah could feel as much as hear; it pressed and eased at him from the back of his skull down to his calves. He moved along with it, with them, until he almost felt he could join in, and then did, the shapes of the sounds making themselves in his chest, loosing themselves from his dry mouth.

They were almost at the village when the *mzee*'s son began breathing in a way that sounded as if the air was ripping in and out of his throat. Noah fell silent. The boy's chest swelled and caved; his eyes went still; he stopped walking. The rest of the group sang louder, more fervently. The boy started to shake. His arrow shafts clattered to the dirt. Noah, his own breath coming short, was about to reach out, touch him, say something, when a white froth erupted from the boy's mouth, spilled over his lips, on to his chin, and his arms flew out—the back of a hand caught Noah at the side of his throat—and he was suddenly crashing through the group, running, head back, arms spread, blindly, straight into the thorn fence; he tore himself free, reeled back and fell convulsing in the dirt.

Two *morani* started after him. Noah ran with them. Dropping to the ground, one *moran* sat on the *mzee*'s son's chest; another grabbed his legs; Noah tried to find his wrists in the flailing, got them, held on. Feeling the boy's body shake, Noah looked at his saliva-smeared face and saw in the trance-struck bliss there all that was to come that night, and the next morning, and in the boy's life that would begin after that. Noah wanted, then, to make the blood kick like that in his veins, to taste the foam rising in his own throat; he could almost feel it spill on his lips, his eyes finally rolling back in his head—almost, but could not. In the boy's sudden wide eyes he thought he could see last night's embers and the *mzee*'s stare, the old man showing how they used to jump up from the grass, how they would cast off the disguising skins.

He had been back in Africa for half a year—living in the Westlands part of Nairobi, with all the other expats, on a road guarded by black men who waved as they dropped the chains to let him through—when he was sent down to the Loyta Hills to get footage of a dead man's family. Loyta was home to some of the last true Masai, and some of the last old-growth forest. The Masai stayed there in part because of the forest—sacred woods, birthplace of spirit tales and terrifier of small children—and the forest had been preserved by the Masai. But now the government wanted stewardship. The Masai refused. Kenyan rangers had shot a *moran* dead.

Be sure to get the wife, the mother, Noah's producer had told him. *Get them in the woods.*

Now he sat in the Land Cruiser next to Peter, his driver-translator, trying to ignore how sick he felt. They had left the last road a couple hours ago and, in the last town, he had bought enough fruit to fill the back seat. It was probably the guavas that did it. Grateful for anything that took his thoughts off his stomach, he was trying to keep Peter talking.

'What's her name?' Noah asked.

Peter pried a wallet out of his jeans, opened it to the plastic sleeve and passed it to Noah. 'She is Prudence,' he said.

A small woman in a bright blue dress surrounded by three boys in yellow shirts and khaki pants. Peter rattled off names, ages, the vocation for which each seemed best suited; the youngest (he was three) was going to be an engineer. Peter himself was going back to school. He must be about my age, Noah thought, at least thirty, though the way the man spoke of life opening up ahead made him seem a decade younger. He tried to compare the driver's face with the children's, but the Land Cruiser lurched through a ravine and Noah had to look away from the picture and hold his eyes on the horizon to keep sickness at bay.

When they got to the village, the elder wanted him to sit with them for tea. He could already see one of the dead *moran*'s sisters cornering a chicken he would have to try to get out of sharing for dinner. He used the old lactose-intolerant excuse, refused even a sit-down in the hut, insisted they all go to the woods right away; the light would be good for only another half-hour.

The truth was it would already be too dark under the trees. But he didn't really care. He had not seen real woods since he'd arrived back in Africa—the land was either in plantations or grazed or eroded—and when he had glimpsed the dark line of trees in the distance he had almost told Peter to drive straight to the forest without stopping at the village at all.

Now the Masai unloaded the fruit he had brought as gifts, and piled in—the whole family from grandparents to baby. After twenty minutes of rolling hills and tall grass, they parked within sight of the paths that entered the woods. Carrying the camera, though he knew he wouldn't use it, Noah followed. He was right; it was already dusk beneath the trees; they'd have to return tomorrow.

Before he left, he and Wes had spent two hours on the phone talking about Africa, about how Wes would have loved to come back, too. *Well*, Wes had said, *I guess it'll have to wait until the old man dies*. His brother was the one with the wife instead of the ex, and the home instead of the rental, and their father needed taking care of now. Noah had offered to help pay for a visiting nurse, and he had paid for the locking bracelet and satellite signal in case their father wandered out of the yard and got lost. But, in the end, he had left the responsibility on Wes, the same way his father had left them with their mother when they had been too young to understand that it was his responsibility to raise them.

Peter was off with the family, talking with them about what even Noah could understand from the gestures and from the reactions of the children was one of the spirit tales that had been born in this woods.

They called it the Forest of the Lost Girl. That morning, when he had asked Peter why, it had made them both uncomfortable—Peter trying to relate the children's fable without talking to Noah as if he was a child, Noah unable to fit himself into the role of one in a way that might have put Peter at ease. In Nairobi traffic, the roadsides thick with men and women who had been walking since dawn to reach jobs still an hour away, the tale had seemed as devoid of magic as the Masai beggars at gas pumps outside the game parks.

Now, watching the elder's sweeping hand, and the children staring wonder-spelled where he pointed, Noah followed their gazes and tried to feel what they must feel. In the depths of the forest the trees thickened. Vines twisted black against the sky. But, no, they were just woods; he had seen thicker trees, lusher foliage, in forests back home.

He tried to remember the story: a small girl (Peter had told him her name, but he had forgotten it) who had wandered into the forest alone. Like all Loyta children, she had been warned away from the woods and, like all children, she had watched the adults go there without her. She was a lucky girl, this whatever-her-name-was, and she had a beautiful mother and a rich father and a sister to sleep with and stay warm at night. Each morning, she kneeled beneath a goat to drink milk warm from its teats. Each night, she had a piece of honeycomb to chew. Already, she was chosen for marriage by a rich *moran* with hair red as sunset and braided down to his buttocks. But as she watched her mother return from the forbidden woods bearing honey and firewood, and her father emerge with sweet-tasting birds or a dead pig slung across his back, she grew jealous. They were postponing her womanhood simply to hoard the wealth of the woods, to keep her from the gifts of a forest spirit who gave to all who entered.

She asked her mother to make her a woman sooner. She begged her father. When they refused, she tried to find the cutter who lived in another village. When she could not, she tried to do it herself. Too afraid, her hand shook. That night, she snuck out of her home and ran in the moonlight to the edge of the woods. Beneath the trees, it was black as the inside of a cow's belly. But she could hear sounds that she had never heard before. They called to her, and she called back her wish, naming the gift that she would ask for when she met the spirit in the woods.

Nobody ever saw her again. It was the same ending he had heard around a dozen campfires on a dozen nights beneath the New England pines of his childhood home, his father telling ghost stories to boys who would soon be too old to feel the chills. But Peter had gone on: you could still hear her. Even today, from the edge of the forest the children of the villages listened to the sounds of work—the hacking of axes, the grunts of men dressing kill—but they knew it was not their parents. A slave to the forest spirit, forever stuck in the body of a little girl, she toiled day and night at jobs meant for grown men, struggling forever to provide the gifts her people demanded of the woods. If you ask the children, Peter said, they will tell you, 'Go there at night, wait at the edge of the trees and listen for her crying.'

Sitting on a half-rotted stump, watching dark fill the places where dusk had been, Noah tried to keep perfectly still. The elder had stopped talking. He could feel them all looking at him. For one more moment, he tried to imagine what sort of noise might come from a small girl grieving the loss of a honeycomb, or the beat of a sister's heart, or the memory of warm goat's milk spilling over too-eager lips.

From beyond the edge of the woods, a car door smacked. Peter was coming back towards the clearing carrying the camera bag. Noah pushed himself up from the stump. He settled the camera on to his shoulder. Through the viewfinder he could see the red glow of the low-light warning, the black woods, the hints of vines and leaves still clinging to the last of the day. The Masai family stood motionless as the branches fallen at their feet. They stared at him, waiting. Noah called Peter over and explained that he wanted to film the family walking away down the path. They went in single file. He followed them with the lens until they had disappeared. In his frame there was just night filling the clearing and the dim memory of the trail. Their sounds came back from the dark—whispers, footsteps—and he listened, pretending to film on, delaying as long as he could the moment when he knew that he would have to call them back. □

GRANTA

IN THE COUNTRY
Tessa Hadley

Tessa Hadley

In a pile of papers on the telephone table, there are two family photographs in an envelope: they are waiting for Karen to find frames for them. The Lavery family like to have photographs taken whenever they all get together. Both of these were taken in the same place in Stella's garden, in front of an old wall grown over with a rambler rose: in both, canvas chairs have been put out on the grass for the adults, the children are sitting on a rug. The photos were taken less than a year apart: the first one was Stella's sixtieth birthday and the roses are blooming, the second was Stella and Jim's thirty-fifth wedding anniversary, and the roses are only in bud. Someone looked it up and found that the thirty-fifth anniversary was Jade, so everyone is wearing something green; Stella begged to be excused horrible jade objects for presents (someone did buy them *crème de menthe*, for a joke). Stella and Jim are Tom's parents, Tom is Karen's husband. Mostly the same people are there in both photographs; the family composition has only crumbled slightly at the periphery. In the second picture Jim's elderly mother is missing, because she is in hospital with a broken ankle; also Tom's sister Cordelia has a different boyfriend. In the first picture Karen has two children, two boys. In the second picture she also has her new baby, another boy. He's too tiny to put on the rug, only a few weeks old. She is holding him almost ceremonially, upright against her chest. Her face is half hidden behind him, glancing away from the camera, as if she's dipping down to kiss his scented scalp, breathe into that mysterious black baby hair which will fall out after the first few weeks. Already, now that her baby is sitting up laughing at his brothers, eating mashed banana, she's forgetting the secret of his first self: contained and pensive, with eyes as dark as blueberries, that seemed to know her.

When Tom and Karen drove into the yard on the morning of Stella's sixtieth, there seemed to be no one around, although the dog came strolling to greet them. They opened the car doors, the boys spilled out, Tom and Karen sat on in the car for a few more moments, subsiding after the stress of the journey from London. The peace of the place, at the end of a no-through road, sifted on to them out of the air. Parts of the old farmhouse were fifteenth century or even earlier; in the stonework the whorls and arcs of lost doors and windows were preserved like fossils, and high in the walls of a ruined stone barn were the niches of a dovecote. Stella was an architect, she knew how to do nothing to spoil it all.

—Go and make sure the boys are safe, Karen said.

She got out and started unpacking the bags of presents and food, and their overnight things; they seemed to need such a huge quantity of stuff these days to go away anywhere. Tom in the passenger seat kept his eyes closed; because he was very long and thin and it was a small car he had to sit with his knees almost up to his chin. He wouldn't learn to drive. He groaned; he always managed to work himself up into a state of tension about these visits home. The dog, an intelligent old collie, pushed its head sympathetically into his crotch. Karen walked around the barn and saw that the boys had found their cousins and that they were all with Jim, who was skimming weeds off the pond with a net on a long handle; he waved at her. Beyond the garden Jim and Stella owned a couple of rough fields where Stella kept her horses and her goats, a copse of beeches, and a tiny two-roomed cottage at the bottom of the hill which Stella used as a studio and for overspill guests. The whole place was hidden away in the intricate folds of red sandstone Somerset hills, reached through lanes just wide enough for one car, between the high hedgerows that were ancient field boundaries. Karen had never stayed in the country in her childhood, but her imagination of it had been something like this.

The double glass doors in the long room at the back of the house were flung wide open on to the paved terrace for the sunny day, but the curtains were pulled across inside, and Karen had to find a way through them; then her eyes took time adjusting to the dim light. Stella was sitting on the sofa at one end of the room with her arms round her two daughters, Rose and Cordelia. They were watching television.

—Daytime television? Karen said. —Is this because now you're sixty you can let yourself go?

—Karen, darling, you've arrived! I didn't hear Tray barking. It's a DVD, Rose recorded it. But that's quite enough for now. It's rather hard to bear.

—No, let Karen see a bit of it.

—It's Mum, in her youth, said Rose. —She's about twenty, on some programme about what young people think. They were showing it as part of a 1960s season. She's on a panel. I just happened to put it on and saw her on it: so we missed the beginning. It's amazing. She's so beautiful.

—I hardly remember doing the panel. I had no idea the footage still existed.

—It's when she was writing for *Spare Rib*.

—No, it's before *Spare Rib* existed.

—Look at her! Isn't she amazing?

Karen could never get used to how Stella's daughters were as intimate with their mother as puppies, always cuddling up and stroking and praising one another, confiding heated-up secrets or developing little tiffs. She had never known anything like this in her own family, although they didn't get on badly. In reaction she held herself back at a satirical cool distance, as if she and Stella were the grown-ups and Rose and Cordelia were lovable children.

They made room on the sofa for her to squeeze in. The film's washed-out colour made it look as if even the light and air were different in the past; Karen realized she was looking at a younger Stella. The girl on the television screen was wearing a paisley-patterned blouse and a fringed suede waistcoat. Her eyes were heavily made up and too dark for her pale perfect face, which was passionately in earnest; her long red-gold hair seemed to crackle with static round her head. For the first moments it was shocking for Karen to connect that girl with the ageing woman beside her. 'I haven't actually taken LSD myself,' the girl said. 'But I can understand anyone dropping acid who isn't ready yet for an engagement with the system at the level of conflict.' Her voice was lighter and her accent seemed much more upper class than Stella's was now: she sounded like a well-brought up schoolgirl on speech day. She wasn't at all awkward with the cameras on her, although there was something polished and brittle about her defiance, as if it was a performance of a part.

—I was twenty-three, said Stella. —Is that any excuse? Did I really once sound that priggish? I refuse to believe it.

—It was you! Cordelia said. —You're just the same!

Stella turned the DVD player off although her daughters protested —That's quite enough of that, she said. —Too lacerating. I want to play with my grandchildren. The day's too lovely. Where's Tom?

She stood up and began to haul back the heavy curtains from the windows. Stella at sixty was Karen's idea of a certain kind of powerful older woman, tall and gaunt, with big bones; there was some pale peppery red colour left in the grey of the frizzy hair, which she still wore long, tied in a pony tail. As usual she was wearing baggy tracksuit bottoms with a man's shirt. Her pale freckled skin was beginning to be age-spotted and slackening on her bones; she was the type to be contemptuous of the idea of cosmetic surgery. Sometimes the nakedness of Stella's face dismayed Karen, sometimes she thought it was beautiful in its decay, like something she might have found in the woods round here, a lacy leaf-skeleton, a piece of bark splotched over with lichen, or a twiggy knot of witch's broom. She wondered if she would have the audacity, when the time came, to let herself go like that. She thought that you would have to think very well of yourself, to bear it.

Stella said something quickly and lightly while she and Karen were hitching up the curtains on the big brass hooks that caught them back: almost as if it was not for her daughters to hear —How can it be so long ago? It was only yesterday.

—It looked very interesting, Karen said carefully.

Tom came in, carrying bags. Whenever he first entered the family home he put on a face of nervous suffering which exasperated Karen, so that she kept her distance from him —Happy birthday, Mother, he said, frowning and blinking: he called her Mother as if he was using the word ironically and it was too ordinary to be adequate to the history that lay between them. Tom was long and gangling like Stella, but he had Jim's eloquent brown eyes—dog eyes, Stella called them— and his red full mouth, that seemed to twist up and down to express all varieties of distress and pleasure.

—My darling boy. Stella held her arms open for him; afterwards he submitted to his sisters' embraces.

—You and Karen are upstairs in the blue room, Stella said. —All the kids in the back attic. I've put Cordy and Seth down in the cottage. She thinks we'll be too much for him.

—Seth? Karen asked. —He's new. Is he nice?

—He's gorgeous, Stella said.

—No, he really is. I'm totally in love.

Cordelia had Jim's brown colouring too, and she was small and plump and soft-skinned like him.

—You'll recognize him when you see him, Rose said. —He's in a soap.

—Karen doesn't watch soaps, said Cordelia.

—Which one is he in? Where is he?

—*Emmerdale*. He's the doctor. And he's gone into Watchet for ciggies.

—Londoners can't seriously believe we don't have corner shops in the country.

–Really he's just trying to escape my clutches, now I've dragged him down to meet my folks.

Karen walked down the garden to find out what the children were doing. Jim was organizing all five of them—Rose had three, a boy and two girls—into a team at the pond, some skimming, some forking the weedy mess, Rose's smallest one importantly shooing the ducks, running at them waving little fat hands. When Karen saw they didn't need her she didn't approach any closer, she let herself drop down on to the rough grass. Unless for a moment she relaxed, she was never aware of being vigilantly on guard with Tom's family. Rolling over on to her face now, with her arms stretched out, she closed her eyes, and felt the hard shapes of the earth pressing up underneath her, unmoulded to her contours. She imagined being buried, having earth in her mouth and nose and ears, insects tickling over her, her flesh turning to a dry brown fertilizing cake.

The men carried out the huge table that was cut from a single piece of oak, and put it on the grass under the apple trees: the double doors had deliberately been made wide enough for this. They brought out the most comfortable armchair, too, for Jim's mum, who was tiny, ancient, perplexed and deaf; everyone took turns to sit and chat with her. The dog lay under the table and the women spread it with a cloth and dishes and flowers; Jim opened some white wine. He had found something special for the occasion because Stella didn't like champagne. Karen didn't know anything about wine, but she loved the zinging hit of the first mouthful out of the cold heavy glass. She put down the glass down very carefully away from the edge of the table. All the ordinary things at Stella and Jim's—glasses, table napkins, carving knife, milk jug—were desirable in a way that Karen hadn't been aware of as a possibility for household items before she came to this house, although Stella handled them without any fuss, and never talked about shopping. If you asked, it would turn out that these things had been bought when they were first married and living in Iran, or that they had been made by some gifted silver designer who had died since, or were in some other way singular and interesting.

Stella changed out of her jogging bottoms into a green linen dress which she wore with bare legs and sandals, and long ropes of pearls. Her daughters crowded her, exclaiming over the pearls. She made a debunking face to Karen across their bent heads. —Don't you think pearls are awfully county? These were my mother's, I've never really worn them.

—They're worth a fortune, Rose said.

—You're wondering which one will get them when I'm dead.

They protested in horror. —We don't want your wretched pearls. We want you.

—You're a wicked old woman to say such a thing.

—Haven't I always told you she was wicked? Jim joined in complacently.

—I'll leave the pearls to Karen then.

They made Karen try them on. She sat very still where she was on one of the canvas chairs, with one leg crossed over the other, while Rose dropped them, doubled up, over her head, still warm from Stella's neck. They all looked smiling at her. Tom was cross-legged some way off under an apple tree, squinting at her over his cigarette. Stella had forbidden him to smoke within twenty yards of the house and he had paced the distance out; Cordelia's new boyfriend, Seth, had insisted he was happy not to smoke at all, though it was he who had driven in the first place to buy the cigarettes. Karen felt herself swallowing against the weight of the pearls.

—Well? Am I very Sloane?

It might be the wrong joke: perhaps the pearls were too good for that. The family Stella came from weren't the Sloane kind of posh. However, they were all looking at her kindly, appraisingly. She had changed out of her jeans for the birthday lunch, and put on a bright red halter-neck dress in a clinging stretch material that crossed over and tied in a bow at the small of her back; when she packed it she had wondered if it might be the wrong thing to wear for an outdoor summer meal, but looking round now she was sure that they approved. She could read their eyes and see herself, she didn't need a mirror, but Rose, kind Rose, insisted on dragging her inside. —You have to be shown how lovely you are, she said. It was nice anyway, to be out of the sunshine for those few minutes, in the empty house. In the dim stone-flagged entrance hall their reflections swam at them out of a tarnished gilt-framed mirror; both of them shuddered in the cool. Karen was always wary, forced to contemplate herself head-on. She hadn't been expected, when she was a child, to look like anything special.

—Aren't you just perfect? See?

Not perfect, ears too big, forehead so high: but something that still surprised her, and which she imagined as if it was to do with keeping a balance, holding those long level eyes and the swing of dark short hair and the bare straight shoulders still, like holding liquid steady in a glass: it might spill if you looked too carefully.

—And I can't believe you've had two babies, Rose said wistfully, putting her hand on Karen's flat stomach.

—Those great boys. I sometimes wonder, where did they come from? Karen twisted Rose's rope of red hair in her hand. —I wish I had this.

—And the freckles that go with it?

—All the lot.

She wound the pearls in with Rose's hair and piled it on top of her head.

—That's very clever, said Rose. —You're good, aren't you? Veronese. I look like a Venetian courtesan. He liked his women ample.

Karen didn't have to ask who Veronese was: Tom had taken her to Venice twice. They went outside with Karen holding up Rose's hair to show everyone. Then Cordelia wanted pearls in her hair too, and Stella had to find hairpins. Cordelia took her top off, to show them she also had Veronese breasts.

—Which really means, she said, —no kind of breasts at all, just little triangular white mounds. Like a boy's. Like custards.

And it was true, her breasts did make Karen remember the ones in some of those huge old paintings, pink-nippled little custards, disproportionate to the goddesses' huge thighs and bottoms; not that anything about Cordelia was huge, she was petite and pliant. Jim took a photograph of his daughter sitting at the table under the apple trees with pearls in her hair and her top off; all this was before they'd even started the food. Karen stole a quick glance at Cordelia's boyfriend and he seemed to be taking it all in his stride, laughing and talking and looking at her breasts quite frankly. After all, he was an actor, he and Cordelia had met in a play, they would be used to this kind of thing.

Only Vera, old Mrs Lavery, who wasn't supposed to understand, seemed embarrassed by Cordelia's nakedness. —Is Cordy all right? she asked no one in particular. Seth was good-looking, dark-skinned with shoulder-length black wiry curls and a strong, compact torso: at first Karen thought he must be Asian, until she worked out from his name and something he said that he was Jewish. If anything, he was trying a bit too hard to charm everyone. Ivan, Rose's violinist husband, was so shy that no charm reached him; he sat locked into the private world of his talent (not such a great talent, Tom thought).

Coming up to the table while she was helping get all the children into their places, Tom said something extraordinary to Karen. —Don't take *your* top off, he said in an undertone, quite seriously, like an instruction: as if he had really thought she might be tempted to. Luckily no one except Karen noticed it.

—Put them away now Cordy, Stella said, bringing out the meat on a plate. —I'd hate them to get splashed with gravy.

Stella and Cordelia were vegetarians, but Stella always cooked meat for the others: this time a leg of Exmoor lamb with garlic and rosemary, the skin crisp and salty and blackened, the inside pink. Karen was concentrating on getting Frankie, her three year old, to sit still in his chair. He was over-excited after a game where all the children had hurled themselves at top speed down a grassy slope on to an old mattress they had dragged out from one of the barns. Frankie's face was red and wet with sweat, he was bouncing crazily and arhythmically in his seat. His cousin Laurence, the gang leader, aged eight, encouraged him from across the table.

—Hey, Frankie!

—Hey, Laurie!

—Frankie, you're a pain, said Tom.

Roland, his older son, who was more obedient, watched Frankie reproachfully. Laurence bounced hard too, Frankie wriggled out of Karen's grip to bounce again, Ivan pleaded with Laurence in an undertone in French. Ivan's mother was French, he and Rose were bringing the children up to be bilingual.

—Hey, Laurence! Stella was a loved grandmother but also fearsome, so that the children watched her carefully. —Stop *now* matey, or you'll be sent inside.

Rose and Ivan blushed and suffered at the threat of punishment.

Stella assessed anxiously what she put on to Tom's plate —Is it cooked?

—It's good, said Tom, eating hungrily: he loved his mother's food. He was relaxing into the family as usual now, after his initial stand-off. He sat next to Stella; Jim sat at the other end of the table between his daughters and his mother. Vera had a white linen napkin tucked in under her chin. Seth was telling them funny stories about working for a theatre director Jim knew.

—So what's this I hear about you being on the telly, Mother? Tom said.

He and his sisters could get away with calling the television the telly, and watching all the worst programmes.

—You mustn't see it, darling, Stella said. —It would be bad for your Oedipus complex. The girls tell me I'm very gorgeous.

—I'm immune, said Tom. —You're not my type. What is it that you're saying, on this programme?

—That's the real mystery. Coming out of what certainly looks like my mouth used to look, are all these words that I'm sure I've never spoken.

—Such as?

Stella forked up a piece of Persian spinach pancake. —How about: 'it's important not to exaggerate the importance of libertarian elements in the processes of revolution'.

—You didn't really say that?

—She did! said Cordelia. —And 'the future is on the streets of Paris and Berlin'.

—That's the question. Was it me? It *looked* like me. But I have no memory of ever owning any such statements. Yet I sounded so certain.

Tom took more of the potatoes roasted in olive oil. —You old Maoist you.

—It's easy to make fun, Stella said. —I don't know which is more desolating: thinking how wrong I was then, or thinking that now I don't believe in anything with that certainty. Nothing political, anyway. Nobody does, do they?

—I don't know what I believe, said Karen, and then thought that she had drunk enough wine, she ought to stop.

—What I can actually remember about making that programme has nothing to do with ideas.

—I thought you couldn't remember it at all, Rose said.

—It's coming back to me. But only that I was meeting someone afterwards. All the time we were hanging about in the studio, having our make-up done, frightening the bourgeois, I was on fire with the boy I was going to meet. The man. I suppose they were men, by then.

—Oh, Mum! You *were* wicked.

—Why did that stuff get saved in my memory, and not what I believed in?

—What she remembers out of that welter of revolutionary fervour is me, Jim suggested, triumphant, from down the table.

Stella shook her head. —Not you. It wasn't you.

Karen looked to see if Jim minded it not having been him, but he didn't seem to, he was still beaming proudly at Stella.

Before Stella brought out the summer pudding, Jim banged his glass with his knife as if he wanted to make a speech.

—Oh, must you? Stella said.

Karen had known Jim from the radio and television, presenting various arts programmes, years before she went out with Tom. His screen persona was hard and rigorous and exact; she was surprised when she met him by how soft and pleased with himself he seemed, as if he only really taxed himself when he was performing; in real life she found him rather inaccessible behind a vague easy friendliness, although he knew lots of interesting things.

—I'm going to sing, he announced, enjoying the chorus of groans. —For Stella's birthday.

—Oh God, said Tom to Stella. —Not his Geordie childhood, please.

—But I love the songs, Stella said.

When she and Jim were first married he was still a singer on the folk circuit.

—Sair fyeld hinny. That translates for you southerners as 'sore failed hinny'. Sair fyeld noo. 'Sore failed now, sore failed hinny, since I knew you.'

—Cheerful, said Cordelia.

—It's a poignant lament for lost youth. An old man sings it to an oak tree.

—Oh dear. Vera smiled round the table in wonder at her clever son.

—To an oak tree? I thought hinny was a girl. His girlfriend.

—Well, that's what he calls the old oak tree. It's an endearment.

Jim's voice was still good, and he sang without any affectation, not putting on the folk style that he had learned in his youth. It made a good moment, the family assembled in the long grass of the orchard under the apple trees, all lightly drunk on the white wine, the children drunk from their play, the song in its power drawing the meaning of the day all together, looping them all into one true feeling that cleared their heads for more spacious and open thoughts.

Aa was young and lusty aa was fair and clear
Aa was young and lusty many's a long year
When aa was five and twenty aa could loup a dyke
Noo a'm five and sixty aa can barely step a syke.

Thus spoke the ould man to the oak tree
Sair fyeld is aa sin a kenned thee!

Karen caught the eye of Cordelia's boyfriend and knew that he was watching them all, uncertain how to fit in with this family and their unashamed grand gestures.

—Do you remember that one, Nana? Tom called to Vera down the table. —Did you use to sing that up in Newcastle when Dad was a kid?

—Oh dear, said Vera vaguely. —I don't think so, pet.

Later, when the children had gone off with Stella to feed the horses, and Karen and Tom were stacking the dishes from the table in a big basket to carry into the kitchen, Tom put his arms around her from behind, and kissed her on her back, naked where her dress plunged down. 'Aa was young and lusty many's a long year,' he imitated, muffled against her skin, so that she knew he had been listening to his father even though he had pretended only to be weary at his showing off. She also knew that he was apologizing for his moodiness earlier, and perhaps for the remark about taking her top off, although he might have just thought that was sensible advice. She wasn't really angry with him; she had talked with Stella about how it was difficult for Tom, trying to make a career as a critic and writer and trying to do it differently to Jim—Tom wanted to be more subtle, more sceptical, less ripe—but always having to operate in the blurring broad shadow of

The perfect gift.

A gift of *Granta* is perfect for friends and relatives who share your love of reading; there is no risk of sending something that they have already read, and the pleasure will extend all year!

Buy today and you can give four issues of *Granta* for only £24.95* – that's a saving of 50% off bookshop prices.

GRANTA

'The most influential literary magazine in the UK'
Observer

Yes,

I'd like to give Granta as a gift.
Please reserve the following subscriptions:

Number of subscriptions	Delivery region	Price per subscription	Saving
☐	UK/USA	£24.95	**50%**
☐	Europe/S. America	£29.95	**40%**
☐	Canada & rest of world	£34.95	**30%**

BILLING DETAILS   All prices include delivery!

Title: Initial: Surname:

Address:

Postcode:

Telephone: Email:

GIFT ONE DELIVERY DETAILS

Title: Initial: Surname:

Address:

Postcode:

Telephone:

Email:

Please start with ☐ this issue ☐ next issue

GIFT TWO DELIVERY DETAILS

Title: Initial: Surname:

Address:

Postcode:

Telephone:

Email:

Please start with ☐ this issue ☐ next issue

PAYMENT

[1] I enclose a cheque payable to 'Granta' for £_____ for _____ gift subscriptions to *Granta*

[2] Please debit my ☐ Mastercard ☐ Visa ☐ Amex for £_____ for _____ gift subscriptions

Card number: ☐☐☐☐ ☐☐☐☐ ☐☐☐☐ ☐☐☐☐   GGSKQ399

Expiry date: ☐☐ / ☐☐   Signed _____   Date _____

**Please return this form to Granta Subscriptions or telephone +44 (0)20 8955 7011
PO Box 2068, Bushey, Herts, WD23 3ZF, United Kingdom**

GRANTA

Please tick if you would prefer not to receive occasional offers from compatible companies by post ☐ by phone ☐ by email ☐

his father. It was no wonder he behaved badly sometimes, returned into his parents' orbit.

A t the end of the afternoon Karen went for a walk by herself. The curtains were pulled shut across the windows in the living room again, and the children were watching a film, something Jim had been sent that was only just out in the cinemas. Stella and Cordelia had taken the horses out, Rose was with the children, Ivan was practising, Tom and Jim both had articles to finish. Karen had only meant to step outside for a few minutes, but once she began to walk down the path that led along the fields and through the copse of beech trees, there seemed no reason to turn back; they could all manage without her for half an hour. Alone, she felt returned with intensity inside herself, aware of the breathing lifting her chest and the suddenly awakened noise of her thoughts rushing in the hollow of her skull. Yellow light slanted low across the path from between the trees; little birds scuffled in the undergrowth or flitted among the leaves like tricks of sight. Her footsteps seemed hardly to belong to her. A woodpigeon took off from a branch with a startling racket, its wing beats like shots. It was a lovely English summer's afternoon: she had longed to escape into it, but as she walked it remained outside of her, as if she was walking through a commercial, or an estate agents' brochure.

Stella and Jim weren't really country people. Ten years ago, not long before Karen first met them, they had given up their London life. Karen and Tom lived now in the converted bottom half of the tall Georgian terraced house in Highbury that had been Tom's childhood home; the top half was let out and the rents went to Rose and Cordelia. As she walked Karen was thinking about the way the young Stella on the television programme had talked about revolution, speaking the word as if it was a knife kept hidden under her clothes, gleaming and glamorous; she could imagine nursing that hope of some violent adjustment, recharging life with its truth. Sometimes Karen was afraid of how experience now seemed thin and used up, as if her children were the only real thing. Because terrible things happening in other places were so close, on the television and the Internet and in the newspapers, even the solidity of these old hills and woods could seem worn paper-thin. Outwardly the countryside looked the same as it did a hundred years ago, as if there was a wholesome continuity preserved here, safe against change; but that was a delusion. For a start, all the cottages that must have once belonged to poor people were done up now and sold for a fortune to people from the cities.

She was nervous when she heard the noise of someone else moving in the woods behind her, twigs cracking underfoot; probably it was someone from the village walking their dog. She should have brought Tray, too, as a pretext for being here: only she'd slipped away without meaning to come more than a few yards. Looking back she saw Seth, the actor, approaching along the path, his white T-shirt flickering in the shade; he called out and waved to her, and she waited, feeling the sun hot on her in a patch of light where trees had been cut down. After lunch she had put on one of Tom's shirts over her dress and she had been glad of it in the cool of the copse. She was pleased, in fact, to have Seth's company; as he came close her sour thoughts drew off some little distance, as if he was surrounded with a stronger force of pleasurable energy. When he asked if he could get through to the cottage this way, she said she would show him. Because he wore his black hair in a glossy mass to his shoulders, his looks reminded her of the Assyrian kings in the lion-hunts she'd taken the boys to see in the British Museum; he had the same slanting cheekbones, although instead of warrior-like he was funny and friendly. He wasn't much taller than she was, not six foot; around one wrist he wore a gold chain, and the brown skin of his arms was speckled with dark pores; he had a warm male smell she enjoyed, like hazelnut-oil. He explained that he'd thought he ought to take a couple of hours out, he had some lines to learn. They walked on together through the trees, and then along the side of a field planted with tall elephant grass for bio-fuel. Seth said he'd thought it was wheat. —Shit, I've hardly ever been to the country before. What are those? He pointed to some sheep in the next field. —Cows? Rabbits?

—Come on, you must have been to the country. At least as a kid, on a trip or something.

—Honestly, I'm only kidding a bit. But I've always been meaning to get round to it.

—It's lovely here, she said. —Look at the view.

The view from the top of the field really was good, they could see all round them: the sea behind, Exmoor to the south, and close at hand the patched cloth of ancient fields, some worn into a corduroy of ridged sheep runs, draped across a relief of steep hills and valleys so convoluted that Karen was never sure which hamlet or which woods she was looking at, although she came here often. They dropped to sit beside the Dutch barn, with a few bleached hay bales left over in it from last year. An unspoken alliance between them had begun at lunch, when their eyes met over Jim's song, the outsiders in the family. Seth smoked a cigarette. —I was too frightened to smoke at the house, he said. — Cordy's old lady's fairly intimidating.

—Do you see the cottage from here? Karen said. —But I'll come down with you, it's on my way back.

—I really just wanted to clear my head, he said. —I'll probably just fall asleep.

—Is this *Emmerdale*? Are you really the doctor?

—There I was thinking you might be a fan.

—Perhaps I'll watch it now, just to see you.

—Do me a favour. I'd rather you didn't. It's so funny. I've just broken up with my girlfriend.

—You don't mean Cordelia?

—On *Emmerdale*. The actress was already in Australia when they decided to write her out, so we couldn't actually have the break-up, I had to do it on the phone, only of course there wasn't anyone on the other end, it was only me all by myself, ranting into nothingness. 'What do you mean, you think I haven't made enough commitment to this relationship?' 'How can you say that I'm a selfish bastard who only cares about his work?'

Lying on his back on the stony margin of the field he laughed delightedly, and she laughed too, at the idea of it.

—What do you do, Karen? When you're not at home with the kids?

—At the moment mostly I'm at home with them.

—They're nice—pretty girls.

—Boys. Mine are the boys. The girls are Rose's.

—Shit. I'm hopeless with kids.

—Why shouldn't you be? she said tolerantly. —I do a bit of freelance accountancy work for charities, because Tom isn't earning much from his writing at the moment. When Tom and I were first together I was working as a PA for a Japanese importer. I don't think he'd ever met anyone before who hadn't been to university.

—They are a bit overwhelming: the family.

—I love them, Karen said. —I really do love them.

—God, I said some idiotic things to Cordy's father over that lunch.

—It won't matter. But you should always keep something of yourself back from them. Keep a few secrets.

Seth propped himself up on his elbows to look at her.

—Is that what you do?

—Just in case they accept everything about you.

—That would be bad?

—I'm just superstitious.

—What sort of secrets? he asked, and she laughed at him.

—Now, why would I tell you?

She stood up, brushing bits of straw off her dress, and they made their way down the side of a stubble field, treading sweetness from the camomile plants that crept underfoot; below them the slate roof of the cottage glinted through a sliver of woodland, where the last of the slanting sun touched the valley bottom. When they stepped in under the trees the light was thick and green; the path followed beside a stream sunk to a summer trickle among mossy stones. The different acoustic in the wood made Karen shiver, as if she could feel the noise of their steps and their breathing on her skin stretched taut.

—Tom knows, for instance, Karen said, —that before I knew him I used to be a Christian. But he doesn't know quite how much of one.

—That's all?

—Really an extreme kind of a Christian. I ran away from home and lived with an evangelical group for about a year. I was engaged to one of them. Quite a crazy kind of group. The women all had to cover their heads with scarves, and only the men were allowed to take prayer at the meetings. The women had to obey the men, and the men had to obey the leaders of the group. The elders, we called them. All the money we earned was collected centrally, we were given allowances.

—You're joking. This was you?

—Amazing, isn't it? Where did that money go? When I think about it now. I was temping in an insurance office: I put in all my wages. Those men who ran the group and the whole hierarchy were completely unelected, there were no checks on them, we never knew how they were chosen, it was a process hidden from us, we didn't question it. We went to lectures proving that evolution didn't happen, that God created the world in seven days.

—Surely Tom's heard about all this stuff when he's talked to your parents?

—My parents don't know the half of what went on. Also, they don't get together with Tom's family very often. They're shy people. They don't talk about very much.

—And what happened? How did you get out?

—It wasn't a prison, we were there of our free choice. I just walked away. Well, actually I caught a train.

The last few yards were a rocky scramble; their feet skidded, sending stones rattling. There was still thick sunlight on the track when they came out beside the white-painted cottage wall.

—I haven't talked to anybody about all that for years, said Karen.

—Do you fancy a beer? There are some in the fridge. The key's under a brick. Cordy says there is no crime round here. Or perhaps just very thick burglars. Otherwise why hide the key at all?

On the ground floor of the cottage there was just one room, with a fridge and sink and cooker and a bed; upstairs was Stella's studio. Seth took the top off a bottle of cold beer for Karen then excused himself and went into the tiny bathroom. She sat down on the bed and took in Cordelia's occupation of the space: her holdall on the bed with clothes half pulled out of it, a couple of paperbacks with their spines broken and pages furred, her Ipod charging, a grubby make-up bag beside the sink spilling over with lipsticks, medicines, contraceptive pills, perfume. The way Cordelia allowed her intimate life to flow over and fill any given space struck Karen as unprotected, childlike, dangerous. The only signs of Seth were a masculine heap of keys and wallet and change emptied from his pocket, and a white jacket on a hanger on a cupboard door. The duvet on the bed was still pulled up over the pillows; they had only arrived this morning. The cottage was all in shadow, its perfunctory furnishings seemed a flimsy shell against the light outside the windows.

When Seth came out of the bathroom he showed Karen a small polythene packet.

—Do you fancy a little bit of charlie?

She hadn't touched any drugs since she was pregnant with Roland, and she'd only ever done coke a few times at parties. —I don't think so.

—We bought it specially for the weekend. I thought this might be a good moment.

—Or maybe, Karen said. —Just a little bit. You go first.

He sat on a rickety cane chair opposite her and put out the lines with a credit card from his wallet, on the cover of a book of British birds. She worried shyly that she might make a mess of doing it after all this time, but copied him exactly and remembered how.

—Nice, he said, sitting back with his eyes gleaming at her, pressing the back of his wrist against his nostril. —It's decent stuff.

Karen felt the blooming of intoxication at the front of her mind like a flare, and breathed cold air in sharply. —I'd forgotten what it was like.

—About that sect, he said —That's fantastic. You weren't making all that up?

—No: why would I?

—It's just very hard to imagine you. You don't look the type. I'd imagined those women would be ugly.

Karen was inspired to show him: she buttoned Tom's shirt up to the neck. She wasn't sure how affected she was by the coke. She'd only had a small amount, but she wasn't used to it, so she stood up cautiously, conscious of herself swaying, not unsteadily but heavily and flexibly, like a tree. All the emptiness she had felt when she was walking alone had vanished; she was densely concentrated in the present. The understanding came to her that these alternating moods were two pulses in life, opposite and yet related, like the expansion and contraction of a heartbeat: one diffusing sensation and sending it flying apart, this one gathering it in to the living centre. She had noticed a blue tea-towel by the sink. She arranged it neatly over her hair, folding it across her forehead and tucking it behind her ears with accustomed fingers. It wasn't quite big enough to make a proper headscarf but it wasn't bad.

Seth appraised her, sprawling and tipping on the little chair, one arm across its back. —I like it.

She sat down opposite him again, on the side of the bed. Their knees were touching.

—You have to imagine the kind of sex life I was having with this man: 'my betrothed'. They used all this phoney Biblical language. He was thirty, I was seventeen. Of course sexual intercourse before marriage was forbidden. The way he interpreted that was that we could do everything else except for actually fucking. And then when we'd worked ourselves up into a fine state, we had to pray together.

—You're kidding.

—Like this. She put her hands together on her lap, bent her covered head, and dropped her eyes; for a few moments she focused deeply, making herself sorrowful and troubled. She was conscious through her knees of Seth's holding himself intently still, she thought she could feel the thudding in his chest.

—Lord, look into my heart, she said in a low voice, urgently. — You know what I am, you know how much sin there is in me.

Once, afterwards, when the boys were at school and nursery and Tom was out, Karen watched Seth on television, in his soap. She couldn't actually sit and watch it concentratedly, she had to be doing something else; she set up the ironing board in front of the television and brought in a pile of Tom's shirts and the boys' clothes to get on with. Seth only appeared briefly in a storyline in the first part of that episode, so she spent most of it keyed up in an anticipation that came to nothing. When the credits rolled and she saw his name she doubled up with a peculiar hollow pain in her abdomen, and then she made herself hold the hot tip of the iron just for a long moment against the skin on the back of her wrist. It raised an ugly blister which didn't heal for weeks, and left a little V-shaped scar. She was feeling all sorts of odd things around that time anyway, early in her pregnancy. After that she didn't ever watch it again, and then later she heard that he'd left *Emmerdale*, and was getting decent parts in the theatre instead.

He and Cordelia split up, fairly amicably. Karen had known that was going to happen, partly from things he said, and partly from the sight of that heap of his keys and money left like a provisional small island in the sea of Cordelia's things. Nothing changed in Cordelia's attitude to Karen, so presumably Seth hadn't told her anything. He telephoned Karen once, after he'd finished with Cordelia, but she said she didn't want to see him. She told Tom that Seth had phoned, because she wanted to mention him aloud; she pretended that he'd wanted a number for a contact they'd mentioned to him over that weekend in Somerset. Tom said he thought it was a bit much.

Tessa Hadley

When Karen had got back to the farmhouse on that evening of Stella's birthday, Stella and Cordelia were just riding into the yard: she stood for a while in the dusk while they dismounted, exultant from their exercise, in the romance of the hot smell of the horses and their stiff-legged sideways dancing, hooves clattering and striking sparks from the cobbles. Rose was dozing inside on the sofa, the film had finished, the children were squabbling and watching cartoons. It was long past Frankie's bedtime, but Rose's children were never put to bed anyway until they fell asleep where they were. No one had even noticed that Karen had gone out. Stella put soup and bread and cheese and homemade chutney on to the oak table; while they were eating Seth came in from learning his lines at the cottage. He and Karen had carried the evening off with perfect calm.

Cordelia said she couldn't keep awake after her ride, she yawned and huddled into an old dressing-gown of Jim's. She put her feet on to Seth's lap and asked him to rub them. The Laverys liked playing games on family occasions: when the younger children were finally asleep the grown-ups first played 'Ex Libris', which was about guessing the first or last sentences of novels, and then the game where everyone writes the names of ten famous people, real or fictional, and mixes them up in a saucepan. Cordelia wouldn't play. Karen felt joyous all evening, although she didn't usually like games. She and Seth were on the same team; whatever clues he gave about the names he got, she seemed to be able to guess them straight away. She took Roland outside to show him the moon while Seth and Tom were rolling up and smoking in the dark garden. Roland was in his pyjamas, he complained that the grass was making his feet wet; she lifted him up on to her hip, although he was seven years old and getting too heavy for her to carry. She could smell rank marijuana. In the dark the child's body hot and heavy against hers seemed to be part of the unfolding sensation of the man's weight against her earlier. That evening all the ordinary things that she and Seth said to each another, all the times they brushed past each other or sat down together, were a code for something else enormously important that had happened, but did not appear.   □

G R A N T A

NAPLES '04
Roberto Saviano

TRANSLATED FROM THE ITALIAN
BY VIRGINIA JEWISS

Italian police arrest Cosimo Di Lauro, son of Camorra boss Paolo Di Lauro, Naples, January 21, 2005

You don't need to count the dead to understand the business of
the Camorra. The dead are the least revealing element of the
Camorra's real power in Naples, but they are the most visible trace,
what sparks a gut reaction. Sometimes I try to recall how many have
been killed here since the day I was born. I start counting: one hundred
deaths in 1979, 140 in 1980, 110 in 1981, 264 in 1982… Since I was
born, the Camorra has been responsible for nearly 3,700 deaths. That
is more than the Sicilian Mafia, more than the Calabrian 'Ndrangheta,
more than the Russian Mafia, more than the Albanian crime families,
more than ETA in Spain and the IRA in Ireland. Imagine a map of
the world that marks places of conflict with a little flame: Kurdistan,
Sudan, Kosovo, East Timor. Your eye is drawn to the south of Italy,
where bodies pile up with every war connected to the Camorra, the
Mafia. But there's no little flame, no sign of a conflict.

This is the heart of Europe. This is where the majority of Italy's
economy takes shape. The huge international clothing market, the vast
archipelago of Italian elegance, is fed by the Camorra in Naples. But
here *Camorra* is a nonexistent word, a term of contempt used by narcs
and judges, journalists and scriptwriters; it's a name that makes
Camorristi smile. The word clan members use is *System*—'I belong to
the Secondigliano System,' for example, after one of the shabby
northern suburbs of Naples. It is an eloquent term, a mechanism rather
than a structure. The Secondigliano System has gained control of the
entire clothing manufacturing chain in Naples. Everything that is
impossible to do elsewhere—because of the inflexibility of contracts,
laws and copyrights—is feasible here. Structured around the
entrepreneurial power of the clans, the area produces astronomical
capital, amounts unimaginable for any legal industrial conglomeration.
And with its companies, men, and products, the System has reached
every corner of the globe.

I've been coming to Secondigliano and nearby Scampia for a while,
cruising around on my Vespa. Secondigliano is a large area whose
nickname, 'Terzo Mondo', says it all, as does the graffiti near the
entrance to the main street: THIRD WORLD, DO NOT ENTER. The thing
I like most about these places is the light. The big, wide streets are airier
than the tangle of the old city centre, and I can imagine the countryside
still alive under the asphalt and massive buildings. After all, space is
preserved in Scampia's very name, which in a defunct Neapolitan

dialect means 'open land'. A place where weeds grow. Where the infamous Vele, or 'Sails', a monstrous public housing project, sprouted in the 1960s. The rotten symbol of architectural delirium, or perhaps merely a cement utopia powerless to oppose the narcotraffic machine that feeds on this part of the world. Chronic unemployment and a lack of social development planning have made the area a narcotics warehouse, a laboratory for turning drug money into a vibrant, legal economy. Scampia and Secondigliano pump oxygen from illegal markets into legitimate businesses. In 1989 the Camorra Observatory, a Camorra-watch organization, noted that the northern outskirts of Naples had one of the highest ratios of drug pushers to inhabitants in all of Italy. This ratio is now the highest in Europe and one of the top five in the world.

On December 7, 2004, I am awakened by a phone call in the middle of the night. A photographer friend is calling to inform me of the blitz. Not any blitz, but *the* blitz, the one that local and national politicians had been demanding in response to a deadly feud within the powerful Di Lauro clan. After several weeks of killings, Secondigliano is surrounded by a thousand officers. It's a huge media operation, an invasion of journalists and television crews. After years of silence the Camorra suddenly lives again.

Among those arrested is Ciro Di Lauro, one of the boss's sons. Some say he's the clan's accountant. The carabinieri break down the door, search everyone, and aim their rifles at kids' faces. All I manage to see is an officer shouting at a boy who is pointing a knife at him.

'Drop it! Drop it! Now! Now! Drop it!'

The boy drops the knife. The officer kicks it away, and as it bounces off the baseboard, the blade folds into the handle. It's plastic, a Ninja Turtle knife. Meanwhile the other officers are frisking, photographing, searching everywhere. Dozens of blockhouses are knocked down. Reinforced concrete walls are gutted, revealing drug stashes under stairwells. Gates closing off entire portions of streets are toppled, exposing drug warehouses.

Hundreds of women pour on to the streets, setting trash bins on fire and throwing things at the police cars. Their sons, nephews, neighbours are being arrested. Their employers. Yet it's not just a criminal solidarity that I sense on their faces, in their angry words, or their hips, swathed in sweatpants so tight that they seem about to explode. The drug market provides a means of support for most Secondigliano residents, but it is minimal. The only ones who get rich, who reap exponential advantages, are the clan businessmen. All the rest, those who work selling, storing, hiding or protecting get nothing but ordinary salaries, though they risk arrest and months or years in prison. The women's faces wear masks of rage. A rage that tastes of gastric acid. A rage that is both a defence of their territory and an accusation against those who have always considered it nonexistent, lost, a place to forget.

This gigantic deployment of law and order seems staged, arriving only after countless deaths, only after a local girl has been tortured and burned. To the women here it reeks of mockery. The police and bulldozers haven't come to change things, but merely to help out whoever now needs to make arrests or knock down walls. As if all of a sudden someone changed the categories of interpretation and were now declaring that their lives are all wrong. The women know perfectly well everything is wrong here; they didn't need helicopters and armoured vehicles to remind them, but up till then this error was their principal form of life, their mode of survival. What's more, after this eruption that will only complicate their lives, no one will really make any effort to improve things. And so those women jealously guard the oblivion of their isolation and their mistaken lives, chasing away those who suddenly become aware of the dark.

At the end of the operation fifty-three people are in handcuffs. The youngest is nineteen. They've all grown up in the so-called Naples Renaissance of the late 1990s, which was supposed to alter people's destiny. They all know what to do as the carabinieri handcuff them and load them into the prison vans: call this or that lawyer and wait till the clan stipend is delivered to their homes on the twenty-eighth of the month along with the boxes of pasta for their wives and mothers. The men with adolescent sons at home are the most worried, wondering what role their boys will be assigned now. They have no say in the matter.

The feud had started when a second-tier Camorra executive, a member of the powerful Di Lauro clan in charge of the Spanish drug markets, fled from Naples to Barcelona with the Di Lauro clan's cash box. At least that's what was being said. In truth he had failed to turn his quota over to the clan, a way of demonstrating that he no longer felt the least obligation to the people who wanted to keep him on a salary. The schism was official. For the moment it involved only Spain, which had always been controlled by the Camorra clans: Andalusia by the Casalesi of Caserta, the islands by the Nuvolettas of Marano, and Barcelona by the 'secessionists'. That's the name the first crime reporters on the story gave to the many Di Lauro men who broke away. But everyone calls them the Spaniards. Without them the Di Lauro clan is weak and disorganized. But the capo, Cosimo Di Lauro, decided: it would be war. It would be the most ruthless war that southern Italy has seen in the last ten years.

After the blitz the war knows no truce. On December 18 Pasquale Galasso, namesake of one of the most powerful bosses of the 1990s, is bumped off behind the counter of a bar. On December 20 Vincenzo Iorio is killed in a pizzeria. On the twenty-fourth the Di Lauros kill Giuseppe Pezzella, thirty-four years old. He tries to take cover in a bar, but they unload a whole magazine into him. Then a pause for Christmas. The guns of war fall silent. Both sides reorganize, try to establish some rules, devise strategies in this most disorderly of conflicts. On December 27 Emanuele Leone is killed with a bullet to the head. He was twenty-one years old. On December 30 the Spaniards murder Antonio Scafuro, twenty-six, and hit his son in the leg. He was related to a Di Lauro area capo.

The neighbourhoods of Lotto T, Vele, Parco Postale, Case Celesti, Case dei Puffi, and Terzo Mondo are a jungle, a rain forest of reinforced concrete where it's easy to disappear, blend in with the crowd, turn into phantoms. The Di Lauros had lost all their top management and area capos, but they'd still managed to trigger a ruthless war without suffering serious losses. It was as if a government, toppled by a coup and without a president, decided that the way to preserve its power and protect its interests was to arm schoolboys and draft mailmen, civil servants and office clerks, to grant them access to the new power centre instead of relegating them to the rank and file.

For the Di Lauros to win, they would have to be less predictable when they strike, to shield themselves among the people and get lost in the neighbourhoods. Before the end they would have to inflict as many losses as possible on the enemy. A kamikaze logic, no explosions.

The only strategy that offers any chance of winning when you're in the minority.

On January 2 the Di Lauros kill Crescenzo Marino. He hangs facedown in his Smart car, the most expensive model, an unusual automotive choice for a sixty-year-old man. Maybe he thought it would fool the lookouts. A single shot right in the centre of his forehead. A thin trickle of blood runs down his face. Maybe he thought it wouldn't be dangerous to go out just for a few minutes, just for a second. But it was. On the same day the Spaniards bump off Salvatore Barra in a bar in Casavatore. It's the day that Carlo Azeglio Ciampi, the president of the Italian Republic, arrives in Naples to ask the city to react, to offer institutional words of courage and express the support of the state. Three ambushes occur during the hours of his visit.

On January 5 the Di Lauros shoot Carmela Attrice in the face. She is the mother of a leading Spaniard. She no longer leaves her house, so they use a kid as bait. He rings the bell. She knows him, knows who he is, so she doesn't think there's any danger. Still in her pyjamas, she goes downstairs, opens the door, and someone sticks the barrel of a gun in her face. Blood and brains pour out of her head as from a broken egg.

When I arrived at the scene in Case Celesti, the body hadn't yet been covered with a sheet. People were walking in her blood, leaving footprints everywhere. I swallowed hard, trying to calm my stomach. Carmela Attrice hadn't run away even though they'd warned her. She knew her son was a Spaniard, but the Camorra war is full of uncertainty. Nothing is defined, nothing is clear. Things become real only when they happen. In the dynamics of power, of absolute power, nothing exists other than what is concrete. And so fleeing, staying, escaping and informing are choices that seem too suspended, too uncertain, and every piece of advice always finds its opposite twin. Only a concrete occurrence can make you decide. But when it happens, all you can do is accept the decision.

When you die on the street, you're surrounded by a tremendous racket. It's not true that you die alone. Unfamiliar faces right in front of your nose, people touching your legs and arms to see if you're already dead or if it's worth calling an ambulance. All the faces of the seriously wounded, all the expressions of the dying, seem to share the same fear. And the same shame. It may seem strange, but the instant before death is marked by a sense of humiliation. *Lo scuorno* is what they call it here. A bit like being naked in public—that's how it feels when you're mortally wounded in the street. I've never gotten used to seeing murder victims. The nurses and policemen are calm, impassive, going through the motions they've learned by heart, no matter whom they're dealing with. 'We've got calluses on our hearts and leather lining our stomachs,' a young mortuary van driver once said to me.

When you get there before the ambulance does, it's hard to take your eyes off the victim, even if you wish you'd never seen him. I've never understood that this is how you die. The first time I saw someone who'd been killed, I must have been about thirteen. It is still vivid in my mind. I woke up feeling embarrassed: poking out from my pyjamas was the clear sign of an unwanted erection. That classic morning erection, impossible to disguise. I remember it because on my way to school I ran smack into a dead body in the same situation. Five of us, our backpacks filled with books, were walking to school when we came across an Alfetta riddled with bullets. My friends were extremely curious and rushed over to see. Feet sticking up on the seat. The most daring kid asked a carabiniere why the feet were where the head should have been. The officer didn't hesitate to respond, as if he hadn't realized how old his interlocutor was. 'The spray turned him upside down.'

I was only a boy, but I knew that 'spray' meant machine-gun fire. The Camorrista had taken so many blows that his body had flipped. Head down and feet in the air. When the carabiniere opened the door, the corpse fell to the ground like a melting icicle. We watched undisturbed, without anyone telling us this was no sight for children. Without any moral hand covering our eyes. The dead man had an erection. It was obvious under his tight-fitting jeans. And it shocked me. I stared at it for a long time. For days I wondered how it could have happened, what he'd been thinking about, what he'd been doing before dying. My afternoons were spent trying to imagine what was in his head before he was killed. It tormented me until I finally got up the courage to ask for an explanation. I was told that an erection is a common reaction in male murder victims. As soon as Linda, one of the girls in our group, saw the dead body slide out from behind the steering wheel, she started to cry and hid behind two of the boys.

A strangled cry. A young plainclothes officer grabbed the cadaver by the hair and spat in his face. Then he turned to us and said: 'No, what are you crying for? This guy was a real shit. Nothing happened, everything's okay. Nothing happened. Don't cry.'

Ever since then, I've had trouble believing those television scenarios of forensic police who wear gloves and tread softly, careful not to displace any powder or shells. When I get to a body before the ambulance does and gaze on the final moments of life of someone who realizes he's dying, I always think of *Heart of Darkness*, the scene when the woman who loved Kurtz asks Marlow what his last words were. And Marlow lies. He says Kurtz spoke her name, when in reality he didn't utter any sweet words or precious thoughts, but simply repeated, 'The horror.' We like to think that a person's last words convey his ultimate, most important, most essential thoughts. That he dies articulating the reason life was worth living for. But it's not like that. When you die, nothing comes out except fear. Everyone, or almost everyone, repeats the same thing, a simple, banal, urgent sentence: 'I don't want to die.' Their faces are superimposed on Kurtz's and express the torment, disgust, and refusal to end so horrendously, in the worst of all possible worlds. The horror.

After seeing dozens of murder victims, soiled with their own blood as it mixes with filth, as they exhale nauseating odours, as they are looked at with curiosity or professional indifference, shunned like hazardous waste or discussed with agitated cries, I have arrived at just one certainty, a thought so elementary that it approaches idiocy: death is revolting.

In Secondigliano everyone, down to the little kids, has a perfectly clear idea of how you die and the best way to go. At the scene of Carmela Attrice's murder I overheard two boys talking. Their tone was extremely serious.

'I want to die like the *signora*. In the head, *bang bang* and it's all over.'

'But in your face? They hit her in the face, that's the worst!'

'No, it's not, and besides, it's only an instant. Front or back, but in the head for sure!'

Curious, I butted in: 'Isn't it better to be hit in the chest? One shot in the heart and it's all over.'

But the boy understood the dynamics of pain far better than I did and explained in detail and with professional expertise the impact of bullets.

'No, in the chest it hurts a whole lot and it takes you ten minutes to die. Your lungs have to fill with blood, and the bullet is like a fiery needle that pierces and twists inside you. It hurts to get hit in the arm or leg too. But in the chest it's like a wicked snakebite that won't go away. The head's better, because you won't piss yourself or shit in your pants. No flailing around on the ground for half an hour.'

He had seen. And much more than just one dead body. Getting hit in the head saves you from trembling in fear, pissing your pants, or having the stench of your guts ooze out of the holes in your stomach. I asked him more about the details of death and killing. Every conceivable question except the only one I should have asked: why was a fourteen-year-old thinking so much about death? But it didn't occur to me, not even for a second. The boy introduced himself by his nickname: Pikachu, one of the Pokémon characters. His blond hair and stocky figure had earned him the name. Pikachu pointed out some individuals in the crowd that had formed around the body of the dead woman. He lowered his voice: 'See those guys, they're the ones who killed Pupetta.'

Carmela Attrice had been known as Pupetta. I tried to look them straight in the face. They seemed worked up, palpitating, moving their heads and shoulders to get a better look as the police covered the body. They'd killed her with their faces unmasked and had gone to sit nearby, under the statue of Padre Pio; as soon as a crowd started to form around the body, they'd come back to see. They were caught a few days later. Retail drug dealers made over into soldiers, trained to ambush a harmless woman, killed in her pyjamas and slippers. This was their baptism of fire. The youngest was sixteen, the oldest twenty-eight, the alleged assassin twenty-two. When they were arrested, one of them, catching sight of the flashbulbs and video cameras, started to laugh and wink at the journalists. They also arrested the alleged bait, the sixteen-year-old who had rung the bell so that the woman would come downstairs. Sixteen, the same age as Carmela Attrice's daughter, who realized what had happened as soon as she heard the shots and went out on to the balcony and started to cry. The investigators also claimed that the executioners had returned to the scene of the crime. They were too curious; it was like starring in your own movie. First as actor and then as spectator, but in the same film. It must be true that you don't have a precise memory of your actions when you shoot because those boys went back, eager to see what they'd done and what sort of face the victim had. I asked Pikachu if the guys were a Di Lauro hit squad, known as a trawler, or if they at least wanted to form one. He laughed. 'A trawler! Don't they wish! They're just little pissers, but I saw a real trawler.'

I didn't know if Pikachu was bullshitting me or if he'd merely pieced together what was being said around Scampia, but his story was accurate. He was pedantic, precise to the point of eliminating any doubt. He was pleased to see my stunned expression as he talked. Pikachu told me he used to have a dog named Careca, like the Brazilian forward who played for Napoli, the Italian champions. This dog liked to go out on to the apartment landing. One day he smelled someone in the apartment opposite, which is usually empty, so he started scratching at the door. A few seconds later a burst of gunfire exploded from behind the door and hit him full on. Pikachu told the story complete with sound effects: '*Rat-tat-tat-tat*... Careca dies instantly—and the door—*bang*—slams open real quick.'

Pikachu sat on the ground, planted his feet against a low wall, and made as if he were cradling a machine gun, imitating the sentinel that had killed his dog. The sentinel who's always sitting behind the door, a pillow behind his back and his feet braced on either side. An uncomfortable position, to keep you from falling asleep, but above all because shooting from below is a sure way to eliminate whoever is on the other side of the door without getting hit yourself. Pikachu told me that as a way of apology for killing his dog, they gave his family some money and invited him into the apartment. An apartment in which an entire trawler was hiding. He remembered everything, the rooms bare except for beds, a table and a television. Pikachu spoke quickly, gesticulating wildly to describe the men's positions and movements. They were nervous, tense, one of them with 'pineapples' around his neck. Pineapples are the hand grenades the killers wear. Pikachu said a basket full of them was near a window. The Camorra has always had a certain fondness for grenades. Clan arsenals everywhere are filled with hand grenades and antitank bombs from Eastern Europe. Pikachu said that the men spent hours playing

Roberto Saviano

PlayStation, so he'd challenged and beat them all. Because he always won, they promised him that 'one of these days they'd take me with them to shoot for real.'

Pikachu and I went for a walk and he told me about the boys in the clan, the real strength of the Di Lauros. I asked him where they hung out, and he offered to take me to a pizzeria where they'd go in the evening; he wanted me to see that he knew them all. First we picked up a friend of Pikachu's, one of the boys who'd been part of the System for a while. Pikachu worshipped him and described him as a sort of boss; the System kids looked up to him because he'd been given the task of providing food for the fugitives and even doing the shopping for the Di Lauro family, or so he claimed. He was called Tonino Kit Kat because he was known to devour masses of candy bars. Kit Kat assumed the attitude of a little boss, but I let him see I was sceptical. He got fed up answering my questions, so he lifted his sweater. His entire torso was speckled with round bruises: violet circles with yellow and greenish clots of crushed capillaries in the centres.

'What have you done?'

'The vest.'

'What vest?'

'The bulletproof vest.'

'The vest doesn't give you those bruises, does it?'

'No, but these eggplants are the hits I took.'

The bruises—eggplants—were the fruit of the bullets that the jacket had stopped an inch before they penetrated flesh. To train the boys not to be afraid of weapons, they make them put on a vest and then fire at them. Faced with a weapon, a vest alone isn't enough to convince you not to flee. A vest is not a vaccine against fear. The only way to anaesthetize every fear is to show how the weapons can be neutralized. The boys told me that they were taken out to the countryside beyond Secondigliano. They'd put the vests on under their T-shirts, and then, one by one, half a clip would be unloaded at them. 'When you're hit, you fall on the ground, you can't breathe, you gasp for air, but you can't inhale. You just can't do it. It's like you've been punched in the chest, you feel like you're dying…but then you get back up. That's the important thing. After you've been hit, you get back up.' Kit Kat had been trained along with others to take the hit. He'd been trained to die, or rather to almost die.

The clans enlist the boys as soon as they're capable of being loyal. Twelve to seventeen years old. Lots of them are sons or brothers of clan affiliates, while others come from families without steady incomes. This is the Neapolitan Camorra clans' new army. The advantages for the clan are many: a boy earns half the salary of a low ranking adult, rarely has to support his parents, doesn't have the responsibilities of a family or fixed hours, doesn't need to be paid punctually, and above all, is willing to be on the streets at all times. There's a whole range of jobs and responsibilities. They start with pushing light drugs, hashish in particular. The boys position themselves in the most crowded streets, and they're almost always issued a *motorino*. They work their way up to cocaine, which they peddle at the universities, outside the nightclubs, in front of hotels, inside the subway stations. These baby pushers are fundamental to the flexible economy of drug dealing because they attract less attention, do business between a football match and a *motorino* ride, and will often deliver directly to the client's home. The clan doesn't usually make them work mornings; in fact, they continue to go to school, in part because if they dropped out, they would be easier to identify. After the first couple of months, the boy affiliates go about armed, both in self-defence and as a way of asserting themselves. The weapons—automatics and semi-automatics the boys learn to use in the garbage dumps outside of town or in the city's underground caverns—are both a promotion on the field and a promise of possibility, of rising to the top of the clan.

When they prove themselves reliable and win the area capo's complete trust, they take on a role that goes well beyond that of pusher: they become lookouts. Lookouts make sure that all the trucks unloading goods at the supermarkets, stores and delicatessens on their assigned street are ones imposed by the clan, and they report when a shop is using a distributor other than the 'preselected' one. The presence of lookouts is also essential at construction sites. Contracting firms often subcontract to Camorra companies, but at times the work is assigned to firms that are 'not recommended'. To discover if work is being given to 'external' firms, the clans monitor the sites constantly, and in a way that is above suspicion. The boys observe, check and report back to the area capo, who tells them what to do if a site steps out of line. These young affiliates behave like and have the responsibilities of adult Camorristi. They start their careers young and charge up through the ranks; their rise to positions of power is radically altering the genetic structure of the clans. Baby capos and boy bosses make for unpredictable and ruthless interlocutors; they follow a logic that keeps law officers and anti-Mafia investigators from understanding their dynamics. The faces are new and unfamiliar.

Pikachu and Kit Kat took me to see Nello, a pizza chef in the area who was responsible for feeding the System boys when they'd finished their shifts. A group came into Nello's pizzeria just after I got there. They were awkward and ungainly, their sweaters puffed out from the bulletproof vests underneath. They'd left their *motorini* on the pavement and came in without saying hello to anyone. The way they walked, with their padded chests, they looked like football players. Boyish faces, thirteen to sixteen years old, a few with the first hints of a beard. Pikachu and Kit Kat had me sit with them, and no one seemed to mind. They were eating and, above all, drinking. Water, Coca-Cola, Fanta. An incredible thirst that they tried to quench even with the pizza; they asked for a bottle of olive oil and then poured large amounts on the pizzas, saying they were too dry. Everything dried up in their mouths, from their saliva to their words. I realized that they were coming off a night shift as watch guards and had taken pills. The clans gave them MDMA pills—ecstasy—to keep them awake, to keep them from stopping to eat twice a day. The German drug maker Merck patented MDMA during the First World War for soldiers in the trenches—those German soldiers referred to as *Menschenmaterial*, human material—to enable them to overcome hunger, cold and terror. Later it was used by the Americans for espionage operations. And now these little soldiers received their dose of artificial courage and adulterated resistance. They cut slices of pizza and sucked them down; the sounds coming from the table were of old people slurping their soup. The boys resumed talking and kept ordering bottles of water. And then I did something that could have been met with violence, but I sensed I could get away with it, that these were kids I was looking at. Padded with plates of lead, but kids nevertheless. I put a tape recorder on the table and addressed them all in a loud voice, trying to catch each one's eye: 'Forza, go ahead and talk into this, say whatever you feel like.'

This didn't strike anyone as strange, no one suspected they were sitting with a narc or a journalist. Someone hurled a few insults at the recorder, then one boy, encouraged by some of my questions, recounted his career. It seemed as if he couldn't wait to tell it.

'First I worked in a bar. I made two hundred euros a month, two fifty with tips, but I didn't like the work. I wanted to work in the garage with my brother, but they didn't take me. In the System I get three hundred euros a week, but if I sell well, I also get a percentage on every brick of hashish and can make up to three hundred fifty, four hundred euros. I have to bust my ass, but in the end they always give me something more.'

After a volley of belches that two of the kids wanted to record, the boy called Satore, a name halfway between Sasà and Totore, two diminutives for Salvatore, continued: 'Before I was out on the street, it annoyed me that I didn't have a *motorino* and had to get around on foot or take the bus. I like the work, everyone respects me, and I can do what I want. Now they give me iron and I have to stay around here all the time, Terzo Mondo, Case dei Puffi. Always in the same place, back and forth. And I don't like it.'

Satore smiled at me, then laughed loudly into the recorder: 'Let me out of here! Tell that to the boss!'

They'd been given iron—a pistol—and a limited territory in which to work. Kit Kat began to speak into the recorder, his lips touching the holes of the microphone, so that even his breath registered.

'I want to open a renovation company or else a warehouse or a store. The System will have to give me the money to get set up, but then I'll worry about the rest, even who to marry. I want to get married, not to somebody from here, though, but a model, black or German.'

Pikachu took a pack of cards from his pocket, and four of them started to play. The others got up and stretched, but no one removed his bulletproof vest. I kept asking Pikachu about the trawlers, but he was starting to get irritated at my insistence. He told me he'd been at a trawler house a few days before, but that they'd dismantled everything; the only thing left was their MP3 player with the music they listened to when they went to do contract killings—what they call 'pieces'. It was now dangling from his neck. Inventing an excuse, I asked if I could borrow it for a few days. Pikachu laughed as if to say that he wasn't offended that I'd taken him for an idiot, for someone stupid enough to lend things. So I bought it. I coughed up fifty euros and he gave me the player. I immediately stuck the headphones in my ears; I wanted to know what trawler background music was. I was expecting rap, acid rock, heavy metal, but instead it was an endless round of Neapolitan neo-melodic music and pop. In America, killers pump themselves up on rap, but in Secondigliano they go off to kill with love songs in their ears.

On January 19, 2005, the forty-five-year-old Pasquale Paladini is killed. Eight shots to the chest and head. A few hours later, Antonio Auletta, age nineteen, is hit in the legs. But January 21 seems to be a turning point. Word spreads quickly, there's no need for a press office. Cosimo Di Lauro has been arrested. According to the Naples anti-Mafia prosecutor's office, Cosimo is the prince of the gang and the leader of the slaughter. According to state witnesses, he's the clan commander. Cosimo was hiding in a hole forty metres square and sleeping on a dilapidated bed. The heir to a criminal association that invoices 500,000 euros a day from narcotics alone, and who had a villa worth five million euros in the heart of one of the poorest regions of Italy, was reduced to hiding in a stinking little hole not far from his alleged palace.

It was a villa that rose out of nothing in Via Cupa dell'Arco, near the Di Lauro family home. An elegant, eighteenth-century farmhouse, restructured like a Pompeian villa, complete with impluvium, columns, plaster decorations, false ceilings and grand staircases. No one knew the official owners. The carabinieri were investigating, but in the neighbourhood no one had any doubts. It was for Cosimo. The carabinieri discovered the place by chance. After breaching the thick walls surrounding it, they came across some workers, who ran off as soon as they saw the uniforms. The war interrupted work on the villa, kept it from being filled with furniture and paintings fit for a prince, from becoming the heart of gold of the decaying body of the Secondigliano building industry.

When Cosimo hears the rumble of the carabinieri amphibians and the clatter of their rifles, he doesn't try to escape. He doesn't even arm himself. Instead he goes to the mirror, wets his comb, pulls his hair off his forehead, and ties it in a ponytail at his nape, letting the curly mane fall on to his neck. He is wearing a dark polo-neck sweater and a black raincoat. Dressed as a clown of crime, a warrior of the night, Cosimo Di Lauro descends the stairs, chest out. A few years earlier he took a disastrous spill on his motorcycle, and the legacy was a lame leg. But he's even thought about his limp; as he walks down the stairs he leans on the forearms of the carabinieri who escort him, so as not to reveal his handicap, and proceeds with a normal gait. The new military sovereigns of the Neapolitan criminal associations don't present themselves as neighbourhood tough guys, don't have the crazy, wide-eyed look of Raffaele Cutolo, head of the Nuova Camorra Organizzata in the 1970s, don't feel the need to pose as the Cosa Nostra boss Luciano Liggio or caricatures of Lucky Luciano and Al Capone. *The Matrix*, *The Crow* and *Pulp Fiction* give a better idea of what they want and who they are. They are models everyone recognizes and that don't need too much mediation.

Spectacle is superior to enigmatic codes of winking or the well-defined mythology of infamous crime neighbourhoods. Cosimo looks straight at the cameras, lowers his chin, and sticks out his forehead. He didn't allow himself to be found out the way Giovanni Brusca did, wearing a pair of threadbare jeans and a shirt with spaghetti sauce stains; he's not frightened like Totò Riina, who was quickly loaded into a helicopter, or surprised with a sleepy look on his face like Giuseppe Misso, the Sanità neighbourhood boss. Cosimo has been brought up in the world of show business, and he knows how to make an entrance. He appears like a warrior who has stumbled for the first time. The expression on his face says this is the price he must pay for having so much courage and zeal. He acts as if he weren't being arrested, but simply moving headquarters. He knew the risk when he triggered the war, but he had no choice. It was war or death. He wants his arrest to seem like the proof of his victory, the symbol of his courage that disdains any form of self-defence as long as it preserves the family system.

The people in the neighbourhood feel their stomachs churn. They set off a revolt, overturning cars and launching Molotov cocktails. This hysterical attack is not, as it may seem, to prevent the arrest, but rather to exorcise any act of revenge. To erase every trace of suspicion. To let Cosimo know that no one betrayed him, no one blabbed, that the hieroglyphics of his hiding place had not been deciphered with their help. The revolt is an elaborate rite of apology, a metaphysical chapel of atonement that the neighbourhood people build from burned-out carabinieri cars, Dumpsters used as barricades, and black smoke from fuming tyres. If Cosimo suspects them, they won't even have time to pack their bags before the axe falls in yet another ruthless condemnation.

Just days after his arrest, Cosimo's haughty gaze stares out of the screen savers of the mobile phones of dozens of kids in Torre Annunziata, Quarto and Marano. Mere provocations, banal gestures of adolescent foolishness. Of course. But Cosimo knew. You have to act this way to be recognized as a capo, to touch people's hearts. You have to know how to work the TV screen and the newspaper, how to tie your ponytail. Cosimo clearly represents the new model of System entrepreneur, the image of the new bourgeoisie, liberated of every constraint, motivated by the absolute desire to dominate every corner of the market and to have a hand in everything. The logic of criminal business, of the Camorra bosses, coincides with the most aggressive neoliberalism. The rules, dictated or imposed, are those of business, profit and victory over all the competition. Anything else is worthless. Anything else doesn't exist. You pay with prison or your skin for the power to decide people's lives or deaths, promote a product, monopolize a slice of the economy, and invest in cutting-edge markets. To have power for ten years, a year, an hour—it doesn't matter for how long. What counts is to live, to truly command. To win in the market arena, to stare at the sun, as the Forcella boss Raffaele Giuliano did, challenging it from his prison cell, showing that he was not blinded even by that supreme light. Raffaele Giuliano, who ruthlessly spread hot pepper on a knife before stabbing the relative of an enemy, so as to make him feel excruciating, burning pain as the blade pierced his flesh, inch by inch. In prison he was feared not for his bloodthirsty punctiliousness, but for the challenge of his gaze. To know you are a businessman destined to end up dead or in jail and still feel the ruthless desire to dominate powerful and unlimited economic empires. The boss is arrested or killed, but the economic system he generated remains, and it continues to mutate, evolve, improve and produce profits. The mentality of these samurai liberalists who know that you have to pay to have power—absolute power— was summed up in a letter a boy in juvenile detention wrote and gave to a priest. It was read during a conference. I still remember it by heart:

Everyone I know is either dead or in jail. I want to become a boss. I want to have supermarkets, stores, factories, I want to have women. I want three cars, I want respect when I go into a store, I want to have warehouses all over the world. And then I want to die. I want to die like a man, like someone who truly commands. I want to be killed.

This is the new rhythm of criminal entrepreneurs, the new thrust of the economy: to dominate it at any cost. Power before all else. Economic victory is more precious than life itself. Than anyone's life, including your own.

The body of Giulio Ruggiero is found on the evening of January 21, the same day on which Cosimo Di Lauro is arrested. A burned-out car, a cadaver in the driver's seat. Decapitated. The head is on the backseat. It hadn't been cut off with a hatchet, a clean blow, but with a metal grinder: the kind of circular saw welders use to polish soldering. The worst possible tool, and thus the most obvious choice. First cut the flesh, then chip away at the bones. They must have done the job right there because the ground was littered with flakes of flesh that looked like tripe. The investigations hadn't even begun, but everyone in the area seemed convinced it was a message. A symbol. Cosimo Di Lauro could not have been arrested without a tip-off. In everyone's mind, that headless body was a traitor. Only someone who has sold a capo can be ripped apart like that. The sentence is passed before the investigations even begin. It doesn't really matter if the sentence is correct or if it's chasing an illusion. I looked at that abandoned car and head in Via Hugo Pratt without getting off my Vespa. I could hear the talk of how they had burned the body and the severed head, filling the mouth with gasoline, placing a wick between its teeth, and setting it on fire so that the whole face would explode. I started my Vespa and drove off.

When I arrive on the scene on January 24, 2005, Attilio Romanò is lying dead on the floor. A horde of carabinieri is nervously pacing in front of the store where the ambush took place. Yet another one. An agitated youth comments as he passes, 'A death a day, that's the refrain of Naples.' He stops, doffs his hat to the dead he doesn't even see, and walks on. The killers had entered the shop with their pistols ready. It is clear that they weren't there to steal but to kill, to punish. Attilio had tried to hide behind the counter. He knew it wouldn't make a difference, but maybe he hoped to show he was unarmed, that he wasn't involved, that he hadn't done anything. Maybe he knew they were soldiers in the Camorra war the Di Lauros were waging. They shot him, emptying their magazines into him, and after the 'service' they left the store—calmly, people say—as if they had just bought a mobile phone instead of killing a human being. Attilio Romanò is on the floor. Blood everywhere. It seems as if his soul had drained out of the holes that riddled his body. When you see that much blood on the ground, you start touching yourself, checking if you've been wounded, if it's your own blood you're looking at. You develop a psychotic anxiety and try to make sure that you haven't been wounded somehow without realizing it. And still you can't believe that there could be so much blood in just one man. You're sure there's far less inside you. And when you've ascertained that it wasn't you who lost all that blood, you still feel empty. You become a haemorrhage yourself, you feel your legs go weak, fur on your tongue, your hands dissolve in that thick lake. You wish someone would look at the whites of your eyes to check if you're anaemic. You want to ask for a blood transfusion, you wish you could eat a steak, if you could just get it down without vomiting. You have to shut your eyes and try not to breathe. The smell of congealed blood, like rusty iron, has already penetrated the plaster on the walls. You have to leave, go outside, get some air before they start throwing sawdust on the blood because the combination smells so terrible it will make you vomit for sure.

I couldn't truly understand why I had decided to show up yet again at a murder scene. But I was sure of one thing: it's not important to map out what has happened, to reconstruct the terrible drama that has unfolded. It's pointless to study the traces of the bullets, the chalk circles drawn around them, like a children's game of marbles. The thing to do instead is to try to understand if something remains. Maybe this is what I want to track down. I try to understand if anything human is left, if there is a path, a tunnel dug by the worm of existence that can lead to a solution, an answer that could give some sense of what is happening.

Attilio's body is still on the floor when his family arrives. Two women, maybe his mother and his wife, I don't know. They walk shoulder to shoulder, cling to each other as they approach. They're the only ones who are still hoping it is not as they know it to be. They understand perfectly well. But they wrap their arms around each other, support one another in the instant before they face the tragedy. And in those very seconds, in the steps that wives and mothers take toward crumpled cadavers, one senses the irrational, mad and pointless faith in human longing. They hope, hope, hope and hope some more that there has been a mistake, that the rumours are wrong, a misunderstanding on the part of the carabiniere official who had told them of the ambush and the killing. As if clinging stubbornly to their belief can actually alter the course of events. In that moment the blood pressure of hope is at its peak. But there's nothing to be done. The cries and weeping reveal reality's force of gravity. Attilio is on the floor. He worked in a phone store and, to make a little extra money, at a call centre. He and his wife, Natalia, hadn't had children yet. They hadn't had time; maybe they didn't have the means; maybe they were waiting for the chance to raise them somewhere else. Their days were consumed by work, and when they were finally able to put a little something aside, Attilio had thought it a good idea to buy into the business where he met his death. But the other owner is a distant relative of Pariante, a Di Lauro colonel who turned against him. Attilio doesn't know or maybe he underestimates the danger; he trusts his partner, it's enough that he's someone who supports himself, someone who works hard, too hard. After all, around here you don't choose your lot, and a job seems like a privilege, something you hold on to once you've got it. You feel fortunate, as if a lucky star had shone on you, even if it means you're away from home thirteen hours a day, you get only half of Sunday off, and your 1,000 euros a month are hardly enough to cover your mortgage. No matter how you got the job, you have to be thankful and not ask too many questions—of yourself or of fate.

But someone has his doubts. And so the body of Attilio Romanò gets added to those of the Camorra soldiers killed in recent months. The bodies are the same, fallen in the same war, but the reasons for their deaths are different. The clans are the ones to decide who you are and what part you play in the game of risk. They decide independently of individuals' wills. When the armies take to the streets, it is impossible to move according to any other dynamic than their strategy; it is they who decide meaning, motives, causes. In that moment, the shop where Attilio worked represented an economy linked to the Spaniards, one that had to be destroyed.

Natalia, or Nata as Attilio called her, is stunned by the tragedy. They'd only been married for four months, but she is not consoled, the president of the Republic doesn't attend the funeral, there's no minister or mayor to hold her hand. Perhaps it's just as well: she is spared the institutional theatre. But an unjust suspicion hovers over Attilio's death, a suspicion that is the silent approval of the rule of the Camorra. Yet another assent to the clans' activities. But the people who worked with Attila—the nickname they gave him because of his fierce desire to live—at the call centre organize candlelight vigils and insist on marching even if other murders occur during the protests and blood still stains the streets. They demonstrate, light candles, clarify, remove all shame, cancel out all suspicion. Attila died on the job and had no ties to the Camorra.

As they were taking away Attilio Romanò, I started to understand why there is not a moment in which my mother does not look at me with anxiety, unable to comprehend why I don't leave, run away, why I keep living in this hell.

I went home, but I couldn't sit still. I went out again and started to run, faster and faster. My heart was pounding, my tongue and teeth were drowning in saliva. I could feel the blood swelling the veins in my neck, flooding my chest, I was out of breath, inhaling all the air I could and then exhaling hard, like a bull. I started running again, my hands frozen, my face on fire. I felt I had absorbed all the blood I had seen on the ground, that all the blood that had gushed out was now pumping through my body.

I ran to the shore and climbed on the rocks. Haze mixed with the darkness so I couldn't even make out the lights of the ships crossing the gulf. The water rippled, the waves were beginning to pick up. It seemed as if they were reluctant to touch the mire of the battleground, but they didn't return to the distant maelstrom of the open sea. The waves were immobile, stubbornly resisting, impossibly fixed, clinging to their foamy crests, no longer sure where the sea ends. □

GRANTA

NONY AND NIXI
Nony Singh

Dayanita Singh, whose photographs appeared in Granta 57 *and* Granta 73, *grew up surrounded by family pictures. Most of them were taken by her mother, Nony Singh, who not only put them into frames, but arranged them, collage-style, under the glass-topped tables of the house and pasted them into albums—one for each of her four daughters. Dayanita—known as 'Nixi'—was her oldest child, and she was photographed the most. About ten years ago, when she was moving, Nony Singh handed Dayanita a box of her photographs and negatives for safe-keeping. This is a ritual that takes place in many households as the family history is passed from one generation to the next. Often such boxes are only opened at Christmas, or when somebody dies, or when a child grows curious about where he or she comes from. Because Dayanita was a photographer, however, she took the negatives to her printer to be developed professionally. When François Hebel, the director of the annual French festival of photography in Arles, came to India last year, looking for pictures for an Indian pavilion in 2007, Dayanita showed him her mother's photographs, with the suggestion that 'domestic' pictures in India might be a rich source. Hebel decided to exhibit Nony Singh's pictures and he invited her to France. It was twenty-five years since she had been out of India, but she and her pictures were received with enthusiasm at Arles. They were exhibited for the first time, many of them in their original square format. A small selection follows, introduced by the photographer.*

At the age of seven I made a portrait of my mother, Mohinder Kaur, in Lahore during a family picnic. It is still one of my favourite pictures. Four years later, after Partition in 1947, we were forced to move to Patiala Punjab in India. I was sent to boarding school in Dehradun, in northern India, where I spent each month's pocket money (twenty rupees) on making photographs with my box camera while my friends spent theirs on sweets. In January 1960, when my husband-to-be announced he had chosen to marry me, his father was so happy he gave me the Zeiss Ikon camera that was slung on his shoulder.

After we were married, I opened a trunk and found it filled with photographs of women, many of them dancing with my husband. He told me these were his girlfriends from around the world, from before he met me. My first reaction was, 'What a way to treat good

My mother, Mohinder Kaur, graceful, dignified and wise, at a
family picnic on the way to Koh Murree, near Rawalpindi
(now Pakistan), 1943.

photographs.' And, 'Is this the respect you show the women you once loved?' So I decided to put them all into an album, 'The Album of My Husband's Girlfriends'. I pasted my own photo on the last page.

I photographed my daughters as they grew. Most of all I photographed my firstborn, Nixi, amazed at the wonder of having created a life—almost like God. After her birth, my husband took us to the Oberoi Hotel in Srinagar, Kashmir, where we stayed in the President's Suite. I put Nixi on the chaise longue and made a picture to prove to my family that I had indeed stayed there. Then I photographed all the light fittings, the beds, the view.

I photographed my family right through our marriage, until my husband died in 1981. After that I took charge of his farm, and I brought up my four daughters.

Nixi was a very artistic child from the start. I still have her sketchbooks, the portraits she did at the age of five. I thought to myself, this is a talent I must ensure does not get smothered in the ups and downs of life. She was always very impatient with my photography, as I counted back the steps to get her in focus. I dressed her as a gypsy for one party and that turned out to be quite prophetic. Even though I dressed her as the Mother Mary, I could tell her life would be far from a conventional one. I had to fight with my husband to send her to design school and once I became a widow I made sure she could follow her passion. My last photo of her, before she became a photographer herself, has my shadow on it.

In 1997, fifty years after Independence, I went back to Pakistan and visited the house I was born in, in Anarkali, Lahore. I saw the room I'd been born in, and I peeped into the tiny forbidden black room next door. It reminded me of my grandmother saying when we were naughty: 'Behave, or I will lock you in the dark room!' Of course, we had all forgotten; my grandfather was a photographer. He died young and so the room was always locked. But that was how the 'dark room' entered our lives.

I still take photographs, though now I use a digital camera that my daughter brought me from abroad. She is the one who took my old negatives and had them printed up. I was so surprised when I saw some of the pictures. The lab had been cropping my square pictures into rectangles. And I thought the camera saw less than my eyes did all this time. ☐

My elder sister, Rajman, with our two cousins in a village in
Pakistan, 1945. Those days it used to be great fun to climb trees
but was not meant for girls. I asked them to go and sit on the
tree to make an unusual picture.

My sister Rajman, newly married, in a romantic pose, on the way to
Kasauli. Her husband was in the army and posted there, 1955

My younger sister, Guddi, who was considered very beautiful, posing as
Scarlett O'Hara from 'Gone with the Wind', Srinagar 1962

Before we married, my husband asked me what two or three things I would wish to do after our marriage. One was to meet Pandit Nehru (which he arranged), the other was to stay in a five-star hotel. So he took me to the President's Suite at the Oberoi Palace. I was very happy that he had made my wish come true, Srinagar 1961

My darling Nixi surrounded by the grandeur of the President's Suite
at the Oberoi Palace Hotel, Srinagar 1961

I was so happy in this suite that I tried to capture every detail of it.
I wanted to remember even the royal lamps on the wall,
Oberoi Palace Hotel, Srinagar 1961

Two single beds and a cot. They did not have double beds,
Oberoi Palace Hotel, Srinagar 1961

I had to capture my baby looking happy in the strong arms of her
father, Srinagar 1962

Nixi used to suck her thumb and pull her hair, so the only way to stop her was to shave her head. But since we are Sikhs, I was terrified of my father-in-law's reaction, Srinagar 1962

Nixi in the Nawabi style of Bhopal, stitched by me, Bhopal 1963

Nixi I dressed as a gypsy and her sister Nikita as an angel. Later in life
they adopted these roles, Play House School, New Delhi 1964

My husband was annoyed with me for fluffing Nixi's hair, but I
thought it made a good pose, Delhi 1964

Nixi, Delhi 1965

Nixi and Nikita in frilly frocks, stitched by me. Nixi never had the patience for posing. Nikita was ever so patient, Delhi 1965

Nixi and Nikita at my husband's family home. My father-in-law, who had gifted me his camera on hearing the news of his son's marriage plans, was standing beside me to receive his two granddaughters from their evening boat ride, Bhopal 1966

Nixi, with her boarding school in the Himalayas in the background,
Kasauli 1976

Nixi wearing the halter-neck top her father had forbidden her to wear,
except for in this photograph, Delhi 1979

Nixi on her way to study at the National Institute of Design in Ahmedabad. I just knew she was talented as an artist and fought with my protective husband to let her go. It was expensive. I had no idea what she would become one day. I just wanted her to be self-sufficient and never have to depend on any man for money, Delhi 1980

GRANTA

WHEELS OF PROGRESS
Gemini Wahhaj

Bakher Khan bought a shell keyring on Cox's Bazaar beach from one of those bare-chested girls who sell trinkets in the dark. He had had the name 'Mohua' carved on the shell. He showed it to Mr Vincent when Mr Vincent climbed in the Jeep the next morning.

'Very nice,' said Mr Vincent. 'Your wife?'

'No, my daughter,' replied Bakher Khan.

Siddiqi the engineer said, 'You have a daughter? In that case there is no question of writing your wife's name.'

Mr Vincent's car was full today. Bakher Khan was pleased that he was driving more people than Robiul, the driver of the other car. Mrs Ann was coming with them, too; she had left her daughter behind in Dhaka. They had flown in the night before to Chittagong Airport, Mr Vincent, Mrs Ann, Mr John and Mr Frans. Bakher Khan and Robiul had driven down from Dhaka to wait for their arrival. Bakher Khan thought they could have made the trip to Sitakunda on the way from the airport to the hotel in Cox's Bazaar—Sitakunda was only thirty-seven kilometres from Chittagong—but the foreigners had been tired.

Geological tour by the exploration department! Bakher Khan had memorized the words. He was good at memorizing, learning, improving himself.

He drove in a trance-like state, thinking about his three-year-old daughter: how she ran about the small flat in Mohammedpur, her bangles tinkling all the time, even when she slept in the dark between Bakher Khan and his wife. He thought especially about her feet, so tiny and fat that they always made him think this moment with her would pass, she would grow, her feet would get bigger and she would no longer run about his little home.

Mrs Ann and Mr Vincent also had babies. Mrs Ann's was just four months old. After some moments of eavesdropping, Bakher Khan gathered that they were discussing what Mr Vincent and his wife and Mrs Ann and her husband did when their babies cried at night. He felt an immense satisfaction in gathering this from the soft laughs; his English had improved vastly since he had become Mr Vincent's driver.

'So Mary says, you get up, and I say, it's your baby,' Mr Vincent was saying, 'and we both lie there groaning. Then it's always me… Mary just can't do it at night.'

Mrs Ann chuckled, said her Bill was quite good at handling little Cara, but she just couldn't let them be. There was more laughter from the back seat, a warmth in the car. Bakher Khan was especially happy to be back in Chittagong, his home town. Siddiqi was also laughing. Then Mr Vincent asked Siddiqi, 'Do Bangladeshi fathers ever take care of their children?'

Siddiqi stopped laughing and said he didn't know, he was not a father yet. Something about Siddiqi's manner and his long face soured the atmosphere in the car. Bakher Khan did not know what was wrong. Siddiqi had seemed cheerful enough when they drove down together. He had come with the drivers to settle on the hotel, buy the supplies, choose locations for the tour. Bakher Khan had driven him in Mr Vincent's car. They had laughed a lot and sat in circles singing popular film songs, but now Siddiqi had ruined the sense of camaraderie. His scowls, his silences and his short replies to the foreign experts disturbed Bakher Khan greatly.

They were stuck in traffic. Mr Vincent gave Bakher Khan directions from the back. Then he said, 'Can you believe that? Look at those cars blocking the shoulders and coming the opposite way. Sure, go ahead, make it worse.' Bakher Khan watched with a sinking heart as the trucks took up the road space that would have allowed the cars to pass by. After a year of driving Mr Vincent, Bakher Khan had become increasingly aware of Bangladesh's shortcomings: drivers who did not follow rules and blocked the roads, police sergeants who did not know their own duties, not to mention the corruption, the greed, the lack of law and order, the dirt everywhere. He now looked at his country, which he had always regarded with a lazy warmth, through new eyes. When he drove Mr Vincent home at night—Mr Vincent worked late every day at the office, after everyone else at the gas company had left—they would have philosophical conversations about Bangladesh.

'I don't know, Ba-ker,' Mr Vincent would say. 'I get depressed every night. This place is so corrupt, I wonder if we can make any progress at all. This country could have been so much. You have so much gas, Ba-ker, if only the officials weren't so pig-headed and corrupt. If you could develop this gas, there would not be one hungry man in your country.'

Bakher Khan honked his horn and Mr Vincent said not to; it wouldn't do any good. Bakher Khan immediately recognized the wisdom of this advice. He was very proud to be working for the gas company. When his old company sold out to this one, he had become an employee instead of a mere contractor. These people were so intelligent, they had so much to teach... Bakher Khan often dreamed, when he was waiting in the car for Mr Vincent, that his country would change; there would be super highways, electricity in every village, high rises for everyone to live in.

At last, the traffic cleared and they began to move. Mr Vincent asked Siddiqi if he had remembered to load all the food for their trip to Sitakunda, and Siddiqi sullenly said yes. Mrs Ann coughed in the sudden gust of exhaust and roadside tar work (which had probably been the cause of the traffic jam). She told Mr Vincent that her little Cara had been ill with breathing problems at least three times since she had been born—the doctors thought it was the pollution in Dhaka. Mr Vincent had the same problem with his boy, who had developed asthma. Bakher Khan felt disappointed that his country was so backward, that Mr Vincent and Mrs Ann were having to make such grave sacrifices to help it progress.

The road was clear now and he sped on, the wind flying against the outside glass, the air inside cool from the AC, and he had to brake only occasionally when he passed a slow rickshaw or van, or a fool of a man walking his cow by the road. Bakher Khan thought that perhaps one day his daughter would attend the local university and become an engineer, too, become what Mrs Ann was: a...reservoir engineer. He loved Mohua so much: her long cotton dresses that reached her ankles, the bell that tinkled around her waist, the drop of kajal on her forehead that protected her against evil.

Mr Vincent's firm was so advanced that when the managers met to decide the company's mission and vision, even the drivers had been invited. It was a long-drawn-out process, with every department making several proposals, and in the end there was a big meeting with lunch—sandwiches from Coopers. In the meeting, the most popular slogan was 'Circles of Progress'. But the exploration manager, who was Mr Vincent's boss, pointed out that progress was linear. Someone joked that circular was a good slogan for their partner company in Bangladesh because all the Bangladeshi officials talked only in circles. Everyone thought hard, and so did Bakher Khan and, finally, when they chose a phrase—something that would appear underneath the company's name—it was 'Wheels of Progress'. Bakher Khan really liked this slogan.

At last they were approaching Sitakunda. They were beginning to climb uphill. The other car, with Mr John and Mr Vincent followed behind.

'Go slow,' said Mr Vincent. 'Ease up on the brake.' Mr Vincent always gave him tips on driving, how to handle the Jeep on dunes and hills, in mud and through water. There were signs announcing that Sitakunda would soon become an eco-tourism park. For now, it was green and quiet: terraced agricultural fields along the steps of hills and little boys who walked with the harvest or with goats up the slopes. Bared walls of hills had been cut for quarries. A quarry was a good place for a geological exploration, Mr Vincent explained. Mr Vincent was always explaining things and educating him.

'Vincent, I think we should park here,' said Siddiqi.

'No, let's go further up,' said Mr Vincent.

They continued on until the stalks of paddy pushed against the windows. The boys who walked along the narrow path had to jump into the ditches.

'All right, let's get out,' said Vincent. 'Siddiqi, bring the equipment. Leave the lunch in the car.'

Mr John and Mr Frans stepped out of the other car. Mr John was the guide. 'Siddiqi, come here,' he would say. The group would stop, measure, look, discuss. The drivers followed behind, and Robiul said to Bakher Khan wasn't it nice to see their Bangladeshi engineer walking alongside the foreign experts? But Siddiqi looked so dark and shrivelled that it was impossible to be proud of him. Bakher Khan hovered close to the group, and from time to time Mr Vincent drew his attention to interesting features in the landscape, pointing with his slender white finger with the gold band. He wore a stylish white hat to keep off the sun and he carried a camera in the pocket of his slim white pants. Bakher Khan repeated the words to himself: shale, sandstone, dislocation, faults, formations. He had once worked for an NGO and he still remembered some of the terms: sustainable, participatory, development. These expressions continued to serve him well; Mrs Ann and Mr Vincent were saying that the development of gas was the means of sustainable development for Bangladesh: 'Think. Now Bangladesh survives only on aid, on other people feeding its people. It's eternal, this giving. But with gas, Bangladesh could feed its own people.'

Bakher Khan was hopeful. He imagined his country making linear progress, Mohua in a slim skirt like Mrs Ann's, long boots, pushing up her glasses to study a quarry.

The local people were now crowding round the group and the drivers had to shoo them away: 'Go, go. There is nothing to see here.' Sometimes a man would ask them what the foreigners were doing and they would explain that these were great technical experts come to get gas out.

'Is there any gas here?' the boys asked. But mostly they stared at Mrs Ann or at Mr Vincent's camera. Mrs Ann smiled sweetly at them, although Bakher Khan could see the staring made her uncomfortable. They stood right behind her when she stopped, followed her when she walked, breathed the shampoo in her hair. When one group of boys chewing on sugar cane disappeared, another soon appeared.

'Are they bothering you?' Mr Vincent asked, and Mrs Ann smiled: *no*.

Mr Vincent explained to him that the sandstone held the gas— he pointed with his finger at the lines of sand—and the shale acted like a cap to hold in the gas. He pointed at lines of shale. Bakher Khan memorized the phrase 'trapped gas'. At last, when he thought there was no end to the information that he should swallow and keep within—as if by being able to keep it all in he could apply his knowledge and help his country move forward on the path of progress in the energy sector—they reached the top of the hill. The temple of Sitakunda appeared suddenly as they rounded the corner. They stood at the edge of a cliff that fell to the valleys of cultivated fields below. Steps led up to the temple where pilgrims had climbed to pay their respects for hundreds of years. For hundreds of years it had stood unchanged and unchanging. Bakher wondered what would happen once the eco-park opened. Mr Vincent and Mrs Ann were discussing the options if they discovered gas or oil under the temple. They joked that they could put a rig there and make it resemble a temple.

The survey was over for now. Mr John lowered himself to the sandstone and sat by the edge of the cliff. Mr Vincent sent Siddiqi back to the car with the other driver to fetch the lunch supplies. Perhaps Siddiqi was sullen because he was a geologist but he was having to do all this menial work. Although Bakher found Siddiqi's twin roles slightly confusing as well, he disapproved of his attitude; he shouldn't look down upon any work as menial; he was the guide on the tour. Without him how would the foreign experts know which hotel to stay at, how to negotiate with boats and ferries for tomorrow's trip to Maheskali? This was the trouble with Bangladeshis: they thought work was beneath them.

Mrs Ann and Mr Vincent stood by the cliff's edge, admiring the scenery. They compared it to Scotland. Bakher Khan felt proud. Mr Vincent had once said Dhaka was all concrete, it was bewilderingly depressing. Bakher Khan had been depressed by Dhaka ever since then: the alleys that clogged up with plastic bags, the children who got wet in the rain, the dirty buses with their black exhaust which choked the lungs of infants. Mr Vincent had once visited Bakher Khan's home when Mohua was very sick. She had pneumonia but Bakher Khan hadn't realized. She would have died if Mr Vincent and his wife had not admitted her to the PG Hospital. Bakher Khan felt sure that the company would bring progress at last to his country. But here, at Sitakunda, he felt happy. Here was something he could be proud of: the open air, the story of Ram and Sita, the temple overhead, the children who walked around with their goats. This was the Bangladesh Bakher Khan had grown up in, the essence of his soul, and he was happy that Mr Vincent also appreciated these surroundings.

The night before, Mr Vincent had asked the two drivers to join them for dinner at the hotel in Cox's Bazaar to which Siddiqi had directed the party. Mr Vincent said he had been happy in his job, until he arrived in Bangladesh. He had had such high hopes at first, but now he had begun to despair. 'Can you even hear birds here in the morning in this place?' he had asked. The party had been silent for a long time, considering this.

There was a cry. Bakher Khan turned to look, his heart trembling a little. Mr Vincent had a protective arm about Mrs Ann's shoulder and was leading her away.

Bakher Khan moved closer to Mr Vincent and Mrs Ann to ask, what happened, what happened?

A group of boys had been standing by them, teenagers wearing Sando shirts and lungis. The boys had been staring at Mrs Ann then they had formed a circled around her and someone had touched her yellow hair. Mr John stood up to console her; she was very shaken. Mr Frans had been studying the sand and the shale a little distance away, and even he answered her call of distress. They all surrounded Mrs Ann to comfort her.

Bakher Khan said to the boys, 'Go! Go! Don't you have anything better to do? Go!' He wanted to explain to Mrs Ann that they had meant no harm. They simply wanted to touch her golden hair, which seemed just as unreal as dreams of gas and wealth seemed to them now. But he knew he could not explain this to Mrs Ann, that he did not possess the English to do so. And it was more than that—it was something he couldn't put into words. So he hovered, feeling sorry for everything.

Then Mr Vincent said to Bakher Khan, 'Just ask them what they're doing for their country, standing around with nothing to do, the silly fools.'

Bakher Khan stood like a statue, unable to move. His chest throbbed with pain. Siddiqi and Robiul were back with the food in ice boxes. From where Bakher Khan stood, he could see the Sitakunda, the mossy steps that led to the derelict temple, and out of the corner of his eye, under the cover of his lashes, he could also see the boys; they reminded him of his own youth, and he felt very downcast about them. He felt that he was a silly fool himself. What had he done with his life after all, what good was he, what good was anybody in his country? Even the professors at the university where Bakher Khan wanted to send Mohua were never trusted to work on the samples the exploration team collected; they had to send everything for analysis abroad. He felt disgusted with the boys, with all the worthless youth of Bangladesh, and with himself; he saw how they all seemed to Mr Vincent—absolutely useless.

'Let's eat,' said Mr Vincent. 'Siddiqi, fetch the food.'

Siddiqi had forgotten to bring a bottle opener. He stood awkwardly with two Coca-Cola bottles in each hand, apologizing. But even when he apologized, he did it resentfully, as if he were about to explode.

Bakher Khan looked away. Robiul tried to help by fumbling inside the bags.

'Not to worry,' said Mr Vincent. 'We can eat our sandwiches dry and swallow our saliva.'

'I can do something, Sir,' said Siddiqi. 'I can open.'

Bakher Khan didn't look to see how he would manage this, but he heard a smash. Siddiqi had broken a bottle trying to open it against a rock.

'Good job, Siddiqi,' said Mr Vincent. But Bakher Khan could feel his anger and he sank further within himself. He wanted to sit down. Mr John held out a sandwich to him and his fingers closed around it weakly. He didn't trust his grip.

Then Siddiqi, dark and sulky in a dirty white shirt, threw the bottle to the ground, and Bakher Khan was astonished to see him standing with his hands on his hips, shaking like a stalk of paddy in the wind.

'Mr Vincent,' he cried in a shrill voice. 'Mr Vincent, I want to quit. I…I have been very unhappy in this company. I get no respect.'

'What kind of respect do you want?' Mr Vincent asked quietly.

'I get ordered about, I don't get a promotion, and you talk to me in that tone.'

'What tone?' asked Mr Vincent. Then enunciating his words slowly, carefully: 'Really, Siddiqi, I have been very patient with you. Your performance in the company has been dismal, but I have waited. The trouble with you people is that you want to climb fast to the top by means other than hard work and competence. So cut your bullshit about tone and respect.'

Siddiqi began to cry like a woman, the way Bakher Khan's wife cried when he scolded her for burning the rice or making the daal too thin. He shook and he cried and he walked away down the hill.

The rest of them finishing their sandwiches in silence.

Then Mr Vincent said, 'Well, I guess we had better pack up. Baker and Robiul, can you manage?'

'Yes, Mr Vincent,' Bakher Khan assured him.

He busied himself with picking up the rubbish and lifting the ice boxes. He waited for Mr Frans and Mr John, Mrs Ann and Mr Vincent to lead the way. As he did so, he stared again fondly at the temple, which was now radiant in sunlight. The pounding in his chest had stopped. The boys began to go on their way, waving their sticks gaily, returning to their work in the fields that would be harvested the same way year after year. Mr John had been explaining last night over dinner the cyclical nature of tides and its importance for geologists, but Bakher Khan could no longer remember that lecture. He watched the children and hoped that their lives wouldn't change too soon.

Siddiqi refused to return with them; he would find his own transport and he was going to hand in his resignation at the office in Dhaka.

'You can't do that, my good fellow,' said Mr Vincent. 'There are procedures. You need to give notice.'

But Siddiqi walked away, childishly. Robiul and Bakher Khan assured the foreign experts that they knew the way back to the hotel. Bakher Khan climbed into the driver's seat and let Mr Vincent advise him down the hill. He drove back on the highway to Cox's Bazaar, taking his time, no longer in a hurry, no longer even listening to the hushed conversation, about Siddiqi no doubt, in the back seat. Instead he admired the scenery around him. Mohua would be home now, playing by the drains, dropping beads down them, or perhaps she would have gone to the river in Mohammedpur with her mother to watch the fishermen and the boats. He thought of Chittagong's great harbours, and its container ships and the ocean. He thought of Ram and Sita and the beautiful stories that he had heard in his childhood, stories that never led anywhere but started again where they had stopped the night before.

When they reached Cox's Bazaar, it was getting dark. Mrs Ann and Mr Vincent sat in the shadows. The two cars pulled up side by side in front of the hotel and Mr John rolled down his window to confer with Mr Vincent. They decided to shower and go on to dinner. The foreign experts went to their rooms, telling the drivers when to meet them again in the parking lot. Robiul and Bakher Khan did not shower or wash. They both sat in silence, thinking of Siddiqi, whose duty it would have been to act as guide for the evening, and to organize the next day's trip. Presently, the four experts came out and Mr Vincent and Mrs Ann, both in clean starched shirts and cotton pants, climbed into Bakher Khan's car. Mr Vincent said, 'Bakher Khan, you have the great honour of choosing where we should eat tonight. Lead us. Onward!'

Bakher Khan was from Chittagong. He had grown up in Chittagong. He had visited Cox's Bazaar many times. Although he had never eaten in the best restaurants himself, he could have led them to any number of good ones, efficiently and expertly, in a straight line. But to his own surprise, he took no initiative. When he reached the busy town centre, where all the restaurants were, he just drove around aimlessly.

Mr Vincent tapped him on the shoulder. 'Ba-ker, you're on the same street we just passed,' he said. 'We're hungry, my man.'

Bakher Khan nodded at Mr Vincent's clean-shaven reflection in the mirror. He thought again of Siddiqi, who would be hungry now, walking still or on some dusty bus, and he thought that he cared nothing for the hunger of these foreign experts. Let them tell him where they wanted to eat, when they wanted him to stop. He just kept driving. His shell keyring jangled, reminding him of his musical Mohua, and he forgot everything else. □

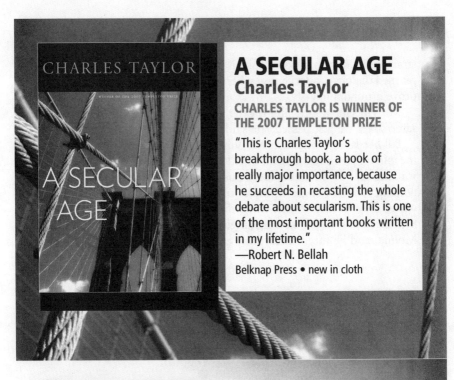
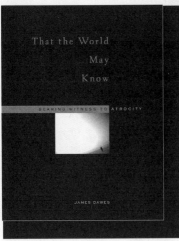

GRANTA

THE CROCODILE LOVER

Helon Habila

Helon Habila

She said, 'Over my dead body,' and so they killed her. The soldiers carried her screaming and grasping at shirt collars, lapels, tablecloth, and hurled her out of the fifth-floor window, and because she was fat and asthmatic, she probably died before she hit the hard tar road in front of the hotel. This was five years ago and I was in America in my second year at NYU and so the story came to me in snippets, a casual line in an email, a paragraph online as I browsed through the home papers. My auntie's death was only referred to in passing by the papers, like a footnote to the lengthy columns about the famous general whose arrest she died trying to stop.

The drive from Abuja Airport at dawn displays the same rubbish heaps by the roadside, the same sketchy, overcrowded junior workers' houses, far away from the city centre, the same sight I waved goodbye to when I was going. Seven years ago. So much remains the same, and yet everything has changed. I was only eighteen when I left for America, just a child, breathless about the new world waiting there for me, too young to know how damaged I was inside, and the nightmares waiting, like some monster behind the clouds outside the plane window, too young to realize that though I was leaving the general in Abuja, his leash was long enough to stretch over the wide blue Atlantic and keep me captive in faraway America.

By 8 a.m. the sun is hot, and I have to lie motionless for almost an hour in the tepid bathwater just to keep cool. My hotel is on a quiet, not-so-central part of Abuja. The whole street is taken up by similar hotels: two-star, medium comfort—which means not being robbed by the management. My taxi driver recommended it. The air conditioning is faulty. I fall into a sweaty half-sleep, weakened by the heat and the jet lag. I have only one friend, Sarah, to call to announce my arrival. She isn't home, so I leave a message.

The general didn't like me having friends, my auntie forbade it. 'What do you need friends for, Dora, when you have me?' he once asked me, pressing his lips upon mine. It was the first time he kissed me. We had gone to visit him in his office. The night before he had given my auntie money and told her to get me new clothes. Now she was here to show me off to the general. He was something important at the ministry of defence; once I heard him boast as he drank in my auntie's restaurant that, in the ministry, only the minister himself was more important than him.

'Wait here. Oga will be with you in a minute,' his secretary said, leading us to a side room screened by a thick curtain. Thirty minutes later he came out, accompanied by a young boy and a girl, holding them by the hands. He patted them on the head and said, 'Goodbye, I'll see you later.'

'His children,' my auntie whispered. And without thinking, I uttered, 'Can she be my friend?' The girl was about my age. My auntie said nothing, because just then the secretary came over and said, 'The general will see you now.'

Later in his office, when my auntie mentioned my remark, he frowned, and then he broke out laughing. 'You innocent thing,' he said, dragging me on to his knee. He bent down and kissed me, his moustache stiff as wire, and said, 'What do you need friends for, Dora, when you have me?'

I watch TV all day, positioning it by the door so that I can sit under the tree in the garden. A slight wind finds its way over the tall, razor-wire-topped walls and stirs the leaves which then stir the soupy heat, bringing a little comfort. I sleep early, waking up in the middle of the night, disoriented, panicking. In the morning the telephone wakes me up. It is Sarah. She says she is coming over at nine.

I met her three years ago when I was working at a Gap store in Greenwich Village. She had stood in a corner, listening to me attend to a customer, and then she came over and said to me, 'You are Nigerian?' I hesitated. Most Nigerians overseas, I discovered, don't like admitting to being Nigerian. I nodded.

'I am Nigerian too.'

We became friends. Her father was a politician, and rich enough to send her to school in America. I did not tell her how I came to be schooling in America—I let her assume that I was on a scholarship. She graduated two years ago and returned home to get married.

'I don't love him,' she once told me about her boyfriend. I didn't ask her why, but I understood with the instinctive understanding of one whose life has been without love.

In the hotel room in Abuja, I tell her everything: about my parents, my auntie and the general. She says nothing, even when I tell her to accompany me to my auntie's house in Garki. In the taxi Sarah finally speaks. 'You don't have to do this, you know. You could just go back to the hotel and pack your bag and return to America.'

'I want to do it,' I say. She takes my hand and smiles.

The taxi driver looks at us in his mirror. He continues to stare archly at me when I catch his eyes in the mirror.

The house has not changed. The ambience, the furniture. The same spacious living room, which doubled as a restaurant during the day; the square courtyard outside with potted plants against the walls, where the restaurant shifted in the evenings to cover the vast concrete space in white plastic chairs and tables. The same iron-and-glass living room door which we would always leave open so that my auntie could listen to her favourite hi-life tune from Beauty's cassette player playing on the table inside; sometimes a drunk customer would stand up to follow the rhythm with his weak legs. One of the doors in the living room leads to the kitchen. That was my station: my eyes on the tripe pepper soup on the fire, my hands up to my elbows in dirty dishes and suds, because I was the cook and also the scullery maid. Another door leads to the second bedroom—our bedroom: Beauty, my auntie's only daughter, and I. She on the bed, I on the floor.

A young, intimidated girl meets us at the door and tells us that 'Madam' isn't home, she has gone to the market. It seems that Beauty has taken over the place—and the business—after my auntie's death. The girl is holding a toddler by the hand. She leaves him and goes into the kitchen to bring us water in a jug. I can see through the open kitchen door: the sink, the fridge, the pots and pans on a table, the basins on the floor.

'That was where I used to work,' I say to Sarah. She is smiling and making faces at the toddler, who stares at her, his expression caught between laughing and crying. The girl is now reaching up, on tiptoe, to the counter over the tall fridge to get the glasses. How old is she? I try to guess. Ten, maybe twelve.

Once, at about the same age, trying to reach the cups on the shelf over the fridge, I dropped a glass on the floor, and in my agitation I also knocked a plate full of rice off the table. I was going to take the rice to a customer. The kitchen door opened to reveal me by the fridge, petrified. Even my tears were suspended. My auntie stood at the door, wordless with anger, and then she lifted a hand—how infinitesimally long the lifting took—and pointed to a pan and duster. 'Make sure you separate the glass from the food, because that will be your meal tonight.' I never dropped a plate after that.

'Sometimes, after a very busy day—mostly on paydays, I would stay awake all night, cleaning the dirty dishes and peeling yam for the next day's meals.'

'Didn't anyone help you?' Sarah asks gently.

'My auntie would mostly disappear with a favoured customer and would only return the next afternoon. And Beauty...she never worked. She'd wake up late in the morning, yawn, have her bath, have her breakfast, then go out shopping with her mother. Sometimes she'd lie in, listening to her CDs or watching a movie. Then, in the evening, when the customers began to arrive, she'd sit outside the living-room door, facing the courtyard, reading a magazine while her mother went from table to table, chatting up the customers, and I'd be in the kitchen.'

Sometimes, her mother would direct Beauty to a particular table, to keep an important customer company—like the general. He was perhaps the most important customer to ever set foot in my auntie's restaurant. I remember the day I first heard his name. My auntie came into the kitchen to cook goat's-head pepper soup for him herself. 'The general is so particular, he wants everything just right,' she said, talking to herself as I handed her the salt, the pepper, the knife. I had never seen her so excited before. From that day I began to hear his name more and more. Sometimes she'd tell Beauty to get ready, that the general was coming to take her shopping. And if she protested, my auntie would really get upset—which was something she almost never did with Beauty. But when it came to the general, my auntie would turn a deaf ear to Beauty's protests.

Beauty was five years older than me. I wore her cast-off clothes, I tried her lipsticks when I was alone in the house, sometimes I went through her picture collections, staring at the faces of her friends from her diploma class, fantasizing about her handsome boyfriend, Aaron, imagining myself in another place, not sure where because I didn't know any other life apart from this one. I had come to live with my auntie when I was only seven, and since then I had seen my real parents only once, when I was nine. They lived in the village in a two-room mud house with six of my younger siblings, who all looked malnourished; my immediate junior sister, Maria, kept looking at me enviously, asking me about life in the city.

The toddler sits on the floor, staring at us.
'He looks like his mother, Beauty,' I tell Sarah.
'Is that her real name?'
I nod.
Beauty returns as we are about to leave. She comes in laden with her shopping in polythene bags, shouting to the girl to take some money from her desk drawer and give it to the taxi driver waiting outside. She stops short at the door when she sees us, and when she recognizes me one of the bags slips out of her hand and on to the doormat.
'Hello, Beauty,' I say. 'It is me, Dora.'
'Yes, Dora. What a surprise.' She doesn't sound surprised, just a bit confused. She passes into the kitchen to put down her shopping, then she returns and sits down, then she gets up and goes back to the kitchen and returns with a glass of water before sitting down again.
'I see she gave you some water. She can be so useless at times. Absent-minded, full of play.'
How like her mother she sounds, I think. Her mother used to describe me in the same words. And how like her mother her fleshy, self-indulgent face is, her thickening waistline, her beer gut, her thick calves. When I first saw her, I had been living with my auntie for almost a month. Beauty had been away at school, in her final year. The day she came home her mother bought a dozen new dresses for her as a graduation present. We waited, I by the kitchen door, her mother and a friend on the sofa, as Beauty went into her room and came out each time in a different dress. Her mother would gushingly praise the dress, and tell Beauty how pretty she looked. 'My baby, my Beauty. You are a model. Ooh, look at that! Just look, look at the way she walks!' and Beauty would strut around proudly, round and round the room and finally come to a stop before the TV, one leg stuck out in front, in imitation of the models on TV. It was that image of her I had in my mind the day she ran away from home. Her mother had walked up and down the room, disconsolate, throwing down her scarf, pulling at her hair, lamenting. I thought of Beauty somewhere forever trying on new dresses, like a display

doll, beautiful, ageless, proudly soaking up admiring glances. But now the beauty has faded. I don't want to ask her about her lover, and if he is the father of the boy.

'I didn't know you were coming,' she says. She sounds sullen, but she has always sounded sullen. I don't hate her, or like her, I say to myself, she has never been kind to me, or overtly unkind. She was simply what her mother had made her.

'It wasn't a planned trip. I just wanted to come. I heard about your mother's death,' I said. 'I'm sorry.'

'They threw her out of the window.'

We sit for a while, in silence, with nothing to say. I want to ask her about my parents, but would she know anything about them, when even I only remember them vaguely?

'I will be going to the village, to see my parents.'

'Is that what brought you?' she asks, and I can see in her eyes that she expects me to ask other questions. I keep quiet, and then finally she says, 'He's been asking after you. He comes here every day, you know.'

I know who she is talking about of course, but almost involuntarily I ask, 'Who?'

'The general. He was released two months ago. He has friends in government and now he is a free man. Just a week ago he said he had been trying your number in America but he had been unable to reach you.'

I turn to Sarah, confusion on my face. She smiles at me. I stand up.

'We have to go now.'

'But what should I tell him? Where are you staying?' she asks, walking us to the door.

'Tell him... I will... Tell him I will come here next week. A week from now.'

'You look frightened,' Sarah says in the taxi.

'I just didn't know he was out...and looking for me. What does he want with me?'

'You have no intention of meeting him, have you?' she asks shrewdly, gazing into my face.

'What do you think?'

'I think he is the biggest of the ghosts you want to lay to rest.'

Helon Habila

That night I do not sleep. My mind detaches itself from my body and ventures by itself into a long-forgotten zone, somewhere in my auntie's house, opening up neglected drawers filled with Beauty's photo albums, hidden closets where I used to keep the laundry, kitchen cupboards full of condiments and spices, and doors forbidden to me. My auntie opens the door and throws a bag of clothes at me. 'Try these on. From today you won't be working in the kitchen. You will be sitting with the customers and taking their orders.' I see the careful lipstick lines on her face, the black arc of the eyeliner. It was a month after Beauty's departure. The lines had deepened on my auntie's face, her lips were permanently tight and she drank more than usual. I saw myself seated beside the general with my auntie on my left side telling me, 'What kind of hostess are you? Can't you see his glass is empty? Pour more drink for him.' I was fascinated by his swagger stick, which was resting between his legs. It was made of crocodile skin, a young crocodile, its head still intact forming the handle. 'I killed it myself, with my bare hands,' the general whispered to me when he saw me staring at it. He took my hand and put it on the head. I shrank. 'Ha ha. It won't bite.'

Once he got very drunk and insisted on dancing with me. Mercifully we were in the living room, not out in the courtyard in full view of the drinking crowd. It was the day he gave my auntie money and told her to buy clothes for me. He twirled me round and round till my head grew dizzy. He had just been promoted to a full general and he was happy. He had brought a case of expensive whisky and brandy for my auntie which his driver had deposited in her bedroom.

'He loves you,' my auntie said later when we were alone. I was in bed; she pulled the sheets over my legs fussily and took me in her arms and squeezed me. 'My pretty, pretty girl. He loves you. You lucky, lucky girl.'

We went to Gambia for a holiday. The general came with his wife and two children. They flew first class while my auntie and I flew economy. She told me to pretend not to recognize him whenever I saw him with his family, to not even look towards him. 'His wife will kill you if she finds out.'

As it turned out I had no need to be that cautious, we saw the general only once in the one week we spent there. We stayed in separate hotels. Our hotel was by the beach, as huge and as extravagant as the ocean itself, and sharing the same name: the Atlantic. I'd spend hours in my room watching the water, the people, mostly white tourists, sunbathing on deck chairs. From the next room I could hear my auntie on the phone describing to her friends back home how expensive and luxurious the hotel was. A day before we left the general came to our room with a friend who introduced himself as Colonel Karfe. My auntie was drunk, and she flirted with the colonel, a big-gutted, bald man puffing on a fat cigar. He was sweating profusely despite the air conditioning. He poured my auntie another drink and as she took it she bent low, letting him have a look at her trussed-up breasts, and when their eyes met they sighed. I stood at the window, turning my back to them. There were seagulls flying near the cliffs that began at the end of the narrow stretch of beach; I watched them rising high in the air, amazed at their freedom.

'My wife thinks I am at a meeting with the army chief of staff right now,' the general said, and they laughed and set up a table in the centre of the room and began playing cards.

'Come and sit here,' the general said, patting the seat beside him. 'Bring me some good luck.' I sat beside him, occasionally getting up to refresh his drink. My auntie sat beside the colonel, a tall glass in her hand. I didn't know when the general took my hand and pushed it under his shirt, but when I resisted his grip tightened on my hand, crushing it. My auntie and the colonel pretended not to notice what was going on under the table despite the plaintive look I kept throwing at them. As the game progressed he opened his zipper and made me hold his penis, moving my hand over it. He was sweating and his voice stuttered as he spoke. My auntie topped up her drink, the colonel puffed harder on his cigarette. The general grew bigger and bigger as the game went on, and at last I felt him explode, washing my hand in semen. From the bathroom, as I scrubbed my hands over and over under the running tap, in futile motions, like Lady Macbeth, I heard his calm voice say to the colonel, 'Your move.'

I kept hearing the words many years later, but amplified a million times, paralysing me, as I lay naked beside my first proper boyfriend in his room in New York. This was after the arrest of the general, after my auntie's death.

'Yo, what's wrong? You frigid?' I remember his name: Rion. He was African-American. 'You must be one of them circumcised Africans.'

I said nothing. I got up from the bed and went to the bathroom to scrub my hand, and the running water disappearing in clear crystal spirals laughed at me, loud, roaring: 'Your move! Your move!' It happened again with the next boyfriend, and the next. But I became really worried when it happened with Andrew, because I loved him more than the others. He was handsome and gentle, and in a way he reminded me of Aaron, Beauty's boyfriend, whose picture I used to daydream about when I was younger.

'Tell me what is wrong,' he said to me one night. I didn't. I couldn't. I was too ashamed. That was when I decided to come home, to retrace my steps over my past, over my crazy history, to seek a cure for my deep-rooted ailment. But I never bargained on meeting the general face to face. I didn't know he was free, walking the streets, looking for me.

When he sent me to America, the general was at the apogee of his power in government. There were rumours that the defence minister would retire and the general take over—the dictator wanted to turn himself into a civilian president and he was carefully selecting a team to cross over with. My general was one of the trusted ones. He was given millions of dollars with which to buy public opinion. He bought my auntie a car, and had her whole house redecorated.

'I'll take Dora to America for a holiday this summer,' he announced one night after a bout of heavy drinking. By the next day he had forgotten all about it. But my auntie hadn't. 'Tell him you want to go to America. Tell him you want to go to school there. Tell him to buy you a house there, a place where he can come for holidays.' She unfolded a plan which, obviously, had been a long time in the making. 'Once you are there, once you have a house, you will allow yourself to get pregnant, and then he will have to marry you. Then I'll come over to take care of you. Talk to him. Today.'

It was the idea of owning a house in America that finally won him over.

But the plan didn't work out exactly as my auntie saw it. He bought the house, he sent me to America, but I did not become pregnant, and neither did my auntie come over to stay with me. Soon after my departure the dictator, Abacha, my general's boss, died. That night, the dictator's close aide, a young, ambitious major, the only one privy to his boss's death, decided to take power himself. They say that with the help of five other majors as ambitious as him, he gathered all the generals on the pretext that the dictator wanted to see them, and when they were all seated in a conference room he locked the doors and sent in his men to arrest them all. Then one by one he picked up the other generals who weren't in the conference room—my general was one of those. He heard the rumour of his impending arrest at my auntie's house, and she, rising to the occasion, advised him to hide out and, knowing how public and unsafe her house was, suggested the hotel next door. She would act as his eyes and ears. He complied—minus moustache, minus martial swagger—disguised as an ordinary civilian. But somehow the soldiers found out where he was hiding and sent their men to arrest him, which they did, in the process entrusting my auntie to gravity via the hotel window. The coup, however, lasted only a week. The majors proved too inexperienced to hold on to power, a group of colonels stepped in and executed all the majors, and released the detained generals—but not all. My crocodile general was among the ones forgotten in prison.

For the next two days I go round the city, to its empty museums and overcrowded markets. I even go to the famous Nicon Hilton Hotel and watch the mostly white clientele and their wives and children jumping into and out of the pool. Sarah calls a few times to find out how I am doing, and if I have decided what to do about the general. I tell her I am still thinking. She says to let her know if I decide to confront him, she'd be happy to come with me. It's funny how the word 'confront' keeps cropping up in relation to the general. A war-like term, and who am I to win a war against a general? No, it won't be a confrontation, just a meeting, a staring hard and long at a monster to see if it still has the power to scare me, to see if I have the confidence to out-stare it. But what if I don't? That is why I hesitate.

But on the fifth day I decide to go. I call Sarah and tell her I want to go alone—it is important for me to go alone. I phone Beauty and tell her to expect me that afternoon, a Saturday, the busiest day at my auntie's. I guess I am trying to hide in numbers.

I arrive late. From outside I can hear him holding court. All voices around him are lowered a few decibels, respectfully, as if to avoid a clash with the general. Beauty sees me at the door and stands up. She is dressed in a lace *bouba*, looking prosperous, lustrous as a star. I remember the day she modelled for her mother and her friend, the first time I saw her. I am dressed in a plain black dress, mid-calf, and flat black shoes. When she takes my hand and leads me to the table I see how heavy her make-up is, as heavy as her tongue, which keeps tripping over her words. She is drunk, and it is only 7 p.m. She seats me next to the general, and then she goes round and sits across from me, as if to keep me in constant view. Although his moustache is gone, the stern and authoritative voice remains, the crocodile swagger stick still remains. He points and waves it to make a point. But somehow without the thick moustache his face looks diminished, empty. He nods briefly at me when I sit down, then turns to the man next to him. I remember that habit, how he'd cut you off in the middle of a sentence and turn to another person for minutes before casually turning back to you to continue the conversation.

'Why did it take you so long to come? I told Beauty to tell you to meet me since last week. How long have you been in town?' he asks when he finally turns back to me.

'Two weeks.'

'Well, then…' he begins, but I cut him off with a question: 'How are your wife and kids…your daughter, what's her name?'

There are lines on his face, but perhaps they are lines of rage. He glares long and hard at me, and then he picks up his drink. I see Beauty staring at me, her eyes glittering; there is disappointment in those eyes. Is she hoping for a public bust-up, a shouting screaming submitting fight, with me doing the submitting? The general has turned away from me once more and is talking loudly to the man next to him. I catch his words even though they make no sense to me.

'…Well, they can't do without us. We are the backbone of this country. See, they brought me out to be a presidential adviser. "General," they said, "we need your expertise… You understand politics more than us, the politicians…" Ha-ha. The incompetent idiots. Bloody civilians.'

'Today an adviser, tomorrow a defence minister, eh?' the man says with a wink.

The general sips his drink. I know he is talking for my benefit, to impress me with his undiminished power, his crocodile virility. Suddenly I feel his hand close over mine, I am too surprised to pull away as he guides it between his legs, forcing it down, still sipping his drink, still not looking at me. I feel his stiff penis beneath his trousers, and suddenly I am fifteen again, helpless, my auntie is seated across from me, pretending not to see what is going on, and all the while the general grows stiffer and stiffer. I look at his face. He is not looking at me, he is still talking to the next man, his face is covered in a sheen of sweat, and his hand is slowly crushing my wrist. I grit my teeth and press down hard into his crotch, grinding his balls against the hard plastic chair. He gasps and splutters, dropping his glass on to the table. He bends over, both hands in his crotch, gasping for breath. Everyone falls silent, waiting. Beauty gets up from her seat and bustles over to him. She holds his head, asking, 'Is everything all right, General? Can I help? Can I get you another drink?' But he can't speak; a thread of saliva is unspooling from the side of his open gasping mouth. She looks at me, questioning.

'I think he got bitten by his crocodile,' I say, nodding at the swagger stick. 'I am not sure.'

'I...I am okay. I just need to go to the bathroom.'

She takes his arm and guides him out of his chair, across the room, and just before they disappear into the doorway she turns and flashes me a look of hate. And suddenly I realize she is sleeping with him. Just like her mother before her slept with him, casually, both before and after he started going out with me. The general is still bowed, one hand leaning on Beauty's arm, the other leaning on his crocodile swagger stick. It is my last view of him. I get up and make my way to the hot, smoky kitchen. The girl is on her knees, peeling yam. She looks up at me, wiping her hand on the hem of her skirt, trying to get up.

'It's okay. Don't stand up for me.' I kneel down beside her and gently pat her on the cheek. 'Tell your auntie I had to go. I have another appointment somewhere. Goodbye.'

At the hotel Sarah finds me staring emptily into the hedge in the tiny courtyard.

'I just wanted to make sure you are safe,' she says.

I tell her what happened. 'It was easier than I had expected. I feel good.'

'When are you going to see your parents?'

'I leave tomorrow. I'll spend only a day there, and then I'll go back to New York.'

'Do you remember them?'

'Only my sister. She was four when I last saw her. She looked like me.'

I used to think of them as strangers in my past, unable to feel any emotions for them. Now I feel my voice growing thick and husky as I talk about my sister. That is how strong I have grown since my victory over the general. Like a god—strong enough to forgive. Strong enough to cry rivers of tears into my pillow after Sarah has gone. □

GrUB

A Novel

Elise Blackwell

Toby

"Some editors are failed writers,
but so are most writers." TS ELIOT

"Elise Blackwell conjures up a universe filled with talentless novelists,
reptilian publishers, unprincipled agents and brain-dead critics. Thank
God any similarity to real life is entirely fortuitous." JOE QUEENAN

Toby   www.tobypress.com   ISBN 190288 136 2

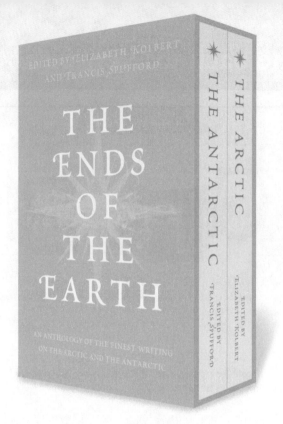

G R A N T A

WHALING
Philip Hoare

Sperm whales off the coast of the Azores in the Atlantic Ocean, 2007

In the early 1970s, we went on a family outing to a safari park, where the star attraction was a killer whale. That day my youngest sister, who was even more enthusiastic about whales than I was, bought a small colour brochure entitled, somewhat apologetically, *Dolphins can be fascinating at Windsor Safari Park*. On the front cover was a grinning Flipper; on the back was an advertisement for Embassy Regal cigarettes, which were 'outstanding value'.

'You will be amused and delighted,' we were told, by 'some facts and figures which might increase your knowledge and enhance your enjoyment of their performance. You might also want to take some pictures of your own—take as many as you like!' After shots of animals lolling at the pool like beauty contestants or leaping in the air like Olympic acrobats, a new player appeared: our other performer. *Ramu: a killer whale.*

'He is growing at the rate of one foot per year'—a fact that raised inevitable consequences, even as we took in the oversized swimming pool in front of us—'and at only four-and-a-half years old he is sixteen feet long, weighs one ton, and eats between eighty and one hundred pounds of herring a day.'

He had been caught for Windsor Safari Park off the coast of North America in 1970 and flown to London by Boeing 707 in a special crate that allowed him to be sprayed constantly with water, keeping him cool and fresh. Eventually, by lorry and crane, he had arrived in the dolphin training pool, and after a short time was ready to commence his training programme.

Only later would I learn that captive whales decline to eat, and are force fed until they do. I was more excited by the thought of a whale about to appear before my eyes. I don't remember how Ramu made his entrance, but as he appeared—this sleek creature with its glossy black-and-white markings redolent of a Hokusai print—it seemed as though his skin had been bleached by the chlorine that kept the pool turquoise-blue in mocking imitation of the ocean.

The whale went through its routine, responding to its trainer's demands like a lapdog. When it leaped in the air and landed with a splash, soaking the thrilled ringside audience, it was as if it were beaten by its captivity, grounded by gravity. Even as its proud dorsal fin flopped impotently over its back.

'Here in their pool at Windsor,' the brochure reassured us, the performers 'should survive for a great many more years than in the sea, to delight and entertain their visitor'. But by 1976, Ramu had grown too big for his tank. That year he was sold to Seaworld in San Diego, where he was renamed Winston, sired four offspring, and died, ten years later, of heart failure—one of more than two hundred orcas to perish in captivity in the last quarter of the twentieth century.

Thirty years later, I was on a bleak stretch of beach south of Skegness in North Yorkshire, a coastline familiar to me from other childhood holidays, walking towards the sea. It was already getting dark, and as I made my way across damp grey sand, I could see something ahead of me that, as I got closer, resolved itself into a comprehensible shape.

But before that, I could smell it; I can still smell it when I look at the pictures. Lying there in the sand was a dead minke whale. Its shiny black skin had been entirely flayed, leaving the fatty layer beneath, a fishy-coloured beige with the texture of latex—except where the blubber had already begun to turn blue.

When I had last seen a minke, it was surfing over Stellwagen Bank in the Gulf of Maine, six miles off Provincetown, snatching breaths at the surface with a brief flash of the sharp-pointed rostrum which gives the whale its Latin name: *Balænoptera acutorostrata*. Its common name, as the whale-watch naturalists delight in telling their audiences, comes from a Norwegian whaler, Meincke, who misidentified it as a much larger (and more valuable) fin whale, and was ribbed by his shipmates for his mistake.

Then, in a rare moment of revelation, a minke had swum by the bow, clearly silhouetted below, the entire animal visible through the grey-green surface of the sea, the flashes emblazoned on its flippers. Now all I saw was a piece of matter that smelled like something between fish and meat. Its flukes were reduced to raw cartilage. There was barely anything to indicate that it had ever been alive— save for its pale little penis hanging from the underside of its flayed belly, flaccid and worm-like.

I fingered it. Everything about it seemed an abuse. Then I walked back in the darkness, with the moon rising behind me out of the North Sea.

Three months later, on Spurn Bight, at the mouth of the Humber estuary, a sperm whale washed close to shore. About thirty feet long, it was, unusually, still alive, struggling on the sand. Helpless onlookers watched the whale's flukes moving frantically, pathetically. As the tide ebbed, thick mud covered its blowhole, hastening an end already inevitable from the pressure put on its internal organs. That winter, four more sperm whales washed up along the east coast, from Aberdeen to Brancaster, their carcasses a rebuke to our shared use of the sea. Even in death, it seemed, whales present us with gargantuan problems.

According to a fourteenth-century decree, every whale, dolphin, porpoise and sturgeon found on English shores is still the property of the monarch. Yet what was once a royal prerogative is now a royal liability. In the twenty-first century, the Receiver of Wreck, based in a Southampton office block, operates, in effect, as whale undertaker to Her Majesty The Queen.

The Receiver, or her Deputy—the current holders of both posts happen to be young women—is alerted by one of nineteen coastguard stations. A dead or dying whale might be out at sea, causing a shipping hazard; or it may present a public nuisance as it is washed up. Sometimes a whale will appear on one beach, only to be carried by the tide to another. In this morbid game of tag, it is the Receiver's job to deal with the prize: a massive carcass. In remote locations, the whale may be allowed to become carrion for birds. Elsewhere, police cordons may be needed—less to shield awed crowds from any zoonotic disease (the reason often given) than to protect them from the heavy plant machinery required to move an animal weighing many tons.

These are expensive disposals. Small whales cost from six to eight thousand pounds to shift; large whales as much as £20,000. A formerly profitable right has become a public expense. It is another paradox: when whales were unprotected, they were valuable commodities, bounties to be claimed by the Crown; now they are treated as managed or even toxic waste, a result of pollution, or of the large doses used to euthanize the animal. And although they soon decay—the paper-thin epidermis peeling, the internal organs breaking down, swelling their bellies with gas—dead whales remain resilient. Their blubber is thick and hard to puncture, and carcasses hang from the claws of plant machinery like Indian mystics suspended from hooks. Sometimes a pair of diggers must join forces to tear them apart; or more modern techniques of dissection are being devised, such as the use of high-pressure water jets. One finback which stranded recently on the Isle of Wight, having drifted there from the Bay of Biscay, required nine truckloads to cart it away, piecemeal, to the local landfill. Another which washed up at Lee-on-Solent was eventually interred in the New Forest.

The Receiver's gallery of stranded whales is a gruesome catalogue of photographs that resemble an insurer's car crash scenes, each more ghastly than the last: a pilot whale lodged in Devon rocks, caught up in the kind of boulders over which children clamber looking for rock pools; a finback washed up at Ventnor, its blubber dripping like wax in the sun, its separated head found yards down the shore; a sei whale, one of the rarer rorquals, lying on Morecambe Sands, victim of its deceptive tides; a humpback in Kent, slumped on its white flippers like an airliner on an emergency landing. An orca in the Mersey. Whales where they should not be.

Many of these may be accidents—ship-strikes, or the result of disease or encounters with fishing lines. But the reasons for other strandings—which can occur en masse—remain unclear. One theory advanced is that the whales are following ancient electrical paths hard-wired into the sea bed, and are deceived by anomalies in the earth's magnetic field which lead them on to the shore rather than through safe deep waters. Certainly, as Thomas Beale observed two centuries ago in his book, *The Natural History of the Sperm Whale*, whales will stay loyally by an ailing or wounded comrade, even though it may mean their own deaths.

More sinister theories suggest they are casualties of naval sonar, developed since the 1960s to detect 'silent' enemy submarines. 'From the US Navy's first deployment of active sonar…tests correlated closely with the strandings of certain whale species,' noted one report. Strandings suddenly became more frequent near naval exercises emitting sounds with drastic effects on diving odontocetes or toothed whales. As they rush to the surface in panic, gas bubbles form in their bloodstreams and induce compression sickness—what a human diver calls 'the bends'. In autopsies, others show massive haemorrhaging around their brain and spinal cord.

In the case of sperm whales, which seem to strand with increasing frequency on Britain's east coast, it is thought they may have taken a wrong turning into the North Sea, their ancient acoustic map of the ocean distorted by centuries of predation. Once, their sonar detected the sounds of other marine mammals, signposting their migratory routes; now, with populations drastically reduced, whales are deceived by noise pollution such as seismic soundings for oil surveys.

According to records kept by the Natural History Museum since 1913, and which document more than 13,000 strandings, incidents have doubled in the past ten years, with eight hundred animals stranded around Britain in 2004. Yet perversely this increase may actually be an encouraging sign. Cetaceans are seen in greater numbers in the Bay of Biscay, and blue whales are swimming through the Irish Sea, a passageway which once proved fatal for the easy access it allowed to British and Irish hunters, a kind of death alley. Now, taking advantage of the modern moratorium on whaling, the great whales are reclaiming their age-old routes. But in the process, they are subject to new threats from their mammalian cousins.

In the past, shore dwellers regarded a beached whale as a gift from the gods. Those less used to such events saw a dead whale as an evil omen, like a comet or an eclipse. When a whale arrived in the Thames during a storm in 1658, it was taken to be an augury of the demise of the Lord Protector, Oliver Cromwell, who died the following day. Incredibly, this was a *Eubalæna glacialis*; a right whale caught in a river with no hope of sustaining its great bulk. John Evelyn noted in his diary:

> A large whale was taken betwixt my land abutting on the Thames and Greenwich, which drew an infinite concourse to see it, by water, horse, coach, and on foot, from London, and all parts.

The interloper was doomed by its unlucky appearance, as if its ugliness itself were a sin. Cornered, it appeared to fight back in a manner with which whalers would be familiar.

> It would have destroyed all boats, but...after a long conflict, it was killed with a harping iron, struck in the head, out of which spouted blood and water.

Philip Hoare

Over the centuries other whales have found their way up other watercourses, from an unidentified whale which swam up the Hudson river from Manhattan in the early nineteenth century, to a narwhal that arrived in York via the Ouse in the 1880s, a medieval apparition beneath the Minster's gargoyles. Yet few could have expected that, in the twenty-first century, a northern bottlenose whale would pass under Waterloo Bridge and alongside the Palace of Westminster, threatening to strand itself on the Battersea embankment within sound of the King's Road.

It was an event that became a kind of circus entertainment, transmitted around the world. An animal used only to the bleeps and clicks of its cousins in the open sea was suddenly subject to the confinement and cacophony of one of the world's largest, noisiest cities. Disorientated and distressed, the London whale moved up- and downstream with the tides, its flukes flapping furiously, its baby-like head rising plaintively out of the water while people shouted at it and boats surrounded it and helicopters filled with film crews buzzed overhead. When I watched these scenes again, months later, the distance served only to make them more upsetting and poignant in the knowledge of what happened next: a hellish death, assailed by the sound of traffic, trains, boats and people, frightened by those who sought to save it, starving and therefore suffering terrible thirst, trying to follow a dead-end river to the ocean.

Inevitably, this visitation was seen as a new omen. A month before, six Arnoux beaked whales, also more habituated to deep water, had made an unusual appearance in Cape Town harbour; with their strange, stubby, protruding teeth, their brown skins and mottled, veined markings, they resembled primeval denizens come to confront the modern world with its sins. Only days before the arrival of the London whale, a dead fifty-foot finback was taken from the Baltic at Bremen and freighted, with a police escort, to be laid at the steps of the Japanese Embassy in Berlin as a protest against that nation's continuing actions in the sanctuary of the Southern Ocean. And in an incident which only later became clear, on the same day that the London whale appeared, four Cuvier's beaked whales were beached in Spain, the result, so subsequent tests would indicate, of naval sonar exercises.

Whatever the fate of its cousins, the London whale was doomed from the moment it entered the estuary, from which it would be carried out in a procession resembling the waterborne funeral of Winston Churchill, televized forty years before. Taken from the river, it lay on its inflated pontoon, watched by news crews and crowds on the Thames bridges. But its frantic muscular movements flagged, and it finally expired at seven that evening. Its tearful attendants asked that the cameras be turned off in respect for its passing.

To some this seemed a kind of collective madness, akin to the reaction to the death of Diana, Princess of Wales. This princess of whales—for it was a she—had become the subject of national and international debate. There were leader columns on how its treatment was a testament to our humanity; and others that claimed, equally, that it was a reminder of the barbarity of the continuing hunts by the whaling nations. Entire newspaper sections were published to commemorate the whale, while others made political capital out of its adventure. One cartoon showed the whale on a flag-draped catafalque in the manner of a lying-in-state—only instead of a quartet of Life Guards with their sabres unsheathed, four photographers stood at each corner with their telescopic lenses down-turned.

By coincidence, the reading at Mass that Sunday was from the book of Jonah, prompting one clergyman to write to a national newspaper, noting that the passage was the one in which 'Jonah says Nineveh, the London or New York of his day, will be overthrown in forty days. The people cut consumption by fasting and wearing the simplest possible garments and renounced violence. With the oil running out and global warming beginning to gallop and the continuing hideous aggression of the United States, perhaps the poor creature was giving us a hint.'

It was not the Yankee whaling fleet—celebrated by Herman Melville in *Moby-Dick*—which reduced the whale population to one-tenth of their pre-whaling numbers. That honour lay with old Europe, rather than the New World.

On Christmas Eve, 1868, Sven Foyn wrote in his diary: 'I thank Thee, O Lord. Thou alone hast done all.' The Norwegian inventor was giving praise for the grenade harpoon he had just patented; a bomb that would implode in a whale's head. Sven Foyn was the herald of a new century of slaughter. The maiden voyage of the whaleship

Philip Hoare

Spes et Fides—Hope and Faith—was equipped with his efficient, terrible weapon. Now no whale, no matter how fast, could escape the cull.

Foyn's invention allowed his fellow countrymen to pursue the giant rorquals which had been beyond reach: blue whales and fin whales, the two largest animals on earth. By the end of the nineteenth century the Scandinavians were killing a thousand finbacks a year. As American whaling declined to just one shore-based station in California, worldwide whaling expanded with the mechanized fleets of Japan, the Soviet Union, Norway, and Britain. Factory ships roamed the oceans, taking an estimated one-and-a-half million whales in the next hundred years. And the twentieth century devised a new use for the whale—in the manufacture of nitroglycerine.

Fifty thousand whales died during the two world wars, victims like the men whose deaths they assisted. Meanwhile, whalemen were celebrated anew, their trade in demand more than ever, as much a part of the war effort as my mother making machine-gun parts in a Southampton factory. And as with the expanding machine of war between man, every kind of device was used to kill whales: exploding harpoons, strychnine, cyanide and curare poisoning (inspired, perhaps, by the Aleutian islanders, who used rotten meat on their barbs to infect a whale with blood poisoning). Even electrocution was attempted: the same method by which the civilized world got rid of its most venal criminals was brought to bear on dumb animals. The hunters came armed with cannon and bomb-lances, ostensibly hastening death, but in practice causing what we can only imagine to be agonizing suffering—an apparent indifference illustrated by the fact that Antarctic whaling stations threw penguins on their fires, using the high oil content of their bodies as living kindling. All the while, the cetacean war was waged from the air as 'planes and helicopters were used to spot their targets.

As early as the 1920s it was becoming clear that this could not go on. Restraint, however, came out of self-interest. Whalers joined forces with conservationists to petition the League of Nations—formed in the wake of the slaughter in Europe—to request restrictions lest the factory fleets depopulate the world of whales. Nevertheless, by the outbreak of the Second World War, thirty-thousand-tonne ships with crews of two hundred and forty were making four-month voyages and catching five hundred thousand tons of whale a year.

Britain had ten such mother ships busy making orphans; Norway ten, Japan six, and Germany six. The global fleet was killing thirty thousand whales a year—ninety-five per cent of them taken by the British and Norwegians. As one Provincetowner, Mary Heaton Vorse, wrote in 1942, 'the destruction has been so great that the size of the huge monsters is becoming smaller each year, and unless international action is taken the whale will become one of the fabulous monsters of the past'.

There was little that was heroic about this new cull, as modern ships fired on whales from the safe vantage point of their high prows. In January 1948, for instance, a Japanese whaling expedition set off for the Antarctic, authorized by the occupying General Douglas MacArthur. Twelve ships sailed six thousand miles south, carrying a crew of thirteen hundred men—enough to populate a small town. The self-sufficient fleet comprised six catcher boats, a ten-thousand-ton factory ship, the *Hashidate Maru*, two processing ships to refrigerate its spoils, an oil tanker, and two vessels for cold storage. Each vessel travelled far apart to avoid collision with themselves or icebergs, using radar to navigate through thick banks of fog until they came upon their appointed enemy: a gigantic blue whale. With other oceans drastically depleted, most whales were now being caught in the Antarctic; those fast rorquals, blue, fin and minke whales which had evaded the early whalers.

A catcher boat was sent ahead, but whenever it had the whale in its sights, the animal sounded; it was two hours before the gunner hit his target. Slowly, they began to reel the animal in, like some oversized tuna.

The first deep cut was made then and there, for fear of the animal's extraordinary metabolism. Marine mammals generate immense body heat; great whales which overexert themselves in pursuit of prey could die of overheating. Thus a whale captured in the Southern Ocean is immediately slit open from throat to fluke, allowing cold water to flush through it. A man might freeze to death in such water, but a whale's insulation is so efficient that, even in these icy seas, its internal heat—usually cooled through blood vessels in the blubber-less flukes—can, in death, cause its very bones to burn.

The whale was towed back fluke first, and up through a ferry-like skidway in the ship's stern, where eighty men worked for four hours to butcher the *Balænoptera musculus*, one of the largest blue whales ever caught. It weighed three hundred thousand pounds—although they only knew this because they were able to slice it into pieces and place it on the ship's scales. The tongue alone weighed three tons. The heart was as big as a car, its vessels large enough for a man to swim in. All reduced to so much offal.

And this accomplished in an atmosphere of outright hilarity: 'Workmen laughed and leaped aboard loins that were skidding toward the loading chute,' observed Lt-Colonel Waldon C. Winston, an American officer accompanying the fleet. 'Others there started a shanty. Over and over, they filled the box on the small platform scales, then emptied the contents down the loading chute.' They might as well have been on a Detroit production line rather than disassembling a whale.

Below decks were huge steel boilers, modern tryworks, where the blubber was reduced to oil and then stored in huge tanks. Nothing was wasted. A special process had been devised to suck vitamin-rich oil from the whale's liver—these were, after all, austere times, when occupied Japan was encouraged by the Americans to feed its schoolchildren fried whale or parboiled blubber. That whale yielded 133 barrels-worth of oil and sixty tons of meat, a harvest valued at $28,000. And the process went on, day by day, month by month, year by year in frozen waters so far from civilization that men wounded in accidents often died, there being no hospital to which they could be taken.

Here, out of sight, off shores belonging to nobody, nobody was responsible. Yet as the ships canned their meat, official observers looked on, and veterinarians and biologists sought to learn about living whales by examining dead ones. It was a uniquely mad situation, belied by its own legitimacy. Although regulations stated that mother and calf pairs were not to be targeted—any gunner who shot them had his pay deducted—pregnant animals were taken. They were the hardest to kill; one blue whale mother caught by a Japanese ship took five hours to die. One scientist who found a five-inch sperm whale foetus had it packed in ice, and back in port at his hotel, used a mixture of vodka and shaving lotion to preserve it overnight. The next morning he dissected the specimen, which had the rudimentary features of the antediluvian animals which became whales; with its pig-like snout, nostrils positioned at the front (before they migrated up the head), its protruding ears and genitals, and its hand-like flippers and residual whiskers, it was as if this whale-in-being might yet become some other creature entirely.

Only in death could man see such whales in detail. Only from these mother ships were the massive animals seen to be colonies in their own right, living cities of crawling whale lice and barnacles fixed for life, only loosening their grip as the blankets of blubber were cut away, the hard shells popping out of the epidermis and clattering to the deck.

Even inside its body, the whale played host to other organisms: the nematode worms that colonized its guts (intestines which, to scientists' amazement, unravelled for a quarter of a mile). Japanese factories ships merely minced up these worms along with the rest of the meat. They were more concerned with the levels of radioactivity to be found in whale flesh, as fallout from nuclear tests and from the devices which had exploded above Hiroshima and Nagasaki turned up as traces in these animals. But then, every man, woman, and child on the planet was absorbing strontium-90 from those explosions into their bones, a legacy for generations to come.

In iceberg-blocked waters, ranks of rorqual whales lay belly up in the dark sea while birds studded about them; captive whales, ready for rendition. The factory ships could cull seventy whales in one day, killing them with weapons that increasingly resembled space-age instruments, flanged and fluked to drive into giant crania, where they exploded. Three hundred and sixty thousand blue whales died in this way in the twentieth century, a martial toll from which they have yet to recover. There are now fewer than fifteen thousand left.

I cannot claim immunity. Within my lifetime, whaling reached its all-time peak. A set of encyclopedias inherited from my uncle, edited by curators from the American Museum of Natural History, and illustrated by photographs of the museum's surreal dioramas, acknowledges the limits of mid-twentieth-century cetology: 'We cannot hope for much success until we know more about these deep-sea mammals,' the authors write. 'We are seriously endeavouring to get this information.'

The book bears witness to a pre-ecological age, but it discerns the stirrings of conscience. A section entitled most important product from the whale declares: 'One recent whaling season in the Antarctic produced 2,158,173 barrels of oil.' And under another headline, 'The whale in danger,' reports that 'whalers took 6,158 blue whales, 17,989 finback whales, 2,108 humpback whales, and 2,566 sperm whales in a single season... This does not include 2,459 whales taken by the Russians.'

The twentieth century saw whaling in numbers that far exceeded the hunts of the nineteenth century. It is salutary to see how sharply the figures escalate. In 1910, 1,303 fin whales and forty-three sperm whales were taken; in 1958, the totals stood at 32,587 fin and 21,846 sperm whales. The cull seemed unstoppable, and it was exacerbated by politics. From 1951 to 1970, the Soviet Union increased its catches outside international agreements, taking 3,212 southern right whales, although only four were reported to the International Whaling Commission. Humpbacks were particular victims of this slaughter: 2,710 dead whales were reported by the Russians; in fact, they had killed more than 48,000.

The Cold War extended even to whales in their ocean fastness. The northern right whales, protected since 1935, were reduced to just one hundred animals by illicit Soviet whaling in the 1960s; southern rights had already reached a low point of tens, off the coast of apartheid South Africa. Bowheads, blue whales and humpbacks all suffered similarly under the disunited nations. An average of 25,000 sperm whales were still being taken each year. And all this despite—or perhaps even because of—the imposition of quotas by the International Whaling Commission. The Antarctic catch for 1967–1968, for example, was set at 3,200 'Blue Whale Units', a limit undermined by the classification of the world's largest animal as a 'unit' and their populations as 'stocks' in bureaucratic, deadly equations:

'1 blue whale unit = 2 finbacks, or $2\frac{1}{2}$ humpbacks, 6 sei whales.'

Not only was the average size of whales in the catch declining, 'which points suspiciously to overkilling,' as one scientist noted, but 'the CDW—take per catcher's day's work—which is a measure of the effort required to take a whale, is also steadily declining, which tells us what we already know, that the whales are disappearing.' An awful but apparently possible outcome led another marine biologist to muse, 'What will be next? Will the orbiting satellite speak through space to tell the hunter where to find the last whale?'

In 1951 alone, more whales were killed worldwide than New Bedford's whaleships—on one of which Melville himself sailed—took in 160 years of whaling. The cull reached its crescendo in 1965, with the death of 72,471 whales. The Scottish port of Dundee, which since the 1860s had prospered by neatly marrying the area's production of jute with the whale oil needed to treat the raw material, still sent out its whaling ships to the Southern Ocean, where the British joined factory fleets from Russia and Japan.

Some of those who accomplished this slaughter are still alive. They describe their work in these open-air abattoirs as something out of Dante's *Inferno*; the remembered noise, the smell, the sights repulse them, retrospectively. If the whales had been able to scream, one said, they would not have been able to bear their work. Instead, silence rendered the whales dumb in the face of destruction. Perhaps they agreed not to protest their abuse, the more to shame their persecutors.

□

'Eloquent and
compulsively readable'
Bill McKibben

ROBERT MACFARLANE

THE
WILD
PLACES

978 1 86207 941 0
£18.99
www.granta.com

GRANTA